Regional Powers and Global Redistribution

Emerging regional powers such as India, Brazil and South Africa pose a challenge to the global order, but it is not always clear what and how fundamental that challenge is. This edited volume highlights various dimensions and interpretations of that challenge, arguing that it is characterised by internal tensions. On the one hand, these states pursue the global redistribution of material, institutional and symbolic resources in the name of promoting global justice. They also promote South-South solidarity by providing modest amounts of assistance to selected least developed states. On the other hand, regional powers gain at least some of their global legitimacy and identities from their largely unacknowledged role as pillars of an order that undermines the opportunities for redistributive change. Their domestic politics and regional policies also place distinct limits on the extent of the global redistribution that they can pursue credibly.

This book was originally published as a special issue of *Global Society*.

Philip Nel is a Professor of Politics at the University of Otago, New Zealand, and Professor Extraordinaire at Stellenbosch University, South Africa.

Dirk Nabers is a Professor of International Political Sociology at the University of Kiel, Germany.

Melanie Hanif coordinates academic initiatives at the Forum Transregionale Studien, Berlin.

Regional Powers and Global Redistribution

Edited by
Philip Nel, Dirk Nabers and
Melanie Hanif

LONDON AND NEW YORK

First published 2015
by Routledge

2 Park Square, Milton Park, Abingdon, Oxfordshire OX14 4RN
711 Third Avenue, New York, NY 10017

Routledge is an imprint of the Taylor & Francis Group, an informa business

First issued in paperback 2018

Copyright © 2015 University of Kent

All rights reserved. No part of this book may be reprinted or reproduced or utilised in any form or by any electronic, mechanical, or other means, now known or hereafter invented, including photocopying and recording, or in any information storage or retrieval system, without permission in writing from the publishers.

Notice:
Product or corporate names may be trademarks or registered trademarks, and are used only for identification and explanation without intent to infringe.

British Library Cataloguing in Publication Data
A catalogue record for this book is available from the British Library

ISBN 13: 978-1-138-83228-2 (hbk)
ISBN 13: 978-1-138-38391-3 (pbk)

Typeset in Palatino
by RefineCatch Limited, Bungay, Suffolk

Publisher's Note
The publisher accepts responsibility for any inconsistencies that may have arisen during the conversion of this book from journal articles to book chapters, namely the possible inclusion of journal terminology.

Disclaimer
Every effort has been made to contact copyright holders for their permission to reprint material in this book. The publishers would be grateful to hear from any copyright holder who is not here acknowledged and will undertake to rectify any errors or omissions in future editions of this book.

Contents

Citation Information	vii
Notes on Contributors	ix
1. Introduction: Regional Powers and Global Redistribution *Philip Nel, Dirk Nabers and Melanie Hanif*	1
2. Rising Regional Powers and International Institutions: The Foreign Policy Orientations of India, Brazil and South Africa *Matthew D. Stephen*	11
3. Rising States and Distributive Justice: Reforming International Order in the Twenty-First Century *Marco Vieira*	33
4. Falling on Fertile Ground? The Story of Emerging Powers' Claims for Redistribution and the Global Poverty Debate *Janis van der Westhuizen*	53
5. Strategies and Tactics for Global Change: Democratic Brazil in Comparative Perspective *Sean W. Burges*	73
6. India's Identity and its Global Aspirations *Karen Smith*	91
7. India and the Redistribution of Power and Resources *Joachim Betz*	109
Index	129

Citation Information

The chapters in this book were originally published in *Global Society*, volume 26, issue 3 (July 2012). When citing this material, please use the original page numbering for each article, as follows:

Chapter 1
Introduction: Regional Powers and Global Redistribution
Philip Nel, Dirk Nabers and Melanie Hanif
Global Society, volume 26, issue 3 (July 2012) pp. 279–288

Chapter 2
Rising Regional Powers and International Institutions: The Foreign Policy Orientations of India, Brazil and South Africa
Matthew D. Stephen
Global Society, volume 26, issue 3 (July 2012) pp. 289–310

Chapter 3
Rising States and Distributive Justice: Reforming International Order in the Twenty-First Century
Marco Vieira
Global Society, volume 26, issue 3 (July 2012) pp. 311–330

Chapter 4
Falling on Fertile Ground? The Story of Emerging Powers' Claims for Redistribution and the Global Poverty Debate
Janis van der Westhuizen
Global Society, volume 26, issue 3 (July 2012) pp. 331–350

Chapter 5
Strategies and Tactics for Global Change: Democratic Brazil in Comparative Perspective
Sean W. Burges
Global Society, volume 26, issue 3 (July 2012) pp. 351–368

Chapter 6
India's Identity and its Global Aspirations
Karen Smith
Global Society, volume 26, issue 3 (July 2012) pp. 369–386

CITATION INFORMATION

Chapter 7
India and the Redistribution of Power and Resources
Joachim Betz
Global Society, volume 26, issue 3 (July 2012) pp. 387–406

Please direct any queries you may have about the citations to
clsuk.permissions@cengage.com

Notes on Contributors

Joachim Betz is Principal Research Fellow at the German Institute of Global and Area Studies in Hamburg, Germany, and Professor of Political Science at the University of Hamburg, Germany. His main research fields are development policy and development theory; political parties in developing countries; and the economic, social and foreign policies of South Asian countries.

Sean W. Burges is based at the Australian National University where he is a Lecturer in International Relations with the School of Politics and International Relations, as well as a Senior Associate of the Australian National Centre for Latin American Studies, Australia. He is the author of *Brazilian Foreign Policy After the Cold War* (2009) and over a dozen scholarly articles and book chapters on inter-American affairs and Brazilian foreign policy.

Melanie Hanif coordinates academic initiatives at the Forum Transregionale Studien, Berlin. She holds a PhD in Political Science from the University of Kiel, Germany. Previously, she was a Research Fellow at the German Institute of Global and Area Studies in Hamburg, Germany. In her dissertation she discussed the changing legitimacy of regions in international relations in the context of the regional powers debate.

Dirk Nabers is a Professor of International Political Sociology at the University of Kiel, Germany. Previously, he has been Academic Director of the Hamburg International Graduate School for the Study of Regional Powers (HIGS) and a Senior Research Fellow at the German Institute of Global and Area Studies (GIGA) at Hamburg. He has published widely on IR theory, global security and regionalism.

Philip Nel is a Professor of Politics at the University of Otago, New Zealand, and Professor Extraordinaire at Stellenbosch University, South Africa. He publishes on the foreign policies of regional powers; the comparative politics of inequality in developing countries; and the political effects of natural disasters.

Karen Smith is a Senior Lecturer in the Department of Political Studies at the University of Cape Town, South Africa, where she teaches international relations courses. She holds a PhD in Political Science from the University of Stellenbosch, South Africa, where she taught for 10 years. She is also a Research Associate at the Institute for Global Dialogue.

Matthew D. Stephen is a Senior Researcher in the Research Unit Global Governance at the WZB Berlin Social Science Center. His research on rising powers in global

NOTES ON CONTRIBUTORS

governance has been published in journals such as the *European Journal of International Relations, Millennium* and *Politics*. He is currently coordinating a Leibniz Association research project on 'Contested World Orders', involving researchers at the WZB, the German Institute for Global and Area Studies (GIGA) in Hamburg, and the Peace Research Institute Frankfurt.

Marco Vieira is a Lecturer in International Relations at the Department of Political Science and International Studies at the University of Birmingham, UK. He is the co-author of *The South in World Politics* (2010). His current research looks at new models of South-South political cooperation and the impact of rising powers on global norms and institutions.

Janis van der Westhuizen is an Associate Professor in the Department of Political Science at the University of Stellenbosch, South Africa. He previously authored *Adapting to Globalization: Malaysia, South Africa and the Challenges of Ethnic Redistribution with Growth* (2002) and other books and articles on South African foreign policy. His current research project compares South Africa and Brazil's role in global redistribution.

Introduction: Regional Powers and Global Redistribution

PHILIP NEL, DIRK NABERS and MELANIE HANIF

So-called "(new) regional powers" such as Brazil, China, India and South Africa have become omnipresent as a topic in the study of international relations (IR).[1] In recent years these regional powers have emerged as significant representatives and interpreters of the long-standing aspirations of the South in global affairs. Actively formulated by Brazil, India, and South Africa, this agenda is also supported by China, albeit less consistently. Contributions to this special section highlight different aspects of these global goals, but share the conviction that 'global redistribution' provides a useful description of what they entail.

As used here, 'global redistribution' refers to the goal of systematically reducing the wealth, power, and prestige differentials between nation states that characterise the modern world. In this usage, 'global' signifies the scope of the inter-state redistribution that is aimed at. As such, the meaning of the term should be distinguished from another. In studies of the distribution of wealth and income across the world as a whole, global redistribution is used to refer to the evening-out of income and wealth differentials between all the citizens of the world, irrespective of nationality.[2] It is important to distinguish between these two usages. The achievement of the first form of global, that is 'inter-state' redistribution, does not necessarily improve distribution in the second sense of the term. In fact, this distinction provides us with an evaluative tool with which to probe the limits of the distributive aspirations of the leaders from the emerging Southern powerhouses.

Over the past two decades, all four of the regional powers mentioned above have made some progress in reducing absolute poverty within their countries. However, apart from Brazil, all have seen wealth and income inequalities increase, thus placing increasing strains on their already vulnerable societies.[3] The reasons for these wider disparities are many and at least some have to do with the consequences of rapid economic growth and modernisation that places a premium on

---

1. See, for example, Nadine Godehardt and Dirk Nabers (eds.), *Regional Powers and Regional Orders* (London: Routledge, 2011).

2. François Bourguignon et al., "Global Redistribution of Income", *World Bank Working Paper*, No. 3961 (Washington DC, World Bank, 2006).

3. For overviews of inequality trends in these regional powers, see OECD, *Tackling Inequalities in Brazil, China, India and South Africa: The Role of Labour Market and Social Policies* (Paris: OECD Publishing, 2010); and OECD, *Divided We Stand: Why Inequality Keeps Rising* (Paris: OECD Publishing, 2011).

skills.[4] However, it is also true that governments can reduce inequalities through the careful combination of labour market flexibilities, investment in education and training, and through social transfers that, as Brazil illustrates, can be an effective tool for social justice.

In addition, wealth and income disparities within the respective regions of these emerging powers have also increased. This may be due to a lack of leadership shown by these states in their regions. Such leadership can be *structural* (i.e. consistently turning preponderant material capabilities into favourable institutions and policy outcomes), *entrepreneurial* (i.e. displaying a preponderance of negotiating skills), and/or *intellectual* (i.e. the ability to shape other countries' understandings of an issue). Regional leadership and redistribution go hand in hand as both rely on mutuality. Potential leaders have to appeal to the motives of potential followers. It must hence be distinguished from domination and coercion. Leaders might be able to get potential followers to see the world through their eyes. In contrast to mere power holders, leaders are effective because they induce change. Leadership, again in contrast to brute power, is inseparable from the wants and needs of followers, but these wants and needs may be changed within the context of international arguing and bargaining. We doubt whether Brazil, China, India, and South Africa have fully developed the capabilities and the political will of regional leadership. Hence, regional redistribution for the sake of a larger degree of equity remains incomplete.

So, it is important to distinguish between the multidimensionality of truly global redistribution and the narrower inter-state redistribution that emerging powers are pursuing under the banner of 'global redistribution'. In what follows, we focus predominantly on India, Brazil, and South Africa's (henceforth IBSA states) roles in processes of global (that is, inter-state) redistribution. These states indeed have much in common, despite their obvious geographic and cultural differences. All three have both a regional and global significance, although one has to be careful not to overestimate either. Brazil is a middle-sized power globally, but it has a continental scale and regional preponderance economically and militarily. It has more than a half of South America's population, territory, and GDP. India is an emerging global power, with one sixth of the world's population and a fast growing economy with a global reach. South Africa is a middle-sized, regionally prominent state, having only 6 per cent of the population of sub-Saharan Africa, but a third of its GDP. The three share the aspiration to shape the agendas and outcomes of their regional settings, with more or less success. All three rely on a preponderance of material and ideational resources and institutional capacities to project their interests and values beyond their immediate borders and provide some cohesion to their respective regions. In all three cases this process is incomplete and uneven.[5]

At the global level, a number of demand- and supply-side factors have increased the importance of the three IBSA states. On the demand-side, the pressures of crisis-prone globalisation have brought the leading states of the North to

---

4. For a discussion of the many determinants of inequality in so-called developing countries, see Philip Nel, "Redistribution and Recognition: What Regional Powers Want", *Review of International Studies*, Vol. 36, No. 4 (2010), pp. 951–974.

5. Philip Nel and Matthew Stephen, "The Foreign Economic Policies of the IBSA States", in Daniel Flemes (ed.), *Regional Leadership in the Global System: Ideas, Interests and Strategies of Regional Powers* (Aldershot: Ashgate, 2010), pp. 71–90.

engage prominent Southern states in at- and beyond-the-border policy coordination and cooperation. This extends across issue areas as diverse as nuclear non-proliferation, financial regulation and management, securing liquidity in a post-recession era, deepening of world trade, and the mitigation of climate change. In all of these issues, and many beyond this list, a number of emerging global or regional powers have developed the capacity to act as spoilers, if not as veto players. While it is in particular China's size and economic presence that makes it an unavoidable partner in the new global governance, the IBSA states are favoured partners due to a number of factors. Apart from their regional (and in the case of India, also global) economic import, decision-makers and voters in G8 states seem to regard Brazil, India, and South Africa as credible global governance counterparts with whom they share a number of norms and values, given their established democratic regimes.[6]

The demand from the G8 for the IBSA states to play a larger role in global governance has been met by the supply-side initiatives of the latter to effect a realignment and redistribution of power, prestige, and privilege in the global political economy. Basing themselves on long-standing aspirations of the global South, and in particular of the Non-Aligned Movement, IBSA states rely on their predominant regional and emerging global stature to try and shape the international economic environment in order to bring it closer to what they perceive as optimal conditions for the domestic and global advancement of the developing world. In their individual capacities, but also collectively through the establishment of the Trilateral Developmental Initiative or Dialogue Forum of IBSA, the three have come to articulate and defend what they perceive to be the common developmental position of the global South. These include a fairer distribution of the benefits of trade and the removal of non-tariff obstacles obstructing access to OECD markets, increased development-focused capital flows from North to South, larger technology transfers from developed to developing countries, and more recently, securing significant financial and technological assistance from Annex I states in terms of the United Nations Framework Convention on Climate Change (UNFCCC) Kyoto Protocol to assist developing countries in the mitigation of climate change and adaptation to its effects.

The demand-side of the IBSA states' role in global redistribution also includes the structural "demands" of a world economy that is caught in an enduring systemic crisis. The survival, and future expansion, of the world capitalist economy depends on the participation and support of the so-called emerging and transition economies of the world, notably the three IBSA states (and China). While regional powers such as the IBSA states are trying to reform the mechanisms of global governance, they themselves are increasingly being incorporated into and transformed by the power structures of the world system. In contrast to earlier generations of post-colonial leaders, the current leadership of the IBSA states are bargaining that this is a risk worth taking. This bargain means, however, that their programme of inter-state redistribution can be no more than mildly reformist in nature.[7]

---

6. Other regional powers of the global South, notably Egypt, Libya, and Venezuela, to name but three, also aspire to play roles on the stage beyond their regions, and these roles include some element of opposition to the hegemony of the global North. However, exactly because these states lack the credibility among their interlocutors that flows from the robust democratic institutions of India, Brazil, and South Africa, they do not deserve to be categorised together with the IBSA states.

Table 1. Dimensions of Global (Inter-State) Redistribution

	Absolute Gains	Relative Gains
Increasing Wealth and Income	"New geography of wealth" GDP crossover in 2011/3 *Increasing technology transfer and access to markets*	Share of foreign reserves 'Steering' currencies to own competitive advantage *Securing additional 'development' funding through Green Climate Fund (for mitigation of and adaptation to climate change)*
Enhancing Relational and Institutional Power	Increased participation in steering of global economy through the G20 De facto veto in WTO	Reform of World Bank and IMF Appointment of preferred candidates (e.g. Secretariat of UNFCCC) *Reform of UNSC*
Establishing Discursive/ Constitutive Power	*Constituting an 'attitude of non-indifference' towards a specific 'Southern' development agenda*	Acknowledgement of prestige

Note: Italics used to depict explicit IBSA aspirations.

Table 1 distinguishes between six different dimensions of global inter-state redistribution, specifically from the viewpoint of the IBSA states. Note that the items in italics refer to explicit redistributive goals on the part of one or more of the IBSA states that have not been achieved yet. A distinction is made between absolute and relative gains. The first refers to outcomes in which states individually or collectively increase their 'share' of a valued good or outcome, but there is not necessarily a decline in the 'share' of other states as a result. Relative gains, on the other hand, involve zero-sum outcomes. We remain agnostic about the question of whether states prefer relative gains, as realists argue, or absolute gains. We believe that both form part of the strategic and communicative behaviour of states. Table 1 also distinguishes between different *desiderata* of global redistribution, again from the viewpoint of the IBSA states. These we summarise as wealth, prestige, and power.

The upper-left cell reflects that, as we write, inter-state redistribution of wealth and income in favour of developing countries is already taking place on a large scale, reflected in the OECD's useful notion of "shifting wealth". According to OECD calculations, the share of world GDP produced by non-OECD members will surpass the share of OECD members somewhere between 2011 and 2013. This contrasts with the early 1990s, when OECD members had a share of 62 per cent of world GDP.[8] Using a similar classification as the OECD, and constant US$ at 2000 exchange rates, it can be shown that the North-South GDP/capita gap narrowed from 22.1 to 15.9 (28 per cent less) between 1990 and 2009, while the gap between the North and the large three emerging powers (China, India, Brazil) narrowed from 39.3 to 16.6 (58 per cent less).[9] Another striking indicator

---

7. Ian Taylor, "The South Will Rise Again? New Alliances and Global Governance: The India-Brazil-South Africa Dialogue Forum", *Politikon*, Vol. 36, No. 1 (2009), pp. 45–58.

8. OECD, *Shifting Wealth - Perspectives on Global Development 2010* (Paris: OECD Publishing, 2010).

9. Jing Wang, Dana Medianu and John Whalley, "The Contribution of China, India and Brazil to Narrowing North-South Differences in GDP/capita, World Trade Shares, and Market Capitalization",

of the redistribution of buying power in today's world is the fact that by 2008, the global South held twice the value of foreign reserves than OECD states.[10] But this redistribution of wealth is incomplete. Relative material gains being sought by the IBSA states and the global South include the continued exhortation that all OECD Development Assistance Committee (DAC) member states meet the expressed goal of donating 0.7 per cent of GDP as official development assistance (ODA). An increasingly salient redistributive demand, which according to some calculations could eventually match the total annual value of ODA dispensed by DAC members, is contained in the notion of "new and additional" funding that has to support the establishment of a climate change mitigation and adaptation fund. The aim of this fund as reflected in the UNFCCC Copenhagen Accord[11] and reconfirmed in the Cancún and Durban Agreements is to assist developing countries to reduce national greenhouse gas emissions, and to help those that are especially vulnerable to adapt to the effects of climate change. It is noteworthy that on the insistence of Brazil, India and South Africa (together with China – the so-called BASIC states), the Copenhagen Accord explicitly made provision for a financing mechanism of US $100 billion by 2020. Representatives of all four BASIC states were represented in the United Nations High Level Advisory Group on Climate Change Financing, which formulated guidelines for the generation and management of the money that has to go into this so-called Green Climate Fund. If/when this fund becomes operational, it will represent one of the most significant vehicles for North-South redistribution in the long history of this divided world.

Table 1 highlights that aspirations towards global redistribution go beyond the economic rise/emergence of the South and new forms of North-South transfers. Leading Southern states are also pursuing changes to the inter-state distribution of prestige and power through the mechanisms of global governance.[12] The remaining four cells in Table 1 summarise these latter dimensions of redistribution, building on a distinction between relational/institutional power, on the one hand, and discursive/constitutive power, on the other.[13] As far as

---

Working Paper, No. 17681 (Cambridge, MA: National Bureau of Economic Research, 2011), available: <http://www.nber.org/papers/w17681> (accessed 12 January 2012).

10. OECD, *Shifting Wealth, op. cit.*

11. Martin Khor, "After Copenhagen, the Way Forward", *South Bulletin*, No. 43 (2010), pp. 1–3.

12. While global governance is generally defined as a process involving both states and non-state actors with formal as well as informal rules and regulations to advance a common goal, Ole J. Sending and Iver Neumann, "Governance to Governmentality: Analyzing NGOs, States, and Power", *International Studies Quarterly*, Vol. 50, No. 3 (2006), pp. 651–672, we restrict ourselves to the roles of regional powers in this process.

13. This distinction refers to a three-dimensional view of power: the first dimension (or face) of power has most adequately been captured by Robert Dahl's classical definition of relational power. According to Dahl, exercising power is bringing somebody to do something that they would not otherwise do, Robert A. Dahl, "The Concept of Power", *Behavioral Science*, Vol. 2, No. 3 (1957), pp. 202–203. Bachrach and Baratz have added a second dimension of power that can be called institutional. From their perspective, an actor can also exercise power by defining the rules of the game and dominating the agenda-setting process within established institutions. Institutional power can exclude certain interests from entering the public sphere without any actual manifestation of relational power, Peter Bachrach and Morton S. Baratz, "Two Faces of Power", *The American Political Science Review*, Vol. 56, No. 4 (1962), pp. 948–950). According to Luke's definition of the third face, the supreme exercise of power, however, inhibits the existence of any conflictive interests in the first place. This most subtle dimension of power can be called constitutional because it influences the constitution of interests before they become

relational/institutional power is concerned, leading OECD states have learnt most forcefully in the breakdown of the WTO negotiations at Cancún in 2003 that norm development and successful trade regime building depend on the cooperation of prominent developing states. Indeed, one is justified in referring to the likes of the IBSA states and China as veto players in the WTO-managed trade regime.[14] As in the case of the evolution of the G20 over the past 24 months, this does not imply that the leading OECD countries have lost in relational/institutional power, but rather that they are now compelled to share power with the likes of the IBSA states and China. As far as the evolution of the G20 is concerned, the sharing of power and responsibility within what Andrew Cooper calls this "hybrid" of "crisis committee and hub of economic global governance"[15] is unlikely to be perceived as a zero-sum game by any of the players involved.

Reform of the World Bank and the International Monetary Fund, and specifically of the allocation of voting quotas, is another matter, however. Here, the gains that the developing countries are pursuing are distinctly *relative*. In the words of Mr. Pravin Gordhan, Minister of Finance of South Africa and Second Vice Chair of the Intergovernmental Group of Twenty-Four on International Monetary Affairs and Development (G24) when discussing a statement released by the Group on 7 October 2010:

> The G24 supports a significant realignment of quotas and emphasised amongst other things that in the realignment of quotas, given the historical context in which we are operating, the realignment must lead to a shift in quotas from the 'haves' of the world to the 'have-nots' of the world.[16]

While some progress has been made with reforming the World Bank,[17] the reallocation of quotas at the IMF has been a drawn-out and frustrating affair for developing countries. India has called for at least a 7 per cent shift in the fund's quotas from developed to emerging countries and also for giving them more seats on the IMF board.[18]

---

manifest and conscious, Steven Lukes, *Power: A Radical View* (Basingstoké: Palgrave Macmillan, 2005 [1974]), pp. 25–29.

14. Amrita Narlikar, "New Powers in the Club: The Challenges of Global Trade Governance", *International Affairs*, Vol. 86, No. 3 (2010), pp. 717–728.

15. Andrew F. Cooper, "The G20 as an Improvised Crisis Committee and/or a Contested 'Steering Committee' for the World", *International Affairs*, Vol. 86, No. 3 (2010), p. 744.

16. See Transcript of G-24 Press Conference, 7 October 2010, available: <http://www.imf.org/external/np/tr/2010/tr100710a.htm> (accessed 10 December 2011). The Intergovernmental Group of Twenty-Four on International Monetary Affairs and Development (G-24) was established in 1971.

17. In April 2010, the Board of the World Bank approved a slight shift of voting shares in favour of developing countries, while agreeing to raise more money for global aid: "Under the new voting structure announced on Sunday, some emerging economies will have a greater say in how the 186-nation bank distributes aid. This represents a total shift of 4.59 per cent to developing and transition countries since 2008, the IMF and the World Bank said in a joint statement after the meeting. As a result, India's voting power has increased from 2.77 per cent to 2.91 per cent while China has emerged as the biggest beneficiary, its rights increasing from 2.77 per cent to 4.42 per cent. The shift places India at the seventh biggest place after the US (15.85 per cent), Japan (6.84 per cent), China, Germany (4 per cent), France (3.75 per cent) and the UK (3.75 per cent)", *Al Jazeera* and agencies (26 April 2010).

18. *The Economic Times* (26 April 2010), available: <http://economictimes.indiatimes.com/articleshow/5cms857435> (accessed 14 July 2010).

The last two cells in Table 1 emphasise that the assertive behaviour of the three IBSA states (and other powerhouses of the South) in a number of institutions of global governance is premised on two deeper constitutive struggles. One deals with the wish of these leading states of the South to gain recognition of their "prestige" in global affairs. We interpret this as a competitive *relative* aim. Prestige according to Robert Gilpin "refers primarily to the perceptions of other states with respect to a state's capacities and its ability and willingness to exercise its power".[19] To a more or lesser degree, all three IBSA states are pursuing prestige in this sense of the word, partly in order to balance against the perceived hegemony of established global powers, such as the United States, and partly to secure leadership within their own regions.[20]

On the positive end, this kind of engagement is in constant need of attracting the support of potential followers. It is a form of power, but it implies mutuality. Prestige-seeking is thus competitive. Followers must be assured that they can count on the leader in a difficult situation. Strong leadership, in this sense, seems to be essential for guiding and directing a group of countries towards collective action. To bring this kind of reciprocity to the point, James MacGregor Burns distinguished transactional from transformational leadership. While "leaders approach followers with an eye to exchanging one thing for another"[21] in the former case, the follower is more fully engaged in the latter scenario: "The result of transforming leadership is a relationship of mutual simulation and elevation that converts followers into leaders and may convert leaders into moral agents".[22]

At the negative end, though, as a relative, zero-sum outcome, pursuit of prestige is bound to lead to rivalry and resentment, particularly within the very regions that the IBSA states are aspiring to lead. This is nowhere better illustrated than in the pursuit of permanent membership of the United Nations Security Council (UNSC), which is the ultimate prestige-prize in international politics. Brazil and India have joined forces with Japan and Germany in the G4 of states actively pursuing their elevation to that status. South Africa has to tread somewhat more cautiously given the African Union's consensus position that Africa's permanent presence on the UNSC must be a rotational one, but it nevertheless supports the candidacy of India and Brazil. Of course, not all of Brazil and India's neighbours are prepared to support their candidacies, and South Africa's ambitions in Africa and on the global stage are treated with suspicion in its neighbourhood. The desire to join and thereby legitimising the hierarchical world security order sits uncomfortably with the assumption that what the IBSA states are seeking is the flattening out of hierarchical patterns of world order.

The second constitutive struggle that is fought by the IBSA states on behalf of the South is aimed at gaining recognition of the specific development needs of the South that are too easily ploughed-under in the spurious universality promoted by institutions of global governance.[23] This perspective is able to challenge

---

19. Robert Gilpin, *War and Change in International Politics* (Cambridge: Cambridge University Press, 1981), p. 31.
20. Daniel Flemes, "Emerging Middle Powers' Soft Balancing Strategy: State and Perspectives of the IBSA Dialogue Forum", *GIGA Working Paper*, No. 57 (Hamburg: GIGA, 2007).
21. James M. Burns, *Leadership* (New York: Harper and Row, 1979), p. 4.
22. *Ibid.*
23. Nel, *op. cit.*

mainstream theories of international relations in that a reading of the problems of the 'South' through a Northern lens is circumvented. This struggle against the invisibility of specific 'Southern' attributes and needs in the processes of global governance continues in a variety of contexts, from keeping the focus on development issues in the Doha 'Development Round' of WTO negotiations, to the forceful formulations by the IBSA partners of the specific needs and concerns of developing countries in the current UNFCCC post-Kyoto negotiations about a global climate change mitigation strategy. In voicing concerns about what is happening in these contexts, the Brazilians have explicitly agitated for an attitude of 'non-indifference' to the concerns of the developing world.

Prospectus

The contributions that make up this Special Issue provide the 'flesh and bones' to fill-out the global redistribution 'skeleton' that we sketched in Table 1 and in the preceding paragraphs. Addressing the cases of all three IBSA states, Matthew Stephen asks about the relevance of these newly emerging powers in the institutionalisation of innovative global governance structures. By employing three well-accepted conceptual lenses – balancing, spoiling, and being co-opted – in the fields of trade, finance, and security, Stephen discusses the heterogeneity of these regional powers' strategies and their highly diverse impact across institutional sub-systems, which at times reflect competing logics of behaviour. Amid all these differences, these states' commitment to and positive development towards global redistribution remains undisputed from Stephen's perspective.

In his contribution, Marco Vieira shows that the IBSA states are not only pursuing redistribution via existing global regimes. They are also creating new regimes, based on the normative reference points around global distributive justice forged by the struggles of the global South over the past 50-odd years. One such new regime is the institutionalisation of South-South development assistance in the form of the IBSA Trust Fund that provides hunger and poverty relief to afflicted nations of the South. In contrast to earlier and largely ineffective attempts at South-South cooperation, the small but effective IBSA Fund forms part of an increasingly assertive presence of donors from the South in the field of official development assistance. It also puts into effect the discursive demands of the IBSA states for recognition of the distinctive needs and contributions of the South in global development.

Yet, the global actions of the IBSA states and their domestic 'reforms' do not necessarily represent a normative breakthrough in all senses of the term. Janis van der Westhuizen takes issue with recent developments in the global poverty debate and the contribution of IBSA states in this regard. In a comparative perspective on South Africa and Brazil his article analyses several initiatives that the governments in Pretoria and Brasilia have launched on the basis of their novel esteem as rising powers. Van der Westhuizen concludes that new coalitions between old and new powers can be seen as a response to the need for a more socially responsible world order. In this context, the IBSA Forum, and, more specifically, the IBSA Fund with its strong focus on development cooperation, is an intra-systemic attempt at ameliorating the worst aspects of global capitalism in crisis, rather than an attempt at replacing the reigning world order. Nevertheless, by opening the normative space for ideas of redistribution and justice to flourish, it is contributing to further delegitimising the neoliberal basis of this order.

The final three articles in this issue each take a deeper look at one of the three IBSA states. While Karen Smith and Joachim Betz focus on India, Sean Burges examines the role of Brazil in processes of regional and global governance. Burges introduces a broad framework for the study of the foreign policy of Brazil, ranging from the passive (avoiding mindless opposition, collectivisation) through the neutral (consensus creation, technocratic speak) to the assertive (building new organisations, propagating new thinking) and finally to the aggressive (principled presidential righteousness). He argues that Brazil profited from the global financial crisis in gaining increased international recognition. On the basis of his systematic survey, a major theoretical argument emerges: Newly emerging powers need to display an ability to act as agenda setters, showing innovative solutions to overcome deadlocks or operating as a broker to gain support for salient solutions. International politics, in a nutshell, is a reflective process, necessitating "a deliberative process of exchanging arguments. In the words of Oran Young, it implies the power of ideas to shape the intellectual capital available to those engaged in institutional bargaining".[24]

Arguing from a constructivist perspective, Smith inquires into the nexus between identity and the promotion of a redistribution of power and wealth in India's foreign policy. Although a liberal view, which advocates working within the prevailing global order to advance India's economic performance, is still dominant within Indian foreign policy discourses, global redistribution may well become a by-product of a foreign policy that is best characterised by rivalling elite identities and resulting inconsistencies.

As Joachim Betz maintains in his contribution, this is due to the influence of a variety of specific interest groups on India's foreign policy strategies. Underlining Smith's argument, Betz contends that India did not challenge the existing international economic order, but was instead more oriented towards carving out a better position for itself. In spite of some minor domestic steps to include the poorer states and sections of society into India's economic and social progress, overall redistributive efforts remain feeble. Regional and global redistributive efforts can be seen as a competitive subterfuge, and are mostly triggered by India's competition with other countries, such as Pakistan and China, which gives us important insights into the dynamics of leadership at the international level: regional powers act under constraints when they use their established and newly acquired power; they are not entirely free to choose their options, for their actions are shaped by followers, by potential challengers, and by circumstances to varying degrees. The redistribution of wealth, power, and prestige is not a smooth process over which emerging powers have ultimate control. It is unpredictable and uneven, and whether it eventually leads to a more equitable and legitimate world order remains to be seen.

---

24. Oran R. Young, "Political Leadership and Regime Formation: On the Development of Institutions in International Society", *International Organization*, Vol. 45, No. 3 (1991), p. 300.

Rising Regional Powers and International Institutions: The Foreign Policy Orientations of India, Brazil and South Africa

MATTHEW D. STEPHEN

How do rising powers relate to international institutions? At the same time as rising regional powers from the South emerge as key players in international politics, they confront a highly institutionalised world order established and maintained by and for the United States and its allies. Traditional perspectives identify three major patterns of behaviour for rising states in international institutions: balancing, spoiling, and being coopted. This article uses these perspectives to ask how the redistributive aspirations of three rising regional powers – India, Brazil, and South Africa (IBSA) – impact on international institutions in the fields of trade, money, and security. The findings indicate that there is strong variation across issue areas. Trade provides support for the spoiling perspective, while the areas of money and security exhibit aspects familiar both to the balancing and cooptation perspectives. A broader picture emerges of IBSA states' general integration into hegemonic norms and being coopted into existing international institutions, but at the same time as balancing the influence of the established powers and reforming these institutions to conform to a more South-oriented, sovereigntist image of world order.

In the 1990s the OECD countries led by the United States were seen as the unquestioned centre of the world political and economic systems, while discussions of global governance could largely ignore developing countries. But recent shifts in the global political economy have seen the emergence of several newly powerful states from the South. Developing countries are now home to about one half of global economic activity as measured by GDP,[1] and Goldman Sachs have influentially predicted that the four BRIC (Brazil, Russia, India and China) economies could outweigh the members of the G7 by 2035.[2] Other projections based on

---

*I would like to thank, while in no way implicate, Melanie Hanif, Philip Nel, Autumn Lockwood Payton, Michael Zürn, and the anonymous reviewers for their comments on earlier versions of this article, as well as acknowledge the useful feedback of participants at a *Berlin Graduate School for Transnational Studies* PhD Colloquium in Berlin, 23 May 2011, and at a panel of the International Studies Association Asia-Pacific Regional Section Conference in Brisbane, 30 September 2011.

1. OECD, *Perspectives on Global Development 2010: Shifting Wealth* (Paris: OECD Publishing, 2010).
2. Goldman Sachs Global Economics Group, "BRICs and Beyond" (Goldman Sachs, 2007), available: <www.goldmansachs.com/our-thinking/brics> (accessed 5 May 2012).

different models all expect a radical and fundamental shift in the centre of gravity of the global economy from North to South.[3]

Mirroring these changes has been a sharp and swift change in tone by scholars of world politics. To (unfairly) single out one author: In 2001 John Ikenberry was simply repeating common knowledge when he wrote that, "American power in the 1990s is without historical precedent. No state in the modern era has ever enjoyed such a dominant global position".[4] Yet seven years later, the same author made this observation:

> Today, a group of fast-growing developing countries – led by China and India – are rising up and in the next several decades will have economies that will rival the United States and Europe. For the first time in the modern era, economic growth is bringing non-Western developing countries into the top ranks of the world system.[5]

While economic expansion has underpinned the emergence of these regional powers, attention is quickly turning to the political implications of their rise. In the eyes of established states, emerging markets have become emerging powers. Prominent in this group are the IBSA states (India, Brazil and South Africa), which share a regional preponderance and certain characteristics and sensibilities in their vision for the emerging world order. The rise of the IBSA states and other powers from outside the Western heartland goes hand in hand with a new Southern multilateralism of the emerging regional powers, such as the diplomatic realisation of a BRICS multilateral forum of emerging economies (Brazil, Russia, India, China, and since 2010, South Africa), and the formation in 2003 of the IBSA Trilateral Forum of India, Brazil, and South Africa, signalling these countries' intentions to "contribute to the construction of a new international architecture, to bring their voice together on global issues and to deepen their ties in various areas".[6] Clearly, the redistribution of economic weight on a global scale is beginning to manifest implications for global governance.

The process of global redistribution alters the relative position of major states, but coexists with changes in the nature of the world order in which this redistribution takes place. A 'Westphalian' order may have always been more of an ideological rather than historical phenomenon,[7] but it has constituted the traditional way in which to conceptualise world politics in practice and in theory. In contrast, rising regional powers today face a world order that is characterised by the increasing importance of international institutions. One indicator of this is their simple quantitative increase, accompanied by an increase in the governing capacities of international

---

3. Deutsche Bank Research Globale Wachstumszentrum 2020, "Formal-G für 34 Volkswirtschaften", *Aktuelle Themen*, No. 313 (Frankfurt: Deutsche Bank, 2005); Uri Dadush and Bennett Stancil, *The World Order in 2050* (Washington DC: Carnegie Endowment for International Peace, 2010); John Hawksworth and Gordon Cookson, *The World in 2050* (London: PriceWaterhouseCoopers, 2008).

4. G. John Ikenberry, *After Victory: Institutions, Strategic Restraint, and the Rebuilding of Order After Major Wars* (Princeton: Princeton University Press, 2001), p. 270.

5. G. John Ikenberry and Thomas Wright, *Rising Powers and Global Institutions: A Century Foundation Report* (New York: The Century Foundation, 2008), p. 3.

6. IBSA Trilateral Forum, "Brasilia Declaration of the IBSA Trilateral Forum", June 2003, available: < http://www.ibsa-trilateral.org/index.php?option=com_content&task=view&id=48&Itemid=27 > (accessed 30 May 2011).

7. Stephen Krasner, *Sovereignty: Organized Hypocrisy* (Princeton: Princeton University Press, 1999).

institutions.[8] Meanwhile, global trends such as societal and economic denationalisation and the prominence of transnational non-state actors and processes have prompted the question of whether Westphalia is still an adequate basis on which to understand world politics, if indeed it ever was. This indicates a complex relationship between a shifting global distribution of power and the changing nature of international politics. The image of a world order in transformation, or an "emerging world order", can be juxtaposed to the image of emerging powers or "emerging societies".[9]

Where authority has been reallocated within global governance, the importance of this authority for the relations between major and regional powers has also grown apace. The noticeable aggregation of political authority away from the traditional national context can be expected to give rise to legitimation problems and resistance.[10] Increasing attention has been turned to the role of new powers and major developing states in challenging aspects of political globalisation and posing new challenges to supranational institutions.[11] The claim particularly that developing countries are more guarded when it comes to sovereignty would lend a North-South dimension to this dialectic of governance/resistance.

As an integral part of the ongoing globalisation of political authority, global governance institutions are also the site of a dynamic process of negotiation between North and South over the constitution of regimes, norms and institutions. It is a widely held view of scholars from many theoretical perspectives, and a frequent political statement by leaders of emerging states, that rising regional powers are portents of change in the world order. But what is the precise nature of this change? Are we heading into a more chaotic period characterised by the emergence of competing regional blocs and the decline in effectiveness and legitimacy of international institutions, or will these tendencies be contained by an expanded system of global management based on existing principles of multilateralism?

After a brief note explaining the rationale for selecting India, Brazil and South Africa (the IBSA states) as regionally-based emerging powers, this article formulates three ideal-typical perspectives through which to understand the orientations of rising regional powers, and applies these perspectives to the IBSA states in three

---

8. Michael Zürn and Matthew Stephen, "The View of Old and New Powers on the Legitimacy of International Institutions", *Politics*, Vol. 30, No. S1 (2010), pp. 91–101.

9. Jan Nederveen Pieterse and Boike Rehbein, *Globalization and Emerging Societies* (Houndmills: Palgrave, 2009).

10. Michael Zürn, "Global Governance and Legitimacy Problems", *Government and Opposition*, Vol. 39, No. 2 (2004), pp. 260–287; Michael Zürn and Mathias Ecker-Ehrhardt (eds.), *Gesellschaftliche Politisierung und Internationale Institutionen* (Frankfurt: Suhrkamp, 2011).

11. Alan Alexandroff and Andrew Cooper (eds.), *Rising States, Rising Institutions: Challenges for Global Governance* (Waterloo: Center for International Governance Innovation and Brookings Institution Press, 2010); Ikenberry and Wright, *op. cit.*; Andrew Hurrell, "Some Reflections on the Role of Intermediate Powers in International Institutions", in *Paths to Power: Foreign Policy Strategies of Intermediate States*, Working Paper, No. 244 (Washington DC: Woodrow Wilson International Center, 2000), pp. 1–10; Andrew Hurrell and Amrita Narlikar, "A New Politics of Confrontation? Brazil and India in Multilateral Trade Negotiations", *Global Society*, Vol. 20, No. 4 (2006), pp. 415–433; Andrew Cooper and Agata Antkiewicz (eds.), *Emerging Powers in Global Governance: Lessons from the Heiligendamm Process* (Canada: Wilfrid Laurier University Press, 2008); Andrew Cooper, Agata Antkiewicz and Timothy Shaw, "Lessons from/for BRICSAM about South–North Relations at the Start of the 21st Century: Economic Size Trumps All Else?", *International Studies Review*, Vol. 9, No. 4 (2007), pp. 673–689; Timothy Shaw, Andrew Cooper and Agata Antkiewicz, "Global and/or Regional Development at the Start of the 21st Century? China, India and (South) Africa", *Third World Quarterly*, Vol. 28, No. 7 (2007), pp. 1255–1270.

institutional areas of global governance. The goal is not to test rival models but to develop conceptual frames through which to interpret the redistributive aspirations of the IBSA states in the three issue areas of trade, money, and security. Empirical material is derived from analysing the countries' public diplomacy and from secondary literature. The final section summarises the findings and implications for global governance. A broader picture emerges of IBSA states' general integration into hegemonic norms and being coopted into existing international organisations, but at the same time as balancing the influence of the established powers while reforming these institutions to conform to a more South-oriented, sovereigntist image of world order. The findings reinforce the need for analyses of rising powers to take account of issue-area variation and to go beyond the standard 'power-transition' or 'balancing' rubrics for understanding their foreign policy orientations.

India, Brazil and South Africa as Rising Regional Powers

The IBSA states occupy a pivotal position in the unfolding power shift that makes them particularly interesting cases to examine. The most obvious of these is the increased share of global economic resources that the IBSA states, along with other rising states, have captured during the latest phase of globalisation.[12] More important however, is the positioning of these states at the centre of non-western multilateralism amongst rising powers, and the self-presentation of India, Brazil and South Africa as being key players in the North-South axis of international politics, which is further boosted by their portrayal as leaders of particular regions of the developing world fostering regional integration projects.[13] The IBSA states therefore appear as states crossing a threshold to be able to actively shape the institutional structures of world politics. For these reasons, the emerging Southern IBSA states in particular have attracted scholarly attention for their perceived importance to the future of global governance.[14]

Nonetheless there remains significant confusion as to whether the IBSA states are best analysed as regional, rising, or middle powers in world politics. Indeed, while the middle power category has gained favour with some,[15] the

---

12. As outlined by Philip Nel, Dirk Nabers and Melanie Hanif, this issue.

13. Philip Nel and Matthew Stephen, "The Foreign Economic Policies of Regional Powers in the Developing World: Toward a Framework of Analysis", in Daniel Flemes (ed.), *Regional Leadership in the Global System: Ideas, Interests and Strategies of Regional Powers* (Aldershot: Ashgate, 2010), pp. 71–90.

14. Chris Alden and Marco Vieira, "The New Diplomacy of the South: South Africa, Brazil, India and Trilateralism", *Third World Quarterly*, Vol. 26, No. 7 (2005), pp. 1077–1095; Beri Ruchita, "IBSA Dialogue Forum: An Assessment", *Strategic Analysis*, Vol. 32, No. 5 (2008), pp. 809–831; Daniel Flemes, "India-Brazil-South Africa (IBSA) in the New Global Order: Interests, Strategies and Values of the Emerging Coalition", *International Studies*, Vol. 46, No. 4 (2009), pp. 401–421; Philip Nel, "Redistribution *and* Recognition: What Emerging Regional Powers Want", *Review of International Studies*, Vol. 36, No. 4 (2010), pp. 951–974; Nel and Stephen, *op. cit.*; Ian Taylor, "'The South will Rise Again'? New Alliances and Global Governance: The India-Brazil-South Africa Dialogue Forum", *Politikon*, Vol. 36, No. 1 (2009), pp. 45–58.

15. For example, Daniel Flemes, "India-Brazil-South Africa (IBSA) in the New Global Order: Interests, Strategies and Values of the Emerging Coalition", *International Studies*, Vol. 46, No. 4 (2009), pp. 401–421; while Ozkan refers to 'pivotal middle powers', Mehmet Ozkan, "A New Approach to Global Security: Pivotal Middle Powers and Global Politics", *Perceptions: Journal of International Affairs*, Vol. 11, No. 1 (2006), pp. 77–95. See also Detlef Nolte, "How to Compare Regional Powers: Analytical Concepts and Research Topics", *Review of International Studies*, Vol. 36, No. S1, (2010), pp. 881–901.

concepts and perceived behavioural traits associated with the 'middle power' category in international relations seem a less useful rubric for an understanding of the IBSA states.[16] Unlike the classical or traditional middle powers,[17] none of the newly emerging Southern powers are allies of the United States, and each has at some point advocated for a different kind of international order.[18] Furthermore, the growth rates and regional autonomy of the new rising regional powers distinguishes them from the traditional middle power category associated with countries such as Canada, Australia, or the Scandinavian countries.[19]

Rather, the IBSA states are better characterised as occupying a dual role as regional and rising powers. India and Brazil can plausibly aspire to the status of global powers (Indian officials already refer to the coming 'tripolar' order), while South Africa has relied on its status as a fast-growing regional power with a global diplomacy to underpin its influence. In a further contrast to traditional middle powers, rather than donning a bridge-building or compromise approach associated with "middlepowermanship",[20] the IBSA states have adopted orientations more consistent with their status as rising powers, and become major antagonists to the established states in several institutional contexts. The IBSA states "have donned the mantle of spokesmen for the interests of developing countries in general",[21] taken on a self-appointed role as leaders in various Southern alliances such as the G77 at the UN and the G20 at the WTO, and built cooperation with other rising powers through initiatives such as the IBSA Trilateral Forum, the BASIC group in climate negotiations, and the now annual BRICS summits. Unlike traditional middle powers, the rising regional powers are seen as challenging the legitimacy of the existing world order and favouring a more multi-polar and pluralist system.[22] But to what extent is this image justified, and how can this be understood through the traditional concepts associated with rising powers?

Regional Rising Powers and International Institutions: Three Perspectives

Rising Powers Balancing the Core through International Institutions

The balancing perspective on rising powers states that as rising powers, such as the IBSA states, gain in power and influence, they will seek to 'balance' the

---

16. The difficulties inherent in the 'middle power' concept are outlined by Andrew Hurrell in his "Some Reflections on the Role of Intermediate Powers", *op. cit.*, p. 1; and Eduard Jordaan, "The Concept of a Middle Power in International Relations: Distinguishing between Emerging and Traditional Middle Powers", *Politikon*, Vol. 30, No. 2 (2003), pp. 165–181.

17. Jordaan, *op. cit.* makes the compelling argument for distinguishing 'emerging' from 'traditional' middle powers.

18. Andrew Hurrell, "Hegemony, Liberalism and Global Order: What Space for Would-be Great Powers?", *International Affairs*, Vol. 82, No. 1 (2006), p. 3.

19. Alden and Vieira, *op. cit.*, p. 1079; Andrew Cooper, Richard Higgott and Kim Nossal, *Relocating Middle Powers: Australia and Canada in a Changing World Order* (Vancouver: University of British Columbia Press, 1993). A *locus classicus* of this issue is George Glazebrook, "The Middle Powers in the United Nations System", *International Organization*, Vol. 1, No. 2 (1947), pp. 307–315.

20. Robert W. Cox, "Middlepowermanship, Japan, and Future World Order", *International Journal*, Vol. 44, No. 4 (1989), pp. 823–862.

21. Nel, *op. cit.*, p. 955.

22. Andrew Hart and Bruce Jones, "How Do Rising Powers Rise?", *Survival*, Vol. 52, No. 6 (2010), p. 66.

power and influence of the established powers. This fundamental dynamic of the international system will then be played out within international institutions. The traditional notion of balancing entails a deliberate attempt at inter-state redistribution both in absolute and in relative terms, but the central mechanism is that this emerges from the need to secure the relative elevation of the rising regional powers compared with their established rivals.

The balancing perspective emerges from a tradition of international thought, which emphasises the fundamentally different organising principles of domestic and international political orders. India, Brazil, South Africa and other regional powers will be assumed by the logic of inter-state competition to engage in a competition for economic and military resources to maximise their own security.

The balancing perspective emerges most clearly in the domain of security, where it is often assumed that security is the most fundamental goal of regional powers and that their power capabilities will determine their foreign policy options.[23] In particular, because rising regional powers such as the IBSA states are still in a precarious developmental position in relation to the developed world, they will be expected to come together against the established powers to secure greater political and economic autonomy: "Secondary states, if they are free to choose, flock to the weaker side; for it is the stronger side that threatens them".[24] The balancing perspective leads us to expect that India, Brazil and South Africa will be part of a broader international move to balance the unstable concentration of power in the United States.[25]

The balancing perspective extends into the realm of international institutions, leading to a form of "soft" or "institutional" balancing.[26] The concept of soft balancing argues that the depth of US military power makes balancing in the military sphere unrealistic, and diverts the balancing mechanism to "soft" means such as foreign economic policy and international institutions, which can increase the costs and the difficulty of the hegemon using its extraordinary power, and encourages gradual multipolarisation.[27] Soft balancing can also rely on "territorial denial, entangling diplomacy, economic strengthening, and signalling of resolve to participate in a balancing coalition".[28] This is compatible with Andrew

---

23. Robert Gilpin, "A Realist Perspective on International Governance," in David Held and Anthony McGrew (eds.), *Governing Globalization* (Cambridge: Cambridge University Press, 2002), pp. 237–248; Stephen Krasner, *Structural Conflict: The Third World Against Global Liberalism* (Berkeley, CA: University of California Press, 1985).

24. Kenneth Waltz, *Theory of International Politics* (Reading, MA: Addison-Wesley, 1979), p. 127.

25. Kenneth Waltz, "Evaluating Theories", *American Political Science Review*, Vol. 91, No. 4 (1997), 913–917; Kenneth Waltz, "Structural Realism after the Cold War", *International Security*, Vol. 25, No. 1 (2000), pp. 5–41; Kenneth Waltz, "Thoughts About Assaying Theories", in Colin Elman and Miriam Elman (eds.), *Progress in International Relations Theory* (Cambridge, MA: MIT Press, 2003), pp. vii–xii.

26. Robert Pape, "Soft Balancing Against the United States", *International Security*, Vol. 30, No. 1 (2005), pp. 7–45; T.V. Paul, "Soft Balancing in the Age of US Primacy", *International Security*, Vol. 30, No. 1 (2005), pp. 46–71; but compare Stephen Brooks, "Dueling Realisms", *International Organization* Vol. 51, No. 3 (1997), pp. 445–477; Stephen Brooks and William Wohlforth, "Hard Times for Soft Balancing", *International Security*, Vol. 30, No. 1 (2005), pp. 72–108; William Wohlforth, "The Stability of a Unipolar World", *International Security*, Vol. 24, No. 1 (1999), pp. 5–41; Randall Schweller, "Bandwagoning for Profit: Bringing the Revisionist State Back In", *International Security*, Vol. 19, No. 1 (1994), pp. 72–107; Randall Schweller, "Unanswered Threats: A Neoclassical Realist Theory of Underbalancing", *International Security*, Vol. 29, No. 2 (2004), pp. 159–201.

27. Pape, *op. cit.*, p. 17.

28. *Ibid.*, p. 36.

Hurrell's observation that in the current order, the problem of unbalanced power lies primarily in allowing the powerful state to "skew the terms of cooperation in its own favour, to impose its own values and ways of doing things, and to undermine the procedural rules on which stable and legitimate cooperation must inevitably depend".[29]

A complement to soft balancing is 'institutional balancing', conceived as "initiating, utilizing, and dominating multilateral institutions, as an overlooked realist strategy for states to pursue security under anarchy".[30] Institutional balancing can seek to bind a target state into international institutions in which they can constrain their behaviour ("inclusive institutional balancing"), or it can consolidate unity against a target state by excluding it from international institutions ("exclusive institutional balancing").[31] The soft balancing perspective on rising regional powers therefore directs our attention to the possibility of IBSA states seeking relative gains in relational and institutional power. IBSA behaviour has indeed been interpreted as conforming to the logic of "soft balancing".[32]

Rising Powers Spoiling International Institutions

At variance to the expectations of the balancing perspective, the spoiler perspective derives from theories of hegemonic stability and power transitions. It states that the arrival of new powers of systemic importance leads, inevitably, to the decline of international institutions.[33] According to this view, as regional powers grow in economic strength they will act as spoilers in the functioning of effective international institutions.

The spoiler hypothesis emerges from hegemonic stability theory. This proposes a correlation between hegemonic dominance of a system and the provision of public goods and functioning international institutions. A liberal international economy characterised by openness and non-discrimination provides the greatest potential for mutual advancement for states, but "a hegemon is necessary to the existence of a liberal international economy".[34] This encompasses an open trading order, a stable international monetary regime, stable flows of capital, a degree of counter-cyclical domestic macroeconomic management, and possibly even international 'security'.[35]

Following this classic formulation of hegemonic stability theory, the spoiler perspective states that the ability of a country (e.g., the United States) or a concert of countries (e.g., the G7) to act as custodians for the global capitalist economy

---

29. Andrew Hurrell, "Rising Powers and the Question of Status in International Society", Unpublished draft paper, (November 2009), pp. 7–8.

30. Kai He, "Institutional Balancing and International Relations Theory: Economic Interdependence and Balance of Power Strategies in Southeast Asia", *European Journal of International Relations*, Vol. 14, No. 3 (2008), p. 492.

31. *Ibid.*, p. 493.

32. Flemes, *op. cit.*, pp. 401–421.

33. A.F.K. Organski, *World Politics* (New York: Knopf, 1968); Robert Gilpin, *The Political Economy of International Relations* (Princeton, NJ: Princeton University Press, 1987).

34. Gilpin, *Political Economy of International Relations, op. cit.*, p. 88.

35. Robert Jervis, "Security Regimes", *International Organization*, Vol. 36, No. 2 (1982), pp. 357–378; Charles Kindleberger, "Dominance and Leadership in the International Economy: Exploitation, Public Goods, and Free Rides", *International Studies Quarterly*, Vol., 25, No. 2 (1981), pp. 242–254.

depends on their relative economic size and consequent ability to assume many of the costs of providing the public good of economic stability, while at the same time internalising many of the benefits for their own economic growth. The opposite effect attends the behaviour of small states: they behave as 'free riders' due to their lack of economic influence.[36] The most destabilising impact, however, emerges from economic rising and middle powers, which are systemically important for the maintenance of the world economy but not big enough to stabilise it:[37] "Since they tend to act as if they were small free riders, middle-sized countries are extremely destabilizing and are the 'spoilers' of the system".[38]

This can be joined to the balancing hypothesis by the argument that new powers' attempts at redistribution in relational and institutional terms further undermine the hegemonic consensus.[39] The hegemonic state can no longer dictate terms to secondary states, and this undermines the strength of international institutions that depend on the power balance that gave birth to them.

This inevitable conflict between rising and declining powers can only be mitigated through the emergence of a new order "that reflects the changed array of national interests and the distribution of military and political power".[40] International governance is most likely to emerge in the sphere of economic exchanges, but will remain subordinate to competing state interests. The spoiler perspective enjoins us to examine whether the IBSA states' redistributive aspirations really do undermine existing institutions and the provision of global public goods. It may be possible for cooperation to continue "after hegemony", "provided that the interests and social purposes of the major economic powers are congruent".[41] This admits of the possibility for continued 'cooperation', but hangs crucially on the foreign policy outlooks of rising powers.

Rising Powers Coopted into Liberal International Institutions

A stark contrast to the balancing and spoiler perspectives is the perspective of rising regional power cooptation: that is, that as regional powers grow in global influence, the institutional structure of the current world order will integrate and coopt them into existing international institutions. The cooptation perspective states that the redistributive aspirations of the IBSA states may imply changes for some limited procedural structures of international institutions, in line with their newly developed capacities, but that the basic liberal principles underlying them will remain intact. There is therefore no contradiction between the supranationalisation of political authority and the rise of new powers.

There are two distinct logics of international order underpinning the cooptation perspective. The first emerges from a functionalist theory of international

---

36. Kindleberger, *op. cit.*, p. 249.
37. *Ibid.*, p. 250.
38. David Lake, "International Economic Structures and American Foreign Economic Policy, 1887-1934", *World Politics*, Vol. 35, No. 4 (1983), p. 519.
39. Gilpin, "A Realist Perspective", *op. cit.*, p. 239.
40. Gilpin, *Political Economy of International Relations, op. cit.*, p. 91.
41. Ibid., citing John G. Ruggie, "International Regimes, Transactions and Change: Embedded Liberalism in the Postwar Economic Order", *International Organization*, Vol. 36, No. 2 (1982), p. 384; compare of course Robert O. Keohane, *After Hegemony: Cooperation and Discord in the World Political Economy* (Princeton, NJ: Princeton University Press, 1984).

institutions, which understands them as expanding the room for 'cooperation' between major powers by reducing the uncertainty inherent in making international agreements. They lower transaction costs, provide information, and furnish mechanisms of enforcement. Order between states arises from the ability to reap joint gains arising from deliberately coordinated action, and international institutions empower states to reach their own egoistic ends.[42] This sits well with authors for whom 'world order' is increasingly maintained not by a balance of power or a hegemonic state but by international institutions, or "the rules that govern elements of world politics and the organizations that help implement those rules".[43] These regimes and institutions are not the product of power, but devices to solve common problems and increase the delivery of governance goods. The mutual interests that rising powers share with established powers therefore expand the scope for cooperation and integration.

The second logic underpinning the cooptation perspective emphasises the benefits for regional powers of the distinctly liberal principles underpinning the post-war institutions created by the West. This emphasises a more historical analysis and explanation of the distinctly liberal characteristic of the order created by the United States after its victory over alternative modes of international politics in the Second World War.[44] In this view, and in contrast to the functionalist logic of the first element of the cooptation hypothesis, international institutions precisely do constrain rather than enable state power and "lock states into patterns of cooperation that acquire their own imperatives".[45]

In contrast to the spoiler hypothesis, whereby the liberal world order and existing institutions are liable to decline with the rise of new regional powers, structural liberalism's cooptation perspective indicates that although the ruling club may expand to include non-Western powers and perhaps demote a few established states, the basic pattern of the existing institutional order will remain untouched.[46]

In this view, although the rise of developing countries will increasingly translate into change in the distribution of rewards from the world institutions for which the US and the West have been the "creators, owners, managers, and chief beneficiaries",[47] the relatively well entrenched and distinctly 'liberal' nature of today's institutions makes the existing order "easier to join and harder to overturn".[48] Existing institutions are relatively non-exclusionary and open to newcomers, with "a wide array of channels and mechanisms that allow the new rising states to join and to be integrated into the governance arrangements of the old order".[49]

---

42. Keohane, *After Hegemony, op. cit.*, p. 13.
43. Robert O. Keohane, *Power and Governance in a Partially Globalized World* (London: Routledge, 2002), p. 27.
44. G. John Ikenberry, *After Victory: Institutions, Strategic Restraint, and the Rebuilding of Order After Major Wars* (Princeton, NJ: Princeton University Press, 2001); G. John Ikenberry, *Liberal Order and Imperial Ambition: Essays on American Power and World Politics* (Cambridge: Polity Press, 2006).
45. Anthony McGrew, "Liberal Internationalism: Between Realism and Cosmopolitanism," in David Held and Anthony McGrew (eds.), *Governing Globalization* (Cambridge: Cambridge University Press, 2002), p. 275.
46. Ikenberry and Wright, *op. cit.*
47. *Ibid.*, p. 3.
48. *Ibid.*, p. 5.
49. *Ibid.*

In a further contrast to the balancing perspective, the cooptation hypothesis can draw on the thesis of a "democratic peace" which indicates that because liberal states are viewed as particularly peace-minded, "Instead of being seen as threatening and prompting balancing responses, concentrations of liberal power will create a liberal version of bandwagoning".[50] In contrast to China and Russia, the IBSA states seem to represent the best hopes for liberal cooptation based on common democratic polities and shared values. This implies that any obstacles to the cooptation of rising powers into existing institutions would likely come not from inherent conflict between rising and established powers but from 'blocking coalitions' of vested interests at a domestic level, who have something to lose from continued liberalisation or the adaptation to Western liberal ideas and ideologies.[51] In this view, "In more benign and consensual hegemonic orders, where restraints on hegemonic power are sufficiently developed... the expected value of balancing is lowered, and the incentives to pursue it are reduced".[52] Due to these unique properties, the international institutions created by the US and its allies after the Second World War provide them with an unprecedented degree of stability. They therefore have a remarkable ability to contain and overcome disturbances that might arise as a result of a shifting distribution of power, the emergence of new major powers, and even "changes in the goals and purposes of states".[53] This perspective therefore concludes that the incentives facing rising regional powers give rise to peaceful cooptation due to their stakes in the existing system.

The IBSA States' Redistributive Aspirations: Spoiling, Balancing, or being Coopted in International Institutions?

The phenomenon of rising regional powers can therefore be conceptualised through three diverging perspectives on their impact on global governance: balancing, spoiling, and cooptation. How well do the three perspectives reflect the redistributive programme of the IBSA states? The assumption of the argument developed here is that analysing the foreign policy orientations of rising regional powers needs to pay careful attention to variation across issue areas. Although rising states may pursue a 'grand strategy' in relation to their rivals, it is more likely that the interaction of rising and declining states gives rise to a complex configuration of competition and cooperation that is issue-specific, reflecting different class structures, societal interests, and domestic and international institutional structures.[54] This section therefore outlines to what extent the redistributive

---

50. Hurrell, "Hegemony, Liberalism and Global Order", *op. cit.*, p. 6.

51. *Ibid.*, pp. 7–8.

52. Ikenberry, *After Victory*, *op. cit.*, p. 28.

53. *Ibid.*, p. 45.

54. For Baldwin, "the notion of a single overall international power structure unrelated to any particular issue-area is based on a concept of power that is virtually meaningless". David Baldwin, "Power Analysis and World Politics: New Trends versus Old Tendencies", *World Politics*, Vol. 31, No. 2 (1979), p. 193. The issue-specific nature of foreign policy formation is also a strong emphasis of liberal international relations theory. See Andrew Moravcsik, "Taking Preferences Seriously: A Liberal Theory of International Politics", *International Organization*, Vol. 51, No. 4 (1997), pp. 513–553; Volker Rittberger, "Approaches to the Study of Foreign Policy Derived from International Relations Theories", *Tübinger Arbeitspapiere zur Internationalen Politik und Friedensforschung*, Working Paper No. 46 (Tübingen, 2004).

achievements and further aspirations of the IBSA states are adequately conceptualised by the three perspectives in the domains of trade, money and security.

Trade

Transboundary flows of goods, services and knowledge are governed by an increasingly institutionalised and constitutionalised network of agreements that cohere in a global regime complex for trade.[55] As rising powers such as IBSA integrate into world flows of trade, they can be expected to take an increasing interest not only in the distributional issues of their shares of world trade and with whom, but in shaping the institutional regime complex that governs these flows.

Given that trade is regarded as a classical positive-sum interaction, in which the best option for all states is liberalisation and mutually agreeing to forgo imposing tariffs through an international agreement, it is somewhat surprising, at least initially, that the area in which the spoiler perspective is most clearly applicable to rising regional powers is in the area of trade. Here the new assertiveness of developing country representatives from the IBSA states, later joined by China, has contributed to deadlock in WTO negotiations during the Doha Round.[56] At the same time, the balancing perspective could help to account for the IBSA states' attempts to offset the institutional and structural dominance of the developed countries in overseeing selective liberalisation of world trade through regionalised preferential trade agreements and increasing emphasis on traditional South-South linkages through technical cooperation and trade facilitation.

The WTO constitutes the central multilateral institution of global trade governance, and a considerable literature now exists on IBSA as a negotiating coalition at the WTO and an aspiring preferential trade area outside the remit of the WTO (PTA).[57] Trade has been one of the most prominent areas in which the

---

55. Kal Raustiala and David G. Victor, "The Regime Complex for Plant Genetic Resources", *International Organization*, Vol. 58, No. 2 (2004), pp. 277–309; Christina L. Davis, "Overlapping Institutions in Trade Policy", *Perspectives on Politics*, Vol. 7, No. 1 (2009), pp. 25–31; Stephen Gill, *Power and Resistance in the New World Order* (Houndmills: Palgrave Macmillan, 2003), pp. 131–135.

56. See especially Andrew Hurrell and Amrita Narlikar, "A New Politics of Confrontation? Brazil and India in Multilateral Trade Negotiations," *Global Society*, Vol. 20, No. 4 (2006), pp. 415–433; Amrita Narlikar, "New Powers in the Club: the Challenges of Global Trade Governance", *International Affairs*, Vol. 86, No. 3 (2010), pp. 717–728; Amrita Narlikar and Diana Tussie, "The G20 at the Cancun Ministerial: Developing Countries and their Evolving Coalitions in the WTO", *The World Economy*, Vol. 27, No. 7 (2004), pp. 947–966; Amrita Narlikar and Rorden Wilkinson, "Collapse at the WTO: A Cancun Post-Mortem", *Third World Quarterly*, Vol. 25, No. 3 (2004), pp. 447–460.

57. Debashis Chakraborty and Dipankar Sengupta, "IBSAC (India, Brazil, South Africa, China): A Potential Developing Country Coalition in WTO Negotiations", CSH Occasional Paper No. 18 (New Delhi: Centre de Sciences Humaines, 2006); Sanjay Kapoor, "Run IBSA, Run", *Hard News*, available: <http://www.hardnewsmedia.com/2010/05/3537>, (accessed 30 May 2011); Francis A. Kornegay, "IBSA: Toward a 'Gondwanan' Strategic Vision", *Synopsis*, Vol. 8, No. 2 (2006), pp. 11–14; Nagesh Kumar, *Trinity of the South: Potential of India-Brazil-South Africa Partnership* (New Delhi: Academic Foundation, and Research and Information for Developing Countries, 2008); Ray Marcelo, "India, Brazil and South Africa Sign Pact to Boost Trade", *Financial Times* (6 March 2004); Amancio de Oliveira, Janini Onuki, and Emmanuel De Oliveira, "Emerging Powers and Global Governance: The Case of IBSA", Paper presented at the International Studies Association 49th Annual Conference, San Francisco, 2008; Lakshmi Puri, *IBSA: An Emerging Trinity in the New Geography of International Trade* (New York: United Nations Conference on Trade and Development, 2007); Paulo Sotero (ed.), *Emerging Powers: India, Brazil and South Africa (IBSA) and the future of South-South Cooperation* (Washington, DC: Woodrow Wilson International Center for Scholars, 2009).

redistributive aspirations of the IBSA states have been targeted, with already significant results. The IBSA states have invested a great deal of diplomatic resources and political capital in developing greater developing country coordination in the negotiations of the Doha Development Round, in opposition to a Northern agenda focused on further extending 'behind the border' agreements concerning investment, competition policy, government procurement and technical issues of trade facilitation (the 'Singapore Issues'), while maintaining extensive barriers to trade in agriculture. This conflict between developed and developing countries, has been invigorated by the increased bargaining power and diplomatic weight of the rising powers, and came to a head in Cancún in 2003, when the 'G20' group of 22 developing countries in favour of agricultural liberalisation put up a coordinated stand, signalling a new politics of "confrontation" in trade negotiations.[58] Since this turning point most global powers seem to have focused their efforts outside the global multilateral system and have focused instead on regional and bilateral agreements, where great power interests are less bound by WTO procedures and allowing greater room for "mercantilist power plays".[59]

The first dimension of the impact of IBSA's redistributive aspirations in global trade governance concerns negotiations at the WTO. The IBSA states played a pivotal role in providing diplomatic leadership in prompting the formation of the G20 group of developing countries at the WTO, and boosted their own positions as the major developing country antagonists to the developed triad in negotiations. The creation of the G20 was particularly significant in this regard, which one Brazilian negotiator described as a "political statement" to the developed countries, while a representative of the Brazilian private sector said it "challenged not only the agricultural policies of the developed countries, but the legitimacy of the model adopted by those countries to negotiate multilateral fora, presenting their agreed position as a fait accompli to developing countries".[60] For the then foreign minister of Brazil, Celso Amorim, "I can state with conviction that the G-20 would not exist without IBSA".[61] Furthermore, underpinning the negotiation position of the IBSA countries, as well as China, is the fact that they are emerging as decisive drivers of global economic growth, equating to a stronger bargaining position at the WTO.[62] The spoiling capacity of the IBSA countries in tandem with other rising powers indicates that the redistributive aspirations of the rising regional powers are unlikely to be subsumed by hegemonic imposition.

The balancing dynamic of the IBSA approach to trade lies in countering the 'hub and spokes' model of international economic and political relations as fostered by the United States. This imperial strategy was formalised firstly under the Clintonite courting of the 'emerging markets' (which included all of the BRICS),[63] while the

---

58. Hurrell and Narlikar, *op. cit.*

59. Robert Hunter Wade, "Feature Review: The Globalizers, by Ngaire Woods", *New Political Economy*, Vol. 12, No. 1 (2007), p. 127.

60. Quoted in Pedro da Motta Viega, "Brazil and the G20 Group of Developing Countries", in Paul Gallagher, Patrick Low and Andrew Stoler (eds.), *Managing the Challenges of WTO Participation: 45 Case Studies* (Cambridge: Cambridge University Press, 2005), p. 115.

61. Celso Amorim, "The India-Brazil-South Africa Dialogue Forum and World Trade", in *The India-Brazil-South Africa Dialogue Forum*, (Brasilia: Ministry of External Relations, Republic of Brazil, 2006), p. 6.

62. Chakraborty and Sengupta, *op. cit.*, p. 74.

63. Alden and Vieira, *op. cit.*, p. 1082; Robert Chase, Emily Hill and Paul Kennedy (eds.), *The Pivotal States: A New Framework for U.S. Policy in the Developing World* (New York: Norton, 1999).

EU has engaged in building 'strategic partnerships' with all of the BRICS except Russia. In contrast, the IBSA Trilateral Forum and associated Trilateral Commission have focused on expanding trade between the IBSA states, by increasing elite business and government connections, sectoral cooperation and exchanges of expertise through a series of trilateral working groups, and introducing new transport linkages between the three countries.[64] This has been supplemented by the active pursuit of free trade agreements between Mercosur and India, Mercosur and SACU, and SACU and India, which are intended to lead to a future tri-continental free trade agreement between India, Mercosur and SACU, which would form the largest trade agreement in the developing world with potentially far-reaching implications for the emerging geography of world trade.[65]

The notion of 'soft balancing' through regional and South-South trade liberalisation may be an appropriate mode for understanding this response to Northern protectionism and trade regionalisation. Indeed, the expansion of an elaborate patchwork of regional trade agreements involving the emerging countries indicates the increasing importance of a global 'non-WTO' regime of trade agreements as the WTO remains deadlocked.[66] Likewise, Taylor identifies that the pursuit of an intra-IBSA free trade deal is part of the regional powers' attempts to foster a new trade geography, which reduces their trade dependence on the members of the G7, and "provide[s] alternative trading axes to the hitherto dominant North-South directions in trade".[67] While the limitations of the prospective gains from an intra-IBSA trade deal have been emphasised,[68] the traditional view that South-South trade agreements are a waste of time due to limited complementarities and small economic size is changing due to the economic rise of the BRICS and the differentiating global division of labour.[69] As trade between non-OECD countries constitutes an increasing share of global trade, political pressures to manage these flows through agreements can be expected to increase.[70] A recent UNCTAD report therefore concluded that comprehensive tariff reductions amongst the IBSA states could double their annual mutual trade levels, based on a common market of 1.2 billion people, US $1.8 trillion of GDP and trade of nearly US $600 billion. "This would make the IBSA partnership of immense strategic value not only in terms of multilateral trade negotiations, but also in terms of shaping the respective roles of IBSA member countries in global economic governance."[71]

---

64. Flemes, *op. cit.*, p. 413–415.

65. IBSA Trilateral Forum, "Brasilia Ministerial Communiqué, September 1, 2009", available: < http://www.ibsa-trilateral.org/index.php?option=com_content&task=view&id=53&Itemid=27 > (accessed 30 May 2011), p. 4. The Southern Common Market (Mercosur) includes Argentina, Brazil, Paraguay and Uruguay, while the South African Customs Union (SACU) includes Botswana, Lesotho, Namibia, South Africa and Swaziland.

66. Agata Antkiewicz and John Whalley, "BRICSAM and the non-WTO", *Review of International Organizations*, Vol. 1, No. 1 (2006), pp. 237–261.

67. Taylor, *op. cit.*, p. 51.

68. Ibid., p. 54; Lyal White, "IBSA Six Years On: Co-operation in a New Global Order", *Policy Briefing*, No. 8 (Johannesberg: South Africa Institute of International Affairs, 2009).

69. Scott McDonald and Dirk Willenbockel, "India, Brazil, South Africa and China: Is the South Big Enough?", Paper Presented at 11th Annual Conference on Global Economic Analysis, Helsinki, 2008.

70. Antkiewicz and Whalley, *op. cit.*

71. Lakshmi Puri, "IBSA: An Emerging Trinity in the New Geography of International Trade", *UNCTAD Policy Issues in International Trade and Commodities*, Study Series No. 35 (New York: UNCTAD, 2007), p. vii.

Rising regional powers have therefore embraced the logic of increasing South-South economic cooperation, i.e. a concerted attempt to overcome the fractured nature of South-South economic relations which are still structured around patterns of comparative advantage engendered by the historical legacy of the (imposed) colonial division of labour. There is remarkably little trade between Africa and the Americas, with both orienting themselves towards the Asian economic boom (trade between Africa and the Americas amounts to only one per cent of total South-South trade). Increased multilateral ties amongst developing regional powers therefore provide a response to the fact that the major part of South-South trade occurs among countries of the same region, with little interregional integration.[72] If current trends were left to continue, South Africa and Brazil would increasingly orient their economies towards trade with Asia while connections between their two continental regions languish. The concerted trilateral initiative to boost tricontinental trade between India, Brazil and South Africa can be accounted for precisely as a political intervention to prevent the further uneven distribution of global trade flows. As the South African trade minister recently put it, "Our membership of BRICS gives us huge opportunities to develop different patterns of trade relationships. We'll seek to building relationships among ourselves".[73] The corollary, however, is the stagnation of the Doha Round and declining relevance of the WTO.

In addition to these redistributive demands in terms of changing the global distribution of trade, the IBSA states have also called for the reform of the institutional structure of the WTO. This consists primarily in expanding developing country participation in the decisive 'Green Room' phases of trade negotiations. The IBSA Brasilia Declaration also called for 'improved' rules in the multilateral trade system.[74] This has already been partly successful, as seen in the shift from the old 'Quad' group of the US, EU, Canada and Japan, to the G4 group of the US, EU, India and Brazil. Nonetheless in June 2007 the Indian and Brazilian foreign ministers declared the G4 'dead' after repeated demands from the EU and US for liberalisation in services and industry. Indian Trade Minister Kamal Nath then referred negotiations back "for the full WTO membership".[75] Despite these critiques, IBSA state representatives have made clear their attachment to the existing basic principles and norms of the world trading order, while seeking to reform some of its more egregious selectivity, include developing countries more fully in its informal negotiation procedures, and perhaps to shift the global trade regime closer to one in which "development really mattered".[76] As a recent IBSA declaration noted:

---

72. Miho Shirotori and Ana Cristina Molina, "South-South Trade: The Reality Check", *UNCTAD Issues in New Geography of International Trade* (Geneva: UNCTAD, 2009), p. 4.

73. Rob Davies to reporters in Cape Town, 30 May 2011, as quoted in Robert Brand, "South Africa Won't Back Scaled-Down Doha Round, Davies Says", *Bloomberg* (30 May 2011), available: < http://www.businessweek.com/news/2011-05-30/south-africa-won-t-back-scaled-down-doha-round-davies-says.html> (accessed 9 June 2011).

74. IBSA Trilateral Forum, "Brasilia Declaration of the IBSA Trilateral Forum", June 2003, available: < http://www.ibsa-trilateral.org/index.php?option=com_content&task=view&id=48&Itemid=27> (accessed 30 May 2011).

75. "Brazil, India declare G4 Dead", *ABC News*, available: <http://www.abc.net.au/news/stories/2007/06/23/1959728.htm > , (accessed 30 May 2011).

76. Dani Rodrik, "The Global Governance of Trade as if Development Really Mattered", *Report Submitted to the UNDP* (New York: UNDP, 2001).

A development oriented, balanced and successful conclusion of the Round at an early date would bolster the credibility of the multilateral trading system in the face of increased protectionist pressures. In this respect, they expressed their concern over the excessive demands made on some developing countries without any indication of adequate additional concessions in favour of developing countries.[77]

Thus while the substance of the global trading regime is criticised, the WTO has avoided calls for fundamental revision, most likely because the consensus principle makes it subject to a status quo deadlock, underlining the IBSA states' preferences for no deal over a perceived illegitimate deal, while the Dispute Settlement Mechanism allows for an element of rights protection for developing countries. Thus while the IBSA states may have taken on a 'spoiler' role in trade, this is likely explained less by the logic of collective action and more by the selectivity and unbalanced structure of the world trade regime. Further, their pursuit of South-South cooperation and a preferential trade agreement between their respective regional trading blocs could be accommodated into a soft balancing perspective.

Money

IBSA states' redistributive programme has implications for the international organisation of credit and exchange in fields including official development aid, currency policy, and the Bretton Woods institutions.

First, IBSA states have lent their voices to the call for developed countries to stick to their commitments for contributing 0.7 per cent of their gross national products as official development aid, as well as calling for unconditional debt relief for the Highly Indebted Poor Countries,[78] thus contributing to pressure for relative redistribution at the inter-state level from North to South.

But these material 'relative gains' are subordinated to the discursive relative gains in prestige by their status as 'rising powers' catching-up on the first world, with democratic credentials to boot. While the IBSA states lend support to the least developed countries in advocating for more first world aid, they reaffirm their own positions as emerging economic successes stories with no need for developmental aid themselves.[79] A related concern for being treated with "respect"[80] attends the IBSA states' statement that South-South cooperation should not be seen as aid, characterised by donors and recipients, but as "a

---

77. IBSA Trilateral Forum, "Fourth Summit of Heads of State/Government Brasilia Declaration", April 2010, available: <www.ibsa-trilateral.org>, (accessed 30 May 2011), p. 4.

78. IBSA Trilateral Forum, "Brasilia Declaration of the IBSA Trilateral Forum", June 2003, available: < http://www.ibsa-trilateral.org/index.php?option=com_content&task=view&id=48&Itemid=27> (accessed 30 May 2011).

79. For example, in several high-profile natural disasters India has rejected aid as unnecessary, while examining the prospect of phasing out development aid in the longer-term. This is despite the Government of India's own estimation that 37 per cent of its population lives in poverty. See, Somini Sengupta, "Pride and Politics: India Rejects aid", *New York Times* (19 October 2005); Government of India Planning Commission, *Report of the Expert Group to Review the Methodology for Estimation of Poverty* (New Delhi: Government of India Planning Commission, 2009), p. 17.

80. Nel, *op. cit.*

common endeavour of peoples and countries of the South, a partnership among equals, and must be guided by the principles of respect for national sovereignty, national ownership and independence, equality, non-conditionality, non-interference in domestic affairs and mutual benefit".[81] The emphasis on non-conditionality means that rising regional powers are coming to be seen as obstacles to conditionality-driven Western attempts at spreading their own ideas of "good governance", and therefore challenging key Western developmental norms.

Second, the IBSA regional powers have also demonstrated a preference for a relative redistribution in global wealth through a change in the structure of the international monetary system. In Sanya in April 2011, the IBSA states joined with China and Russia at the BRICS summit in moving from using US dollars to their own currencies in intra-BRICS credit and grant transactions. At the same time, the head of the China Development Bank would begin loaning in yuan to the other BRICS countries as part of the overall effort to reduce the use US dollars in bilateral trade and investment.[82] Crucially, the rising powers declared their support for "the reform and improvement of the international monetary system, with a broad-based international reserve currency system providing stability and certainty. We welcome the current discussion about the role of the SDR in the existing international monetary system including the composition of SDR's basket of currencies".[83] This coincides with calls from the IMF for greater use of Special Drawing Rights (SDRs) instead of US dollars as reserve assets, while re-examining the basket of currencies of which SDRs are made up (currently limited to US dollars, euros, yen and British pounds). SDRs would need to be greatly expanded for them to become a viable reserve asset,[84] but given that the rising powers are expected to dominate the world economy within the next decades, a gradual shift away from US dollars as a store of value would reduce the US advantage of *seigniorage* and undermine US structural monetary power.[85] This has been accompanied by calls for better and deeper regulation of transnational capital flows, to subordinate them to developmental needs.[86]

---

81. IBSA Trilateral Forum, "Fourth Summit of Heads of State/Government Brasilia Declaration", April 2010, avaiable: <www.ibsa-trilateral.org>, (accessed 30 May 2011), p. 5.

82. "BRICS Give Credit to Local Currencies", South Africa Info, available: <http://www.southafrica.info/global/brics/brics-140411b.htm> (accessed 30 May 2011).

83. BRICS, "Sanya Declaration, 3rd BRICS Summit in Hainan, China", available: <http://netindian.in/news/2011/04/14/00012494/sanya-declaration-brics-leaders> (accessed 30 May 2011).

84. International Monetary Fund, *Enhancing International Monetary Stability: A Role for the SDR?* (Washington, DC: International Monetary Fund, 2011), p.1.

85. See Eric Helleiner, "Structural Power in International Monetary Relations", *EUI Working Papers*, No. 10 (Florence: European University Institute, 2005). Although the economic benefits of minting the world's reserve asset are debated, see Richard N. Cooper, "Prolegomena to the Choice of an International Monetary System", *International Organization*, Vol. 29, No. 1 (1975), pp. 69–73, the overall political and economic benefits cannot be dismissed, Jonathan Kirshner, "Dollar Primacy and American Power: What's at Stake?", *Review of International Political Economy*, Vol. 15, No. 3 (2008), pp. 418–438; and Kathleen McNamara, "A Rivalry in the Making? The Euro and International Monetary Power", *Review of International Political Economy*, Vol. 15, No. 3 (2008), pp. 441–443.

86. IBSA Trilateral Forum, "Brasilia Declaration, June 6, 2003", available: <http://www.ibsa-trilateral.org/index.php?option=com_content&task=view&id=48&Itemid=27> (accessed 30 May 2011); IBSA Trilateral Forum, "Delhi Agenda for Cooperation, March 5, 2004", available: <http://www.ibsa-trilateral.org/index.php?option=com_content&view=article&id=154&Itemid=86>, (accessed 30 May 2011); IBSA Trilateral Forum, "Delhi Summit Declaration, October 15, 2008", available: <http://www.itamaraty.gov.br/temas-mais-informacoes/temas-mais-informacoes/saiba-mais-ibas/documentos-emitidos-pelos-chefes-de-estado-e-de/3rd-ibsa-summit-declaration/view>

Third, at the institutional level, the Bretton Woods institutions have become a subject of rising regional powers' redistributive aspirations. The Bretton Woods institutions face challenges both from new powers and from broader changes that undermine their legitimacy even in their own narrow technocratic terms. For many in the developing world, these institutions have become identified with principles associated with market-driven poverty and even state breakdown.[87] What were once seen as technocratic interventions by the International Monetary Fund (IMF) to restore economic fundamentals based on impartial expertise are now widely seen as having aggravated economic difficulties and implemented policies favourable to Washington. Most rising powers have sought as much autonomy as possible from the IMF by setting up regional equivalents or simply stockpiling foreign reserves.[88] The rapid accumulation of foreign reserves was enabled by the broader absolute redistribution of economic resources to the emerging powers, but this also allows them to avoid the prospect of conditionality and the damage this would do to their prestige.

The participatory or input legitimacy of the Bretton Woods institutions in the eyes of developing countries has always been tempered by their plutocratic voting systems, which also serves to enforce a *de facto* US veto because of the requirement of an 85 per cent majority.[89] In fact the relative increase in tranche votes at the IMF has seen the voting rights of the developing world as a whole actually decrease since its creation, although the increased financial clout of the IBSA states and other emerging powers has also been translated into relative gains at the World Bank and IMF for them. Meeting in South Korea in November 2010, finance ministers and central bank governors of the G20 resolved to redistribute the voting powers of the IMF as well as the International Bank for Reconstruction and Development (IBRD) in favour of major emerging countries. This resulted in a further shift in voting shares for developing countries of 4.59 per cent, and was described by the IMF managing director as the most significant change to the governance of the IMF since its creation.[90]

One month earlier at the World Bank, China and India increased their voting rights at the IBRD branch of the World Bank, while those of the developing world as a whole have reached nearly a half at 47.19 per cent, which the Bank's President Robert Zoellick said better reflected a multipolar global economy.[91] At the same time, changes have occurred to the distribution of executive positions. For the first time in its history, both the World Bank Chief Economist and the three Managing Directors all came from developing countries, and a third seat

---

(accessed 30 May 2011); IBSA Trilateral Forum, "Fourth Summit of Heads of State/Government Brasilia Declaration, April 2010", available: <http://www.ibsa-trilateral.org/index.php?option=com_content&view=article&id=154&Itemid=86> (accessed 30 May 2011).

87. Peter Vale, "Engaging the World's Marginalized and Promoting Global Change: Challenges for the United Nations at Fifty", *Harvard International Law Journal*, Vol. 36, No. 2 (1995), pp. 283–294.

88. Ikenberry and Wright, *op. cit.*, p. 19.

89. John Glenn, "Global Governance and the Democratic Deficit: Stifling the Voice of the South", *Third World Quarterly*, Vol. 29, No. 2 (2008), pp. 217–238.

90. IMF Survey Online, "G-20 Ministers Agree 'Historic' Reforms in IMF Governance", available: <www.imf.org/external/pubs/ft/survey/so/2010/NEW102310A.htm> (accessed 30 May 2011).

91. World Bank Group, "Election of Third Sub-Saharan African Chair for World Bank Group Board", *Press Release No. 2011/126/EXT*, available: <http://web.worldbank.org/WBSITE/EXTERNAL/NEWS/0,contentMDK:22730003~pagePK:64257043~piPK:437376~theSitePK:4607,00.html> (accessed 30 May 2011).

for Sub-Saharan African countries was added to the World Bank Group's Board of Executive Directors, which resulted in developing countries holding the majority of seats at the Executive Directors' table. For Robert Zoellick, "The voices of developing countries are vital to delivering effective development and to reflecting the realities of today's world".[92] Nonetheless, not all moves by the rising powers have been successful, with the IBSA states and China and Russia being notably unsuccessful in ending the European prerogative over the leadership of the IMF in 2011, despite their stated preferences for doing so.

In contrast to the issue-area of trade, the IBSA states approaches to international institutions in the domain of money and finance are clearly at odds with a spoiling approach. Rather, these powers call for greater intergovernmental cooperation and regulation in order to limit development-unfriendly instability in global finance.[93] At the same time, cooptation is reflected in calls for reform of the global financial architecture that are interpreted so as to conform to the basic institutional architecture and their neoliberal norms, while seeking a redistribution of voting rights and leadership positions in the Bretton Woods institutions in their own favour. Calls to boost the role of alternative currencies to US dollars and redenominate SDRs amount to a balancing of the structural privilege attendant on the status of the dollar as the *de facto* world reserve currency. The cooptation orientation is complemented by balancing behaviour.

Security

In the area of the international institutions governing world security we see again that the three perspectives on rising powers' orientation to international institutions are not competitive, but rather complementary. State representatives of the IBSA states have of course invested enormous political capital into the goal of reforming the UN Security Council with themselves as leading contenders as 'representatives' of their respective regions, although South Africa cannot do so explicitly due to commitments within the African Union. Rather than shunning and therefore 'spoiling' this institution, the IBSA states want to be integrated and coopted into it, which would inevitably balance the influence of the established group of permanent members. The IBSA states have made no secret of their aspirations in this regard, declaring at every IBSA Trilateral Forum the goal of making the Security Council more "democratic, legitimate, representative and responsive" by including more developing countries from Africa, Asia, and Latin America as permanent members.[94] To this end, India and Brazil have also joined forces with Germany and Japan as part of the G4 in endorsing each other's bids for permanent membership. At the third BRICS summit in Sanya, the IBSA states even secured some support from China and Russia, with them

---

92. World Bank Group, "Election of Third Sub-Saharan African Chair for World Bank Group Board", *Press Release No. 2011/126/EXT*, available: <http://web.worldbank.org/WBSITE/EXTERNAL/NEWS/0,contentMDK:22730003~pagePK:64257043~piPK:437376~theSitePK:4607,00.html> (accessed 30 May 2011).

93. BRICS, "Sanya Declaration", *op. cit.*; IBSA Trilateral Forum, "Brasilia Declaration" (2003), *op. cit.*; IBSA Trilateral Forum, "Delhi Agenda for Cooperation", *op. cit.*; IBSA Trilateral Forum, "Delhi Summit Declaration", *op. cit.*; IBSA Trilateral Forum, "Brasilia Declaration" (2010), *op. cit.*

94. IBSA Trilateral Forum, "Brasilia Declaration" (2003), *op. cit.*, p. 1; "Delhi Summit Declaration", *op. cit.*, pp.1–2; "Brasilia Declaration", (2010), p. 1.

formally recognising the need to reform the UN and the Security Council, in order to make it more "representative and effective". The BRICS declaration signalled (vague) support for the IBSA states as having an important 'status' in international affairs, declaring that they "understand and support their aspiration to play a greater role in the UN", but falling short of endorsing permanent Security Council membership.[95]

This is consistent with the regional rising powers' insistence on an inter-governmental, UN-based vision for the future world order. The rising regional powers often articulate a desire to strengthen aspects of international institutions with an egalitarian redistribution of political decision-making authority, while at the same time championing their own case for special representation. Rising powers tend to equate a more equitable multilateralism with their own relative elevation.[96] Most rising powers see the UN General Assembly and its related institutions as more legitimate and representative because they adhere to a one state, one vote procedure, and therefore restrict the ability of Western countries to dominate the agenda or to get their way in the endgame.

This stands in contrast to the selective humanitarianism of established powers. The United States has been the power most likely to favour intrusive interventionism by the UN Security Council, while the European Union has been the most consistent champion of new norms, which emphasise the legitimacy of international institutions in defending human rights and favouring conditional ideas of states sovereignty. US-led interventions with or without a UN mandate have meant that international institutions have been associated with selective rather than impartial application of the rules. The identification of international institutions with the interests of Western states undermines their legitimacy and reinforces the scepticism of the IBSA states and others to the authority of international institutions and new norms of liberal interventionism and majoritarian decision-making. In contrast to the European Union, new powers tend to favour national sovereignty as the primary norm of international society.

Russia and China are identified as the major representatives of the traditional Westphalian view, but what is more interesting is the role played by major democratic powers such as the IBSA states. As a European Council on Foreign Relations policy paper noted recently, while the IBSA states should be "natural partners for Europe", the conflict over the basic norms of the UN and the security system means that they end up clashing with the EU. "They do not feel they are accorded the respect and organisational status they deserve, and thus prefer to stand with the G77 or regional groups as a way to increase their leverage."[97] While not identified completely with the "axis of sovereignty", India and South Africa are two of the most consistent critics of selective interventionism and defenders of third world sovereignty.[98] Far from representing a case of cooptation into the values

---

95. BRICS, "Sanya Declaration", *op. cit.*

96. Nel and Stephen, *op. cit.*; Stefan Schirm, "Leaders in Need of Followers: Emerging Powers in Global Governance", *European Journal of International Relations*, Vol. 16, No. 2 (2009), pp. 197–221.

97. Richard Gowan and Franziska Brantner, *A Global Force for Human Rights? An Audit of European Power at the UN* (London: European Council on Foreign Relations, 2008), p. 16.

98. Leaked American diplomatic cables refer to India, Brazil, and South Africa (along with Egypt and Pakistan) as countries which "routinely oppose the United States in multilateral debates [at the UN] despite strong bilateral ties to the U.S.". See Wikileaks Cable 66945, "Pak-US Ties Not Reflected in Multi-Lateral Fora", *The Hindu*, available: < www.thehindu.com/news/the-india-cables/the-cables/article2042826.ece> (accessed 5 May 2012).

of the dominant powers, rising regional powers tend to side with each other. In the UN General Assembly, the positions of China and Russia on human rights issues typically attract more votes than the EU or US.[99]

At one and the same time, the IBSA states' desire for integration into the UN Security Council through permanent representation seems to reflect the cooptation hypothesis, but this is a far cry from integration into the transnational liberal "security community",[100] which would signify the idealised form of cooptation. As the regional powers become more influential in this forum, they are likely to pull it back from the selective interventionism and consistent double standards adopted by powers such as the US. Where IBSA states are successful at redistributing seats in the UN Security Council in their favour, this is likely to exacerbate the tension between the increasing political authority of international institutions and the principle of non-intervention.[101]

Conclusion

How do these findings relate to the broader question of the impact of the IBSA states' general aspirations for international institutions? There is strong variation across issue areas. The impact in trade has contributed towards deadlock at the WTO and therefore conforms to the spoiler perspective, while greater South-South cooperation and the pursuit of trade agreements with other Southern and rising powers reflects a balancing logic. The rising powers are committed to the rules-based system of the multilateral trade regime, but resist further liberalisation in the absence of greater concessions from developed countries. Changes in distributional outcomes in the organisation of credit and money, as well as procedural reforms in international financial institutions, reflect a reformist project that is, however, restricted to the bounds of existing institutions, substantiating a cooptation process. Meanwhile, IBSA states have oriented themselves towards gaining permanent Security Council seats, an aspiration traditionally associated with cooptation, while siding *against* the established powers over the regulative norms of the global security governance. This reflects both the aspirations for enhanced global prestige associated with this "ultimate prestige prize in international politics",[102] as well as active resistance to ham-fisted attempts of the United States to pioneer new norms of pre-emptive war and selective interventionism, or more subtle European attempts to foster notions of conditional sovereignty.[103] This no doubt also relates to the desire of post-colonial states for respect as full members of the society of states with sovereign equality.[104]

While the increasing authority of international institutions has become an object of concern for the IBSA states in the area of security, the opposite has been the case in the economic domains of trade and money, where stronger regulation and

---

99. Gowan and Brantner, *op. cit.*
100. Karl Deutsch, *Political Community and the North Atlantic Area* (Princeton, NJ: Princeton University Press, 1957); Thomas Risse, "US Power in a Liberal Security Community", in G. John Ikenberry (ed.), *America Unrivalled: The Future of the Balance of Power* (Ithaca, NY: Cornell University Press, 2002), pp. 260–283.
101. Zürn and Stephen, *op. cit.*, p. 97.
102. Philip Nel, Dirk Nabers and Melanie Hanif, this issue.
103. Hurrell, "Hegemony, Liberalism and Global Order", *op. cit.*, p. 6; Flemes, *op cit.*, p. 409.
104. Nel, *op. cit.*

institutions are preferred and which are seen as requiring greater developing country involvement. Overall, a complex image emerges where the IBSA powers are integrating into existing institutions while attempting to utilise their new-found influence to pursue an institutionally reformist (or limited revisionist) agenda, and even-out some of the power imbalances favouring the developed North within these institutions.[105] The approaches of contemporary rising regional powers are therefore difficult to comprehensively encapsulate through any of the traditional conceptual perspectives, whose foreign policy orientations are highly differentiated across institutional sub-systems, and sometimes embody competing logics of behaviour.

Accounting for this behaviour will therefore have to move beyond the traditional approaches to rising powers. Consistently, the commitment of rising states to international regimes has been analysed as if participation is an indicator of acquiescence. Studies in this vein see 'separation' or efforts to 'overturn' international institutions as counter-posed to the strategy of involvement,[106] wherein a state's satisfaction with the rules of a world order can be measured simply by its participation in international organisations.[107] Instead, this study of the IBSA states indicates an alternative orientation: integration in order to change international institutions. In this orientation, the IBSA states chart the middle course between the Charybdis of liberal cooptation and the Scylla of counter-hegemonic spoiling of existing institutions.

The findings of this and the other contributions to this special issue therefore confirm that the rise of Southern regional powers will occasion a shift in the procedures and outcomes of global governance favouring redistribution between the states of the North and South.[108] In contrast to previous rising powers, the IBSA states are multilateral activists strongly involved in international institutions, which they try to reform from the inside in their own favour. Their further integration into the institutions of global governance can be expected to perpetuate a process of restructuring which will be forced, even on a limited functional logic, to increasingly consider the needs of emerging developing countries. In this respect even Goldman Sachs can endorse the integration of new powers into the fold of global economic governance.[109] This gives ample reason to conclude that an understanding of the outlooks and preferences of rising regional powers will be increasingly important as they shape the contours of the emerging world order.

---

105. Nel and Stephen, *op.cit.*; Taylor, *op. cit.*; Zürn and Stephen, *op. cit.* See also similar conclusions regarding China in Gregory Chin, "China's Rising Institutional Influence", in A.S. Alexandroff and A.F. Cooper (eds.), *Rising States, Rising Institutions* (Waterloo: Center for International Governance Innovation and Brookings Institution Press, 2010), pp. 83–104.

106. Alastair Iain Johnston, "Is China a Status Quo Power?", *International Security*, Vol. 27, No. 4 (2003), pp. 5–56, p. 11; Jeffrey W. Legro, "What China Will Want: The Future Intentions of a Rising Power", *Perspectives on Politics*, Vol. 5, No. 3 (2007), pp. 515–534, p. 517.

107. Steve Chan, "Can't Get No Satisfaction? The Recognition of Revisionist States", *International Relations of the Asia-Pacific*, Vol. 4, No. 2 (2004), pp. 207–238.

108. See also Leslie Elliott Armijo, "The BRICs Countries (Brazil, Russia, India, and China) as Analytical Category: Mirage or Insight?", *Asian Perspective*, Vol. 31, No. 4 (2007), pp. 7–42.

109. Goldman Sachs, *op. cit.*, p. 5.

Rising States and Distributive Justice: Reforming International Order in the Twenty-First Century

MARCO VIEIRA

Contrary to predominantly materialist accounts of the impact and implications of rising powers in shaping the global order, the present study explores how ideas related to South-South solidarity formed the interests and directed the collective actions of emerging states. It specifically looks at attempts by India, Brazil and South Africa (IBSA), through their trilateral development assistance mechanism, the IBSA Fund, to challenge traditional normative frameworks of best behaviour associated to Western/liberal development models. I argue that contemporary South-South initiatives in general and the India, Brazil and South Africa partnership in particular, are promoting changes in the current political-normative configuration of international relations. Unlike South-South coalitions of the early post-colonial era, such as the Non-Alignment Movement (NAM) and the G77, when newly independent states in Africa and Asia had moral leverage but were economically weak, leading Southern states have achieved economic gains that have significantly raised their normative pull. However, their actual impact cannot be fully understood detached from the historical process by which Southern norms were first created and that later guided the foreign policy agendas of these emerging powers. This article shows the resilience of perceptions, values and ideas, which have been translated into conceptions of 'distributive justice' promoted by Southern powers through initiatives such as IBSA.

> A consensus founded upon the great powers alone, that does not take into account the demands of the Asian, African and Latin American countries, who represent the majority of states and of the world's population, cannot be expected to endure. (Hedley Bull)[1]

This article builds upon the premise that ideas matter in understanding the role of rising states in current global politics. The ideational legacy of South-South activism is a relevant and uncharted dimension of the current academic debate on emerging powers. I argue that contemporary South-South initiatives in general and the India, Brazil and South Africa partnership (IBSA) in particular, are promoting changes in the current political-normative configuration of international relations. Unlike South-South coalitions of the early post-colonial era, such as the Non-Alignment Movement (NAM) and the G77, when newly independent

---

*An earlier version of this paper was presented at the 4th Regional Powers Network Conference held in Stellenbosch, South Africa, 6–7 September 2010. I am grateful to conference's participants for their feedback. I would also like to thank the anonymous reviewers whose comments have strengthened this article greatly.

1. Hedley Bull, *The Anarchical Society* (Basingstoke: Palgrave Macmillan, 2002), p.303.

states in Africa and Asia had moral leverage but were economically weak, leading Southern states have achieved economic gains that significantly raised their normative pull. However, their actual impact cannot be fully understood detached from the historical process by which Southern norms were first created and later guided the foreign policy agendas of these emerging powers. This article shows the resilience of perceptions, values and ideas, which have been translated into conceptions of *distributive justice* promoted by Southern powers through initiatives such as IBSA.

The last 10 years have witnessed a remarkable emergence of academic and policy work on the new powers and their South-South coalitions. Since 2001, following the publication of Goldman Sachs' influential report on Brazil, Russia, India and China (BRICs), and with particular intensity since the establishment of the G20, as a result of the unified and confrontational stance presented by developing countries at the 2003 Cancún Ministerial Conference, a proliferation of authors have begun to explore the likely impact of new Southern powers on the international economic/political order. Although these accounts cover a wide range of diverse research inquiries, they are firmly placed in the analytical categories given by either liberal institutionalist or realist approaches to international relations. The former explore issues related to conditions for inclusion of key Southern states in the exclusive group of Western great powers and the institutions they control. They also focus on South-South diplomatic negotiating strategies, bargaining coalitions, and the individual and collective behaviour of Southern powers within key multilateral settings.[2] The latter look at soft balancing strategies, the role of emerging powers as regional hegemons and changes in the configuration of structural power given the global ascendancy of emerging states such as China, India, Brazil and Russia.[3] Generally, they all assume that the rise of Southern states is dependent upon their adaptation to and acceptance of the norms and decision-making structures of liberal internationalism.[4]

The recent literature on Southern powers mostly dismisses the long-standing links of these states with the normative agenda of the South and the issues that identify them with the wider struggles and moral claims of post-colonial nations regarding a radical reform of international governance structures. Unlike these perspectives, I argue that liberal solidarist norms and the traditional global governance structures they legitimise are under challenge from a coterie of influential developing nations. The underlying and long-term aspect of this challenge, which cuts across issues ranging from nuclear proliferation to the

---

2. Andrew Hurrell and Amrita Narlikar, "A New Politics of Confrontation? Brazil and India in Multilateral Trade Negotiations", *Global Society*, Vol. 20, No. 4 (2006), pp. 415–433; Chris Alden and Marco Vieira "The New Diplomacy of the South: South Africa, Brazil, India and Trilateralism", *Third World Quarterly*, Vol. 6, No. 7 (2005), pp. 1077–1095; Andrew Cooper, Timothy Shaw and Agatha Antkiewicz, "Global and/or Regional Development at the Start of the 21st Century? China, India and South Africa", *Third World Quarterly*, Vol. 28, No. 7 (2007), pp. 1255–1270.

3. Andrew Hurrell, "Hegemony, Liberalism and Global Order: What Space for Would-Be Great Powers?", *International Affairs*, Vol. 82, No. 1 (2006), pp. 1–19; Daniel Flemes, "Emerging Middle-Powers' Soft Balancing Strategy: State and Perspectives of the IBSA dialogue Forum", *Working Paper*, No. 57 (Hamburg: GIGA, 2007).

4. John Ikenberry, "The Rise of China and the Future of the West: Can the Liberal System Survive?", *Foreign Affairs*, Vol. 87, No. 1 (2008), pp. 23–37; Zakaria Fareed, *The Post-American World and the Rise of the Rest* (London: Penguin Books, 2009); Amrita Narlikar, *New Powers: How to Become One and How to Manage Them* (London: C Hurst & Co, 2010).

management of the global economy, is the issue of *distributive justice*. India and Brazil, for example, have traditionally been outspoken critics of Western-dominated international power structures, especially within the United Nations, and the lack of Northern commitment to economic and social development in the South. The proactive stance of these countries' diplomacies on issues related to peace, development and disarmament was realised in initiatives such as the New International Economic Order (NIEO), the Non-Aligned movement and the G77.[5] In this sense, the IBSA partnership follows a long tradition in South-South coordination, aiming at revising international institutions and norms according to well-established ideological/moral arguments.

I use the concept of distributive justice loosely. For the purpose of the present analysis, it refers to the contestation by the most influential Southern states of the 'unjust' or 'unequal' distribution of wealth, influence and security in a number of dimensions of international politics. According to these countries' perceptions, the structure and management of global governance reflects a particular normative/power hierarchy, which reifies and legitimises the hegemony of Western powers. The empirical focus is on the role of the IBSA partnership – and its individual members – as a provider of development assistance to poor countries. The aim is to understand the normative impact of the rise of these new donors and development partners on traditional development models established by Northern donors.[6] Despite the self-serving economic and political aims of IBSA states and other Southern donors, they share a common identity with their recipients of development assistance, coming from historical experiences with colonialism and their shared interest in reforming global governance structures according to principles of South-South solidarity. The current aggressive expansion of Southern powers' economic interests and normative agendas in developing states in Asia, Africa and Latin America has already created alternative international mechanisms, like the IBSA Trust Fund and the Chinese Official Development Assistance, that challenge conventional Western modes of development co-operation. Woods, for example, notes that:

> The world of development assistance is being shaken by the power shift occurring across the global economy. Emerging economies are quietly beginning to change the rules of the game. China, the United Arab Emirates, Saudi Arabia, Korea, Venezuela, India, Kuwait and Brazil, among others, have been increasing their aid to poorer countries. They are giving aid on terms of their choosing.[7]

It is important to mention at the outset that the central argument presented here does not put emphasis on the alleged ambiguity of leading Southern states' model

---

5. Joao Augusto de Araujo Castro "The United Nations and the Freezing of the International Power Structure", *International Organization*, Vol. 26, No. 1 (1972), pp. 158–166.

6. The notions of Northern donors and Western donors are used here interchangeably. They refer to the developed countries, who are members of the OECD's Development Assistance Committee (DAC), and have their contributions to development assistance anchored in Western liberal values such as democratic rule and human (civil) rights. For more on the composition, goals and financial pledges of OECD's DAC, see, Peter Kragelund, "The Return of Non-DAC Donors to Africa: New Prospects for African Development?", *Development Policy Review*, Vol. 26, No. 5 (2008), pp. 555–584.

7. Ngaire Woods, "Whose Aid? Whose Influence? China, Emerging Donors, and the Silent Revolution in Development Assistance", *International Affairs*, Vol. 84, No. 6 (2008), p. 1205.

of development assistance, even though it is acknowledged as a relevant aspect of these countries' involvement in the developing world.[8] Moreover, the article neither qualifies nor compares the distinctive belief systems and moral values behind different approaches to development assistance from traditional and new donors. Instead, the analytical focus is on the claim that a normative framework based on principles of 'distributive justice' has (re-)emerged as a significant alternative to conventional Northern-led development models. Finally, a note on concepts is in order. The interchangeable use in this article of the notions of ideational, moral, principled and normative refers to the shared systems of inter-subjective meaning that historically have organised, constrained and animated the foreign policies of Southern states. These ideas are associated with their long-standing claim for 'distributive justice' in international relations. As shown later, the substantive content of 'distributive justice', as an underlying notion informing IBSA states' foreign policies, is based on the Bandung principles first established in the historic Asian-African Conference of 1955.

The paper is divided in four sections. After this introduction, I examine different conceptions of order and justice in international relations. It is followed by an historical exploration of change in the international order culminating with the current rise of Southern powers in global politics. The third section deals with distributive justice as a unifying idea around which IBSA states built a common political agenda in international affairs. More specifically, I assess the IBSA Trust Fund as a trilateral mechanism aimed at promoting a new model of development cooperation based on the principles of South-South solidarity. Finally, in the conclusions, I sum up the argument, showing the growing influence of IBSA states in changing patterns of relationships with Northern powers.

Order and Justice in International Relations

This section identifies and critically reviews three broadly defined approaches to the relationship between justice and order in international politics:

- First, there is an exploration of cosmopolitan and liberal perspectives that claim the universal validity of Western values, institutions and economic models. They generally assert that the strengthening of liberal international institutions will inevitably lead to a just and stable international order based on a moral system of rules agreed by all members of the international society.

---

8. China's foreign aid policies in Africa have been harshly criticised for not complying with what are considered 'good practices' by the international development community. For more on this, see, Naim Moises, "Rogue Development Aid", *The New York Times* (15 February 2007). Similarly, some authors have noted that India's decisions to provide development assistance are associated with other less altruistic interests, such as diplomatic influence, access to natural resources and markets for Indian goods. The Indian government's refusal to sever cooperation and trade agreements with the Burmese Junta is one such example. For more on this, see, Subhash Agrawal, *Emerging Donors in Development Assistance: The India Case*, Presented to the International Development Research Centre, Government of Canada, December 2007, available: < http://web.idrc.ca/uploads/user-S/12441474461Case_of_India.pdf> (accessed 20 June 2011). It is worth noting, however, that the main argument presented here does not intend to evaluate the sincerity of donors' moral commitments. As further explained later, tensions/contradictions between moral values and the imperatives of economic development and security are a common (and rather expected) trend in the foreign policies of both Northern and Southern states.

- It is followed by the realist emphasis on economic statecraft and national interest. Realists identify an inherent incompatibility between the values of order (peace and security) and justice (human rights and economic/social development). For them, order, understood mostly in terms of balance of power, should have priority over justice in international relations.
- Finally, critical approaches to distributive justice based on a critique of Western dominance/ideology are examined. Broadly, this view asserts that distributive justice based on economic development and sovereign equality should be the overarching value in international politics even if it will lead to further international disorder and later readjustment to a new world system or historic bloc.

It is worth mentioning that this particular categorisation is approximate and it does not imply a rigidly defined and mutually exclusive set of ideas. What I intend to demonstrate by outlining and discussing these different theoretical positions is how Southern states have combined, at times conflictingly, aspects of these three approaches to justify their views on the reform of global governance structures. The conventional academic work on emerging/middle/pivotal powers draws almost exclusively on realist and liberal institutionalist approaches. It has nonetheless failed to notice ideational and moral motivations behind initiatives such as IBSA. In this sense, the term 'South', 'Southern' or 'South-South solidarity' defines a source of shared identity among developing states which is reified by the continuous formation of Southern coalitions, whose founding rationales were informed by a persistent critique of the global order.[9]

Potent moral claims, spanning the period from decolonisation struggles in the aftermath of WWII into Cold War interventionism in developing countries and the more recent socio-economic impact of IMF's structural reforms in Latin America, Africa and Asia, have provided a rallying point for solidarity and activism. Moreover, the solidified inequities of international institutions and regimes from the UN's Security Council to the IMF, GATT/WTO and the World Bank, the unjust environmental toll posed upon developing states as a result of Northern-promoted industrialisation, and the parochial application of Western universalism through military intervention, have also underpinned the shared experiences and common concerns of Southern nations.[10] I argue that these normative elements, which are analytically packed together in this article under the concept of 'distributive justice', have traditionally permeated and consistently legitimised South-South cooperation initiatives from the creation of the Non-Aligned Movement (NAM) and G77 to contemporary arrangements such as IBSA. In this regard, and without denying the powerful economic and geopolitical constraints that have historically pulled leading Southern states apart, this article is essentially concerned with the understudied ideational elements that have brought them together.

Cosmopolitan/Liberal Approaches

Despite the great variety of liberal approaches to international order, they generally fall into two main categories, derived from the work of two of the most

---

9. Chris Alden, Sally Morphet and Marco Vieira, *The South in World Politics* (Basingstoke: Palgrave Macmillan, 2010), p. 3.
10. *Ibid.*, p. 4.

influential liberal philosophers, Hugo Grotius and Immanuel Kant. The former greatly influenced English School authors in international relations theory, particularly Martin Wight and Hedley Bull, and their work on a rule-based international society. The latter provided the philosophical and ethical foundations for contemporary authors working on the idea of global government beyond the inter-state system.[11]

Grotius and his followers promoted the view that international anarchy should be made subject to law rather than fear.[12] States should be bound by rules and their relationship should be based not only on conflict but mostly defined by regulated cooperation. This system would most likely lead to a highly institutionalised international system, nevertheless still centred on nation-states as its main legal authority. Also borrowing from a Grotian tradition, complex interdependence scholars assert that international institutions are catalysts for inter-state cooperation and a fundamental feature of world politics. They perceive institutions as impartial frameworks of norms and rules created to facilitate negotiation and decrease political uncertainty.[13] This framework put forth the idea that 'international justice' will be only achieved through the unrestricted incorporation of all states, regardless of their particular national cultures, religions or political ideologies into the liberal institutions of global governance.

Hedley Bull's idea of 'ideological homogeneity' defines the second model of liberal internationalism under scrutiny here. Bull writes, "the exponents of political ideologies frequently maintain that the triumph of their doctrines throughout the state system as whole would reduce the sources of war and conflict, and lead to a more orderly world".[14] Kant prescribed an international system based on universal morality and the gradual progress towards a system of perpetual peace among a global federation of nations. According to his moral philosophy, war of conquest should be a legitimate tool to reform 'unjust' states that violate the fundamental rights of the citizens. Bull noticed that generally the two models of liberal international order were integrated into single international doctrines such as in the case of Woodrow Wilson's hopes that the League of Nations should be also a league of liberal democracies. It can be also exemplified by Francis Fukuyama's 'end of history' thesis and the idea that liberal internationalism had prevailed after the end of the Cold War as the only viable world doctrine for international order and its institutional frameworks. The US foreign policy doctrine under George W. Bush was also embedded in a neo-conservative liberal ideology that envisaged world peace as a result of (forcefully) spreading liberal values such as democracy, human rights and trade liberalisation into illiberal societies. The current UN doctrine of the Responsibility to Protect (R2P), which controversially sanctions external military intervention in some situations of mass atrocities, is clearly indebted to this tradition in Western liberal thought.

These liberal readings of international order do not take into account the processes by which states in the South negotiate their membership in the international

---

11. David Held, *Democracy and the Global Order: From the Modern State to Cosmopolitan Governance* (Stanford: Stanford University Press, 1995).

12. Michael Doyle, *Ways of War and Peace* (New York and London: W. W. Norton & Company, 1997), p. 258.

13. Robert Keohane and Joseph Nye, *Power and Interdependence* (Harrisonburg: R. R. Donnelley and Sons Company, 1989).

14. Bull, *op. cit.*, p. 237.

society. They assume post-colonial states as passive, rather than reactive, recipients of Western norms and only those capable of incorporating them should be accepted as full members of the international community. Furthermore, Southern states have consistently argued that, despite its humanistic credentials, liberal internationalism has not adequately brought about economic and social distributive justice into the wider international society, which includes newly independent states in Africa and Asia. As shown later, one key feature of contemporary international politics is the growing pluralism of norm-creating processes. In this sense, the new role of Southern powers in articulating norms and values, which are then assimilated in international governance structures, demonstrates their capacity to mount a revisionist challenge to Western norms and institutions.

These rising powers' conceptions of international order and distributive justice have already affected key areas of global governance, namely in multilateral deliberations to tackle climate change, where the group formed by Brazil, India, South Africa and China (BASIC) has played a leading role, and in the G20 negotiations to establish a reformed global financial system. Similarly, as shown below, IBSA has successfully set up, together with other Southern powers, a new paradigm for development assistance and foreign investment in poor countries.

Realism

The realist tradition understands states as autonomous and independent units with a sharp instinct for survival in a volatile international system. In this kind of conflictive and violent international context, global morality, and its corollary, distributive justice, are either unattainable or detrimental to the security and economic welfare of individual states. This particular view assumes states as self-contained economic and political units in which nationals assume moral priority over foreigners and issues of equality and distributive justice can only be legitimate at the domestic level. Conversely, the international system is a space of conflict and competition whereby the states' main goal is to protect and advance the interests of their particular political communities.

According to realist assumptions on structural power, normative/ideational motivations are only epiphenomenal in understanding the behaviour of South-South coalitions such as IBSA. As Krasner puts it, referring to third world's international behaviour during the Cold War: "Third World states want power and control as much as wealth. One strategy to achieve this objective is to change the rules of the game in various international issue areas". For some realist authors, the current shift in economic and political power from the West to the emerging economies of the South, which has been exacerbated by the global financial crisis of 2008–2009, could be understood in terms of historical cycles of hegemonic ascendancy and decline in the inter-state power structure.[15]

Liberal/cosmopolitan authors perceive the inter-state system as strongly bound by common understandings and conceptions of values and principles. Yet, some realist authors claim that the prevailing norms and institutions that any international society relies on reflect the particular domestic preferences and moral systems of the major powers. The material conditions the realists describe

---

15. Robert Gilpin, *War and Change in World Politics* (Cambridge: Cambridge University Press, 1981); Paul Kennedy, *The Rise and Fall of the Great Powers* (New York: Random House, 1987).

explain the dominance of a particular set of international norms in any given historical period. According to this logic, the contemporary changing balance of global material power could represent the opening of new political spaces for the normative reform of international relations based on the aspirations and values of Southern great powers and their coalitions.

Contemporary realist and liberal scholars perceive the rising clout of so-called 'illiberal' powers in quite distinct ways; even if they generally agree that the stability of the liberal international order depends largely on US hegemonic leadership. According to the theory of democratic peace, the expansion of a "zone of liberal democratic regimes" towards illiberal states should be intrinsically linked to the promotion of Western interests.[16] Following the September 11 attacks, the Bush administration started to systematically articulate, quite often inconsistently, the realist precept of military strength with this liberal internationalist idea to justify two controversial wars and a unilateral foreign policy of global war on terror.[17] For Kagan, the emergent power of "authoritarian" states such as China and Russia, poses a significant threat to the expansion of the "liberal pacific union". Kagan foresees a new ideological division of the world between conventional liberal democracies and varied forms of autocratic regimes, which are skilfully adapting their undemocratic political systems to Western capitalist modes of economic development.[18] John Ikenberry, on the other hand, concedes that liberal internationalism faces a crisis of authority as a result of the US' declining hegemonic dominance. Ikenberry argues, however, that the US leadership crisis does not fundamentally threaten the liberal institutional/normative apparatus of global governance that has been developing since the end of WWII.[19]

These arguments clearly underpin the analysis of Southern powers. Their basic assumption is that countries such as Brazil, Russia, India, China and South Africa will face growing pressure to adapt to the normative demands of the international society. They perceive the soft power of particular Southern ideas/ideologies/cultures, which are often embedded in the foreign policy rationale of Southern governments, as stumbling blocks to their full incorporation in the liberal international community. The clash between universal norms and particular cultures is clear in debates over human rights violations in developing countries, the right to prosecute state officials by international courts and the growing acceptance of humanitarian wars in the twenty-first century. The difference with IBSA states though is that, as fully consolidated democracies, they are generally regarded as 'good citizens' of the international liberal community. Their democratic credentials further increase the legitimacy of their claims for distributive justice through the reform of the key decision-making structures of global governance.

---

16. This perspective in IR theory uses empirical evidence and philosophical arguments to defend the proposition that liberal democracies do not engage in war with one another. M. Doyle, "Kant, Liberal Legacies, and Foreign Affairs", in M. E. Brown, S. M. Lynn-Jones and S. E. Miller (eds.), *Debating the Democratic Peace* (Cambridge, MA: MIT Press, 1996).

17. It is worth noticing that prior to 9/11 and during the presidential campaign, the Bush government used a realist rhetoric to articulate the US' foreign policy goals. See for example, Condoleezza Rice, "Promoting the National Interest", *Foreign Affairs* (January/February 2000).

18. Robert Kagan, *The Return of History and the End of Dreams* (New York: Knopf, 2008).

19. John Ikenberry, "The Liberal International Order and its Discontents", *Millennium*, Vol. 38, No. 3 (2010), pp. 509–521.

Critical Perspectives

Some critical theories have historically distanced themselves from cosmopolitan views that assume individuals as the main referents of global morality and international institutions as neutral frameworks to promote inter-state cooperation. Post-colonial and post-structural authors claim that the liberal universalism underlying these perspectives is driven by Western ideology and hence a reflection of dominant discourses/narratives, which claim superiority over alternative cultural identities, economic models and political systems. In this sense, the international institutional arrangements created after WWII would embody the perceptions, value systems and interests of the dominant states and reproduce/legitimise a given hierarchy of power in international politics.[20] These authors recognised that the perpetuation of economic dependence in the South after decolonisation led to new forms of colonialism and stalled development.[21]

Dependency theory authors have emphasised core/periphery relations as a central feature of the global economic system. They claim that self-determination through state-led economic development and political sovereignty are still the best guarantees against Western interventionism and economic dependence.[22] In fact, from the 1930s and 1940s dependent states in Latin America begun to nationalise production and devise policies to limit foreign control of domestic financial markets and the industrial sector. Furthermore, in the 1960s, newly independent states in Asia and Africa, together with their Latin American counterparts, created multilateral mechanisms such as the United Nations Conference on Trade and Development (UNCTAD) to collectively influence the norms that govern international trade to obtain more favourable relations vis-à-vis the hegemonic centres in the North.[23]

It is my contention that the common Southern identity created as a result of the politics of resistance, carried out by key developing countries during the early decades of the Cold War, is an important constitutive element of contemporary South-South coalitions such as IBSA, albeit not fully explored in the current academic debate on rising powers. The debate is framed by a rationalist ontology that views rising powers as unitary actors functionally undifferentiated from their 'declining' Western counter-parts. It downplays, as epiphenomenal or entirely instrumental, the distinctive identities of emerging states and their normative claims for distributive justice in international relations. Dissenting viewpoints among those authors are limited to empirical disputes over the actual goals of rising powers and the political/security/

---

20. Tom Farer and Timothy D. Sisk, "Enhancing International Cooperation: Between History and Necessity", *Global Governance*, Vol. 16, No. 2 (2010), pp. 1–12.

21. For example, Patrice Lumumba once affirmed that by the time of Congo's independence from Belgium colonialism, "we do not have an economic option". By this, Lumumba meant that, even after political decolonisation, the instruments of economic and social control were still well placed in the hands of the colonial masters and their local representatives. In this context, independence was nothing but an empty word. J. P. Sartre, "The Political Thought of Patrice Lumumba", in J.P. Sartre (ed.), *Colonialism and Neo-colonialism* (Abingdon: Routledge, 2006), p.176.

22. T. Dos Santos, "The Structure of Dependence", in C. R. Goddard, P. Cronin and K.C. Dash (eds.), *International Political Economy* (London: Lynne Rienner, 2003).

23. *Ibid.*, p.122.

economic implications of a reconfiguration of power relations in the early twenty-first century.[24]

Critical theorists from a Neo-Gramscian tradition claim that three broad categories of force – material, ideational and institutional – are the main constitutive elements of global political systems. They reinforce and legitimise a particular "historic bloc" which, in turn, defines the "standards of appropriateness"[25] among participants in any given international political order.[26] The hypothesis left unexplored by the literature on rising states is precisely whether the current international circumstances are conducive to the emergence of a new "historic bloc" led by a coterie of Southern states, who have been collectively promoting alternative models of multilateral governance. According to this interpretation, rising powers should be also defined in terms of their increasing capacity to use 'counter-hegemonic' ideas in order to promote global normative change.

The Historical Context of a Changing International Order

The global expansion of European international society began in the late fifteenth century, instigated by maritime exploration overseas. It was successfully consolidated overland with colonial settlements in the Americas, Asia and Africa.[27] At the apex of European imperialism, just before the outbreak of WWI, Britain, the Netherlands, Belgium and France controlled around one third of the world's land. The devastation provoked by two world wars was followed by the ideological and geostrategic conflict between the US and the Soviet Union. In tandem with the rise of the Cold War system, the decolonisation process led to the creation of a large non-aligned bloc of newly independent nations. The Bandung Conference of 1955 encapsulated the growing political articulation between post-colonial nations in Asia in Africa.[28] In his inaugural speech at Bandung, President Sukarno of Indonesia conveyed the sense of moral purpose that was generated among nations that had just emerged from colonial rule:

> What can we do? We can do much! We can inject the voice of reason into world affairs. We can mobilize all the spiritual, all the moral, all the political strength of Asia and Africa on the said of peace. Yes, we! We, the peoples of Asia and Africa, 1,400,000,000 strong, far more than half the human population of the world, we can mobilize what I have called the Moral Violence of Nations in favour of peace.[29]

---

24. See, for example, A.S. Alexandroff and A.F. Cooper (eds.), *Rising States, Rising Institutions: Challenges for Global Governance* (Washington DC: Brookings, 2010). Cooper's analysis of the IBSA partnership is the only attempt in this volume to discuss the normative power and shared identities of rising states. A.F. Cooper, "Labels Matter: Interpreting Rising States through Acronyms", in A.S. Alexandroff and A. F. Cooper (eds.), *Rising States, Rising Institutions, Challenges for Global Governance* (Washington DC: Brookings, 2010).

25. James G. March and Johan P. Olsen, "The Institutional Dynamics of International Political Orders", *International Organization*, Vol. 52, No. 4 (1998), pp. 943–969.

26. R. Cox, "Gramsci, Hegemony and International Relations: An Essay in Method", in S. Gill (ed.), *Gramsci Historical Materialism and International Relations* (Cambridge: Cambridge University Press, 1993).

27. Adam Watson, *The Evolution of International Society* (Abingdon: Routledge, 1992).

28. Alden, Morphet and Vieira, *op. cit.*

29. President Sukarno, Address to Bandung Conference, 18 April 1955, in *Africa-Asia Speaks from Bandung* (Jakarta: Ministry of Foreign Affairs, 1955), p.20.

By the late 1960s, however, and in spite of the continued development of the Non-Aligned Movement, domestic political instability and economic collapse in many parts of the developing world frustrated the aspirations of Southern leaders to build a solid third world front. In 1962, the Sino-Indian border war was a first major setback to the Bandung aspirations of peaceful relations between Southern nations.[30] In spite of that, South-South organisations, such as NAM and the G77, and the principles that underpinned their creation, have survived crises and are still today fostering the ideals of South-South solidarity. The role of the G77 as a locus of South-South coordination in multilateral climate negotiations is a clear example of the institutional resilience and political relevance of these groupings in contemporary international politics.

During the 1970s, the US demise in the Vietnam war compounded by the impact of two oil crises and the economic rise of both Japan and an increasingly integrated Western Europe, seemed to signal the decline of North American dominance. In a turn of events, however, Reagan's hard-line foreign policy of the mid-1980s reasserted the US upper hand in the Cold War conflict. From the early 1990s, Washington bounced back with 15 years of uninterrupted economic growth and uncontested global military and ideological supremacy.[31] The result of this was the unprecedented dominance of Western-liberal ideas in the constitutional structure of global governance in the early twenty-first century with the US as its only maintainer and guardian. The unipolar context of the early 2000s led to academic speculations about the new role of the US as a global empire given its dominance of almost all dimensions of power in international politics.[32]

Yet, the unilateralist US foreign policy that emerged after the 9/11 – based on the doctrine of pre-emptive war and regime change, outside the accepted international mechanisms of collective security – undermined Washington's leadership role in the liberal international society. The war against Afghanistan and the invasion of Iraq in March 2003 strained relations with traditional Western allies and increased anti-American sentiment in developing countries, particularly in the Middle East.[33] Moreover, the failure of international institutions to deal with the pressing problems of climate change, the liberalisation of trade, human rights and nuclear proliferation has also shown the vulnerability of Western international order in the twenty-first century. In this sense, global expectations that the new Obama administration would champion liberal international ideals and restore the US position as the "indispensible nation"[34] were not fulfilled.

This process of growing fragmentation of multilateralism accelerated the emergence of alternative sources of interstate co-ordination/governance. Spearheaded by rising states in the South, the 'Bandung Spirit' seemed to be alive and well 50 years after its inception. Palat, for example, noted that "rapid economic growth

---

30. Odd Arne Westad, *The Global Cold War* (Cambridge: Cambridge University Press, 2007), p. 107, 108.

31. N. Bisley, "Global Power Shift: The Decline of the West and the Rise of the Rest?", in M. Beeson and N. Bisley (eds.), *Issues in 21st Century World Politics* (Basingstoke: Palgrave Macmillan, 2010), p. 67.

32. Michael Cox, "The Empire's Back in Town: Or America's Imperial Temptation – Again", *Millennium Journal of International Studies*, Vol. 32, No. 1 (2003), pp. 1–27.

33. Roger Burbach and Jim Tarbell, *Imperial Overstretch: George W. Bush and The Hubris of Empire* (London: Zed Books, 2004).

34. On various occasions, Madeleine Albright, US Secretary of State during Bill Clinton's administration, described the US as the world's indispensable nation.

registered by, and greater cooperation over a broad spectrum of issues among states of the global South have revived the hope (or spectre) of a 'new Bandung'".[35] The recent phenomenon of South-South partnerships provides a good measure of the changing configuration of power relations and associated normative challenge to traditionally Northern-controlled international diplomacy. This process of growing interaction among emerging Southern powers has been further consolidated in three main groups: 1) the Brazil, South Africa, India and China (BASIC), which emerged as a way out of the quagmire in the December 2009 Climate Change negotiations in Copenhagen; 2) the Brazil, Russia, India, China and South Africa (BRICs), most influential in financial and economic issues within the G20; and 3) the India, Brazil, South Africa Dialogue Forum (IBSA), which most clearly resembles a collective initiative based on a 'shared post-colonial identity' grounded on common normative claims for 'distributive justice' in international relations.[36]

IBSA differs significantly from early modalities of South-South cooperation. Although it retains the sense of like-mindedness which animated past Southern initiatives, particularly with regards to promoting an equitable and rule-based multilateral economic and political system, these Southern powers changed tactics by establishing a smaller grouping of advanced developing nations, aimed at strengthening their collective capacity to negotiate with Northern powers on key issue-areas. Unlike the loose political bonds and broad ideological scope of past coalitions of Southern states, such as NAM, IBSA states recognise that to translate common normative aspirations of South-South solidarity into effective political action, they need to explore political synergies where they exist, such as in multilateral trade and climate governance and in their more general calls for reform of the decision-making structures of international institutions.[37]

Western powers are already adapting their foreign policies to this new international realignment. In July 2010, for example, the British government led by David Cameron released its blue print for international action stressing precisely the need to engage more forcefully with Southern powers. According to the British Foreign Secretary, William Hague:

> The world has changed and if we do not change with it Britain's role is set to decline with all that means for our influence in world affairs [...] Economic power and economic opportunity are shifting to the countries of the East and South; to the emerging economies of Brazil, India, China and other parts of Asia [...] The views of these emerging powers are critical to our ability to tackle global economic reform, nuclear proliferation, climate change and energy security.[38]

---

35. Ravi A. Palat, "A New Bandung? Economic Growth vs. Distributive Justice Among Emerging Powers", *Futures*, Vol. 40, No. 8 (2008), p. 721.

36. Cooper, *op. cit.*

37. For more on this, see, Abdul Nafey, "IBSA Forum: The Rise of 'New' Non-Alignment", *India Quarterly: A Journal of International Affairs*, Vol. 61, No. 1 (2005), pp. 1–78; and Chris Alden and Marco Vieira, "The New Diplomacy of the South: South Africa, Brazil, India and Trilateralism", *Third World Quarterly*, Vol. 26, No. 7 (2005), pp. 1077–1095.

38. William Hague, "British Foreign Policy in a Networked World", Presented at the Foreign and Commonwealth Office, 1 July 2010, available: <http://www.fco.gov.uk/en/news/latestnews/?view=Speech&id=22462590> (accessed 7 July 2010).

This is indication that industrialised states are coming to terms with the fact that the stability of contemporary international order depends to a large extent on establishing a viable and reformed system of norms and institutions that are widely accepted among a growing number of leading states in the international system. In this respect, the unprecedented economic rise of Southern powers has created an historical opportunity to reshape international relations according to the core principles of South-South solidarity. These principles were sketched out during the Bandung Conference of April 1955 and reaffirmed 50 years later by 42 Asian and African leaders, including India, China and South Africa, in commemoration of the golden jubilee of Bandung's historic gathering. The Bandung principles (also known as *Panch Shila*) were accepted as the non-aligned guiding rules to regulate relations between post-colonial nations in the context of the Cold War system.[39] These were:[40]

1. Respect for fundamental human rights and for the purposes and principles of the Charter of the United Nations.
2. Respect for the sovereignty and territorial integrity of all nations.
3. Recognition of the equality of all races and the equality of all nations large and small.
4. Abstention from intervention or interference in the internal affairs of another country.
5. Respect for the right of each nation to defend itself singly or collectively, in conformity with the Charter of the United Nations.
6. Abstention from the use of arrangements of collective defence to serve the particular interests of any of the big powers; abstention by any country from exerting pressures on other countries.
7. Refraining from acts or threats of aggression or the use of force against the territorial integrity or political independence of any country.
8. Settlement of all international disputes by peaceful means.
9. Promotion of mutual interests and co-operation.
10. Respect for justice and international obligations.

The above ideals are analytically encapsulated in this article by the single notion of 'distributive justice'. It refers to the expansion of international political representation, social equality and economic opportunity to include nations traditionally at the margins of global governance mechanisms. The present argument claims that the trilateralist initiative between India, Brazil and South Africa places the emphasis on the realisation of at least part of this normative agenda.

IBSA and Distributive Justice

Since the formal establishment of IBSA in 2003, following discussions among the respective Heads of State/Government during the G8 meeting in Evian, the leaders of IBSA states have repeatedly spoken of global development, which is unequal and thus needs to be readdressed in a reformed system of international

---

39. Alden, Morphet and Vieira, *op. cit.*, p. 41.
40. *Ibid.*, p. 233.

institutions. They share a vision of international order which envisages a system organised in a way that developing countries will have a fairer participation in global politics and the major powers among them will closely engage in the top management of international institutions. Contrasting with the North's modes of engagement with the South, generally based on the universal validity of their own particular values, ideologies and social/political systems, IBSA's model of South-South cooperation is sensitive to the particular social, cultural and economic contexts of Southern states.

Joao Augusto de Araujo Castro, Brazilian Ambassador to the United States and author of the thesis of the freezing of world power structure, stated in 1972 that:

> The less developed countries are seeking to transpose into the international field certain principles of social justice and re- distribution of wealth that have been gradually gaining ground within the domestic systems of the more politically advanced countries. Ultimately, the objective is to obtain international recognition of the principle of "collective security in the economic field", a principle analogous to that which we are trying to encourage in the field of peace and international security.[41]

According to this view, distributive justice would imply the reorganisation of international governance structures in a way that they would promote a more equitable distribution of wealth and political participation of the developing world. This understanding of distributive justice has been one of the foundational principles of the IBSA partnership. In a previous study, I asserted that "it is the linkage between the notion of South as identity, bound to material dimensions of international political economy that provides the basis for an understanding of both its significance and durability".[42] A further elaboration of this assertion is that South-South arrangements in general and IBSA in particular, embody perceptions, values and interests that are essentially defined by Southern states' common claims for distributive justice.

The IBSA Facility for Poverty and Hunger Alleviation (IBSA Fund), created in 2004, shows an interesting, and rather novel, facet of South-South relations in the early twenty-first century whereby emerging Southern powers effectively engage in development assistance towards least developed nations in line with principles of South-South solidarity set forth during the 1950s and 1960s. Each IBSA member contributes US $1 million annually to the Fund, which is managed by the United Nations Development Programme (UNDP). The approved projects are executed by the national/local governments of the recipient states in partnership with UNDP's special unit for South-South cooperation. The Fund has already sponsored development projects in several vulnerable states such as Haiti, Guinea Bissau, Cambodia, Cape Verde, Burundi and the occupied Palestinian territories.[43] In September 2010, the IBSA Fund received the Millennium Development Goals Award for its contribution to achieving the international development goal of eradicating extreme poverty and hunger by 2015; the first of

---

41. Castro, op. cit., p. 162.
42. Alden, Morphet and Vieira, op. cit., p. 5.
43. "The IBSA Fund", available: <http://www.ibsa-trilateral.org//index.php?option=com_content&task=view&id=29&Itemid=40> (accessed 22 April 2010).

eight key development objectives agreed by the 192 UN member states following the Millennium Summit in 2000.

In recent years, IBSA states have been gaining importance in the international development system. India, Brazil and South Africa, both individually and as a group, have significantly increased their financial, technical and advisory involvement in Least Developed Countries (LDCs), particularly in Africa.[44] It is estimated that official international development funds doubled in Brazil during the period 2007 and 2008 and tripled between 2009 and 2010.[45] According to the Brazilian Institute of Applied Economic Research (IPEA), the Brazilian government spent around US $1.43 billion for development assistance between 2005 and 2009.[46] The India Development Initiative (IDI) has also allocated substantial resources for development projects, totalling an estimated US $800 million.[47] The Techno-Economic approach of the African-Indian Movement (TEAM-9) has donated US $50 million for the purchase of an Indian satellite system, as well as debt reduction for five African countries amounting to US $24 million. The Indian government has launched a number of other programmes that have been channelling financial resources and technical expertise, such as the Special Commonwealth Assistance for Africa Programme (SCAAP).[48] During the latest Africa-India Summit, the Indian government made a commitment of US $5 billion credit line to various development projects in Africa and measures to assist African states in infrastructure and capacity building.[49] Although still dwarfed by India and Brazil's financial pledges to international development, the South African government through its African Renaissance Fund has also allocated substantial human and financial capital to other African nations. In the financial year 2008–2009, the South African parliament approved the dispensation of an estimated US $100 million to international development cooperation.[50]

In line with the utilitarian bias of conventional approaches to rising powers, these initiatives have been interpreted as a strategic effort to increase rising IBSA states' soft power influence in the developing world as well as within the UN, which would help to garner support for their bid for a permanent seat in the UN Security Council. It has also been claimed that the financial commitments of IBSA members to the Fund are not sufficient for the purpose of attending the most basic requirements of the targeted recipients.[51] However, the important

---

44. For an empirically rich analysis of the role of these emerging donors in Africa, see, Kragelund, *op. cit.*

45. Overseas Development Institute, "Brazil: An Emerging Aid Player: Lessons on Emerging Donors and South-South Cooperation", 2010, available: <http://www.odi.org.uk/resources/download/5120.pdf> (accessed 5 June 2011).

46. IPEA, *Brazilian Cooperation to International Development: 2005-2009*, Brasilia, Brazil, 2010, available: <http://www.ipea.gov.br/portal/images/stories/PDFs/Book_Cooperao_Brasileira.pdf> (accessed 7 June 2011).

47. Kragelund, *op. cit.*, p.575.

48. *Ibid.*, p.576.

49. "India Announces USD 5 billion Credit Line for Africa", *Business Line* (25 May 2011), available: < http://www.governancenow.com/news/regular-story/india-announces-usd-5-billion-credit-line-africa> (accessed on 20 June 2011).

50. Department of International Relations and Cooperation, Republic of South Africa, "African Renaissance and International Cooperation, Accounting Officer's Report for the Year Ended 31 March 2009", 2009, available: <http://www.dfa.gov.za/department/report_2008-2009/annualreportarffinal08-09.pdf> (accessed 6 June 2011).

51. "Brazil's Foreign-Aid Programme: Speak Softly and Carry a Blank Cheque", *The Economist* (15 July 2010).

missing point is that, by establishing a new development-aid framework, IBSA states are promoting change in the normative context of North-South (or core-periphery) relations.

The IBSA Fund does not require Western-style conditions on good governance on receiving states. They instead link the money to projects that would promote positive social and economic impact through "replicable and scalable projects that can be disseminated to interested developing countries as examples of best practices in the fight against poverty and hunger".[52] For IBSA, the issue of political autonomy and ownership of programmes are fundamental principles. In fact, IBSA defines the Fund in terms of development partnership rather than assistance aid or development assistance. The novelty of initiatives such as the IBSA Fund is precisely that it tries to overcome hegemonic Northern discourses about Southern social and economic problems by offering vulnerable developing nations the opportunity to articulate their own development priorities. This is in line with the influential report of the South Commission, which clearly sets out what 'development' actually means from a Southern perspective and the policies needed to achieve it:

> Development implies growing self-reliance, both individual and collective. The base for a nation's development must be its own resources, both human and material, fully used to meet its own needs. External assistance can promote development. But to have this effect, this assistance has to be integrated into the national effort and applied to the purposes of those it is meant to benefit.[53]

I argue here that IBSA's development approach is based on a particular narrative, which draws on the non-aligned ideology of South-South solidarism. As Woods puts it, "India's aid programme, which began in the 1950s, has centred on respect for territorial integrity, mutual non-aggression, mutual non-interference in domestic affairs, equality and mutual benefit, and peaceful coexistence".[54] In a similar vein, the Brazilian government has integrated development assistance to its South-South foreign policy strategy.[55] The Brazilian Agency for Development Cooperation (ABC in Portuguese) is run by the Brazilian Foreign Ministry, which, since Lula da Silva came to power in 2003, has been consistently infused by a third worldist ideology.[56] This foreign policy vision has been also pursued by Lula's designated successor, Dilma Rousseff. Likewise, South-South solidarity principles, embedded in the foreign policy doctrine of 'African Renaissance', have guided South Africa's international development initiatives. The African Renaissance Fund established in 2000 places importance on:

> [...] an economic and social development agenda for Africa. It is a comprehensive and far-reaching global plan of action to tackle poverty and the developmental needs of Africa [...] In order to achieve the social

---

52. "The IBSA Fund" op. cit.
53. The South Commission, *The Challenge to the South, The Report of the South Commission* (Oxford, Oxford University Press, 1990), p. 10–11.
54. Woods, op. cit., p. 13.
55. Kragelund, op. cit., p. 570.
56. Alden and Vieira, op. cit., p. 1086.

and economic regeneration and development of the Continent, the pre-eminent issue of poverty alleviation, through sustained people-centred development, must be vigorously pursued, so as to provide an improved quality of life for all Africa and her people.[57]

This shared model of development cooperation questions the traditional Western concept based upon Europe's civilizational mission towards post-colonial states. The predominant notion of development has been determined by historical patterns of unequal relations between 'colonisers' and the 'colonised'.[58] This 'development paradigm' has served as the guiding principle for economic co-operation between the Northern and the Southern countries. Six argues that, "in spite of the political rhetoric of ownership and partnership, the West still considers itself the standard-setter for any development model (the universalistic element) and the South or the East (with capital letters) as the essential Other (the essentialised particular)".[59] Similarly, Easterly criticises the Western humanitarian system, and its existing aid programmes, for the lack of full involvement of recipient states as a result of the donors' conviction that, like the old colonial powers, they know what is best for developing countries.[60]

There is, however, a certain ambiguity in the IBSA states' interactions with other developing countries, especially on their regional contexts. The limited recognition of India, Brazil and South Africa as regional leaders by states that make up their respective regions puts a significant brake on the fulfilment of their aspirations individually and through IBSA, as well as contradicting internationally held expectations as to their status. Moreover, the growing economic standing of Brazil, India, South Africa and China, and the expansion of their influence beyond their traditional geographical backyards adds complexity to the trilateral relationship in terms of intra-group competition for regional markets, natural resources and political influence.[61] These emerging powers probably already have more in common with the traditional powers (if the latter even succeed in preserving their great power status into the twenty-first century) than the developing countries whose ranks they are now breaking away from. In this sense, their political claim to represent the aspirations of the entire South is increasingly disputable. This is the result of their unavoidable ambivalent position as emerging economic powers, with a growing global status and self-serving interests, while at the same time, developing nations that face social and economic challenges similar to those of their least developed neighbours in Asia, Latin America and Africa.

This apparent contradiction highlights a common feature among great powers, regardless of either their rising or declining status. In spite of whatever common ideational vision governments of leading states are associated with, they need to

---

57. Department of International Relations and Cooperation, Republic of South Africa, "Establishment of the African Renaissance and International Cooperation Fund", 2000, available: <http://www.dfa.gov.za/foreign/Multilateral/profiles/arfund.htm> (accessed 8 June 2011).

58. Clemens Six, "The Rise of Postcolonial States as Donors: A Challenge to the Development Paradigm", *Third World Quarterly*, Vol. 30, No. 3 (2010), p. 1103.

59. *Ibid.*, p. 1106.

60. William Easterly, *The White Man's Burden: Why the West's Efforts to Aid Have Done so Much Ill and so Little Good* (London: Penguin Books, 2007).

61. Marco Vieira and Chris Alden, "India, Brazil, South Africa (IBSA): South-South Cooperation and the Paradox of Regional Leadership", *Global Governance*, Vol. 17, No. 4 (2011), pp. 507–528.

cultivate economic cooperation, manage political conflict and maintain regional stability in an international system composed of complex and differing political communities. Inconsistencies at the core of the Western project of expanding liberal internationalism, such as in the US government's attempts to promote democratic rule and human rights in the Middle East at the same time cosying up to the authoritarian rulers of Saudi Arabia, are evidence of the difficulties states face while trying to balance order and justice in international relations. Phillips addresses this dual challenge by offering an innovative realist-constructivist explanation of how international orders are created and sustained. According to him, "international orders rely equally on shared visions of the good and accepted practices of organised violence".[62] He interestingly borrows from Machiavelli's image of a centaur, part human and part beast, to explain this dualistic character of international orders.[63]

It is my contention that, in spite of the (expected) *realpolitik* component in the foreign policy rationale of IBSA states, there is clearly a coherent narrative that expresses common moral concerns that have been translated into 'shared visions of the good'. These have been codified into the broad concept of distributive justice, which informs the foreign policy of leading Southern powers. Their shared goal is to overcome the core-periphery logic of international relations by increasing their collective activism in multilateral organisations. This has been expressed by Brazil and India during the 1960s and restated by IBSA partners on numerous occasions. In this sense, the Brasilia Declaration of June 2003, followed by the establishment of the IBSA Trust Fund in 2004, and further compounded by bilateral and multilateral initiatives spearheaded by the governments of the three IBSA partners, provided the foundation for a broad development cooperation framework shaped by deep-rooted principles of South-South solidarity.

Conclusions

The academic analysis of emerging powers and their coalitions has been characterised by a general assumption that defines them as status quo powers either attempting to adapt/accommodate to Western normative frameworks and institutions or trying to increase their relative power and influence vis-à-vis the North. According to these perspectives, the establishment of the IBSA partnership should be generally understood as a kind of soft balance strategy by middle powers to increase their bargaining position within international organisations. They define India, Brazil and South Africa's international identity/personality in terms of these countries' particular material capabilities and political influence as middle powers, regional hegemons or bridges between the developed and developing worlds. Similarly, the IBSA Trust Fund is seen as an attempt by key Southern states to increase their soft power leverage among the poorest developing states and hence boost their chances to be accepted into the select group of the Security Council's permanent members.

---

62. Andrew Phillips, *War, Religion and Empire, The Transformation of International Orders* (Cambridge: Cambridge University Press, 2011), p. 4.
63. *Ibid.*, p. 15.

Notwithstanding the relevance of the current literature on contemporary South-South coalitions, I argued in this article that the scholarly work on their impact and implications to international order should go beyond narrow assessments of distribution of material power and collective negotiating strategies within multilateral settings such as the WTO. As shown earlier, the rise of Southern powers as alternative sources of economic assistance, particularly in the case of China, but also in relation to IBSA, is bringing about a more fundamental rupture in Western-defined normative standards of appropriate economic and political behaviour. Effectively, the novelty of contemporary North-South relations is that new 'post-colonial donors' are influencing long-standing patterns of economic relations between Western powers and their recipients of aid in the South. A new development agenda has been set up by states such as China, India, Brazil and South Africa whereby civilisational hierarchies based on the modern North vs. pre-modern South are been replaced by horizontal models of development partnership.

Theoretically, India, Brazil and South Africa, through their IBSA partnership, show a political mixture of realist, liberal and post-colonial elements. They seek to revise their foreign relations with the North along realist assumptions of power politics and interest-orientation. Similar to realist thinking, they are inhospitable to ideas of cosmopolitan justice that could justify foreign interference in their sovereign authority. They nonetheless support the norms of liberal internationalism and its main multilateral institutional structures based on the fundamental rules of sovereignty and equality among states. At the same time, foreign policy principles associated with post-colonial ideology are frequently outlined in the political rhetoric of Indian, Brazilian and South African decision-makers. Here, the 'Bandung' idealism of 'non-alignment' deserves particular notice. These "principled ideas"[64] still play a relevant role in mobilising South-South support, especially when it comes to strengthening multilateralism, confidence building and economic co-operation. Nevertheless, these ideas should not be mistaken as cosmopolitan demands on universal human justice. Although this is a fundamental moral goal for most developing countries, Southern governments are generally wary of the actual intentions behind Western military interventions based on universalist/humanitarian goals.

IBSA partners have consistently supported the norm of peaceful coexistence and political equality among independent, territorially-based nations. Yet, they add a moral imperative whereby fairer economic and political distribution of economic and political power among states, rather than individuals or economic elites, would promote a more stable order in international relations. This paper therefore puts forth the hypothesis that IBSA, through its trilateral assistance Fund, represents a political/ideological attempt to promote the norm of 'distributive justice' at the international level. It combines two major claims namely political independence and economic development through a fairer participation in global economic/political relations. Drawing from the 'Bandung Spirit' of the early post-colonial period, they criticise the hierarchy of economic/political power that renders autonomy, equality, and non-intervention elusive norms in international relations.

---

64. Judith Goldstein and Robert O. Keohane (eds.), *Ideas and Foreign Policy* (Cornell, NY: Cornell University Press, 1993).

Falling on Fertile Ground? The Story of Emerging Powers' Claims for Redistribution and the Global Poverty Debate

JANIS VAN DER WESTHUIZEN

Drawing on a neo-Gramscian perspective, it is argued that considerable policy convergence at both the level of international organization and the state has made a significant contribution towards generating the required global sentiment within which emerging powers' redistributive demands are more likely to receive a sympathetic hearing. These dynamics are illustrated with reference to the global poverty debate. The recent "rediscovery" of global poverty seems symptomatic of various ongoing processes whereby a basis for a coalition between the privileged powers and those not so privileged (the emerging powers) is being constituted as a response to the need for a more socially responsible world order. After considering some broad parallels between the policy convergence process in South Africa and Brazil, this paper concludes by highlighting some of the initiatives state elites in Pretoria and Brasilia have launched in reaction to the newly emerging policy space within which their esteem as rising states can be demonstrated.

In November 2010, Seoul hosted the G20 Summit. A novel innovation of the summit was the first creation of a G20 Working Group on Development, an initiative driven by the Korean hosts who insisted that developing countries should lead with the design and implementation of strategies suited to their own circumstances—and given Korea's phenomenal developmental success—sought to play a bridging role and enhance the conditions for generating consensus on global development at a time when considerable ideological differences continue to persist.[1] In the aftermath of the global financial crisis of 2008–2009 and the extent to which major rising states have been relatively unaffected by a crisis so severe many compare it to the 1930s Depression, it is clear that the old trans-Atlantic power base imposes its development orthodoxy with increasing difficulty.

At least until the attacks on the World Trade Centre in New York in September 2001, many egalitarian social movements pushed the agenda for a more

---

* An earlier version of this article was delivered at "The Leading Scholars Programme", ASERI, Universita Cattolica del Sacro Cuore, Milan, April 2010; at the 4th Regional Powers Network Conference, 6–7 September 2010, Stellenbosch Institute for Advanced Studies (STIAS), Stellenbosch; and to the German Institute of Global and Area Studies, Hamburg, June 2011.

1. Gregory Chin, "G20 Development Plan Bridges Old and New", Seoul G20 Commentaries (November 2010), Center for International Governance Innovation (CIGI), available: <www.cigionline.org> (accessed 7 July 2011).

redistributive global order—such as those concerned with debt relief in Africa and Latin America and the multitudes that protested against globalisation in London, Seoul, Johannesburg, and Washington. Bono (and his project RED), Bob Geldof's Live 8 concerts, those involved in the "Make Poverty History" campaign and even Kofi Annan, the UN Secretary-General appointed a host of UN goodwill ambassadors in support of the UN Millennium Development Goals (MDGs): Brazilian football star Ronaldo, Harry Belafonte, Nobel Prize for Literature winners Nadine Gordimer and Seamus Heaney, Angelina Jolie, David Beckham and many others—all in the name of poverty eradication, mostly in the developing world.[2] Moreover, according to some estimates the MGD target of halving the rate of global poverty by 2015 from its 1990 level, may already have been achieved. Between 2005 and 2010, the total number of extremely poor people (those living on less than US $1.25 per day) fell by nearly half a billion people, from over 1.3 billion in 2005 to under 900 million in 2010.[3] In fact, in 2005 supplementing the income of the poor to bring their daily income up to US $1.25 would have cost US $96 billion or the total volume of foreign aid given that year.[4]

How does one explain this "rediscovery" of global poverty? In this article it is argued that the rediscovery and popularisation of global poverty reduction coincided with a decided shift towards something of a centre-left or global "third way" context both at the level of multilateral organisations as well as the state, thereby creating a basis for a coalition between the privileged and those not so privileged (the emerging powers). These *reformist* (rather than transformative) impulses which underlie the incorporation of the emerging powers seeks to create a more socially responsible world order. However, one should not over-estimate the scope for global redistribution the incorporation of these powers suggest, as it is unlikely for proposals that threaten the continued survival of the liberal international system to be adopted.

Drawing on Craig Murphy's analytical approach, this article illustrates how multilateral organisations played a key role in constructing consensus, particularly from the 1990s and how that consensus was also replicated at the national state level, with reference to the cases of South Africa and Brazil in relation to the global poverty debate. I contend that the ensuing policy convergence at the global and domestic level has, in ideational terms, helped set the stage for the return of redistribution to the agenda of global politics—be it in terms of the reconfiguration of power within institutions of global governance, negotiations over climate change or simply greater recognition of the need for various social policies to tackle inequality at the domestic level in the advanced developed, emerging and least developed economies. This article focuses not on the *outcome* of this interaction with the advanced industrialised world, but rather

---

2. For more on the Make Poverty History campaign as political spectacle, see K. Nash, "Global Citizenship as Show Business: The Cultural Politics of Make Poverty History", *Media, Culture and Society*, Vol. 30, No. 2 (2008), pp. 167–181.

3. Poverty reduction rates are, however, very regionally bound. By 2015 Sub-Saharan Africa will be by far home to most of the world's poor at 39.3 per cent, followed by a distant South Asia at 8.7 per cent, largely because of the prevalence of fragile states in Sub-Saharan Africa. L. Chandy and G. Gertz, *Poverty in Numbers: The Changing State of Global Poverty from 2005 to 2015* (Washington, DC: The Brookings Institution, 2011), p.4.

4. *Ibid.*, p.3, 13.

as a *process* of persuasion, including the process of framing,[5] and more specifically, the conditions that have helped to make for more fertile ground in which emerging powers' claims have been planted. The article concludes by briefly highlighting some of the initiatives state elites in South Africa and Brazil have launched in reaction to newly emerging policy space within which their esteem as rising states can be demonstrated.

International Organisation, Expanding Markets and Social Change

According to Neo-Gramscians, the economic logic of capitalism forces industrialists to produce more goods that can be sold to larger markets in order to increase profits. International cooperation among industrialised states seeks therefore to extend the market for international goods beyond the confines of national borders. International organisations have been crucial means for the formalisation of international cooperation, with membership open to most states in international society. International organisations promote not only the physical infrastructure of international markets such as transport systems and telecommunications that make it possible to buy and sell goods and services, but also the monetary and financial systems that support trade; set industrial standards and the protection of intellectual property, as well as securing wider international markets by making it easier for states to cooperate by overcoming many obstacles or resistances to globalisation. These could include the creation of international agencies or initiatives such as the International Labour Organization (ILO) in reaction to industrial workers' fear of losing control over production and the introduction of new production techniques.[6] Larger markets are the outcome of vast technological innovations and investments triggered by new lead industries that characterise each industrial era. For example, the Industrial Revolution of the ninteenth century involved large public investments in power systems for mills; the mid-century Railway Age required similarly large investments in railway networks and the turn of the century Second Industrial Revolution needed huge investments in electrical power and telephone systems. The Automobile Age of the mid- to late-twentieth century required even larger investments in roads, railway networks, airports and mega-factories, and marketing and research facilities, while the Information Age required even larger investments, such as in the Internet.[7] Yet the transition between different industrial eras is marked by conflict between those more likely to benefit from the emerging new industrial order and their opponents (such as industrial labour); or those who benefited from the existing order (older economies and older sectors and regions in the developing world that did not experience all the benefits of the new lead industries); or those who are likely to provide low wage labour and

---

5. A frame is a "persuasive device" used to "fix meanings, organize experience, alert others that their interests and possibly their identities are at stake, and propose solutions to ongoing problems...[and] provide a singular interpretation of a particular situation and the indicate appropriate behaviour for that context". R.A. Payne, "Persuasion, Frames and Norm Construction", *European Journal of International Relations*, Vol. 7, No. 1, (2001), pp. 37–61. Thanks go to Leslie Wehner at GIGA in Hamburg for suggesting this point.

6. C.N. Murphy, *International Organization and Industrial Change: Global Governance since 1850* (Oxford: Polity Press, 1994).

7. C.N. Murphy, *Global Institutions, Marginalization and Development* (New York: Routledge, 2005), p.60

resources (natural and agricultural) for the industrial core and rival industrial centres. For example large regions of the world that have provided raw materials and labour for the centre and that have not received corresponding degrees of new technology and high levels of investment in industry have prompted international organisations to help reduce conflict through the UN's support for decolonisation and development assistance.[8]

International organisations thrive and then whither and need to be reformed or are replaced by entirely new organisations. Such transitions often coincide with economic crises that create space for the emergence of egalitarian social forces directed at a reformation of the existing order. However, not all social forces necessarily succeed in convincing the powerful of the need for reform of the evolving new order. Rather, those social forces that are least implicated or blamed by the powerful for the economic depression of the previous era are likely to be accommodated in the emerging order.[9] Yet the *world time context* that characterise these dynamics also *requires a considerable degree of policy convergence between erstwhile contending groups or positions to make a coalition between the privileged and less privileged possible*. I contend that South Africa and Brazil—lead by formerly "radical" parties such as the African National Congress (ANC) and the Worker's Party (PT)—have become "rising powers" not only because of economic considerations, but also because they have emerged at a time of crisis, creating space for their emergence as social forces clamouring for the reform of the existing order. Accordingly, the rest of the article illustrates how multilateral organisations played a key role in constructing consensus, particularly since the late 1990s and how that consensus was also replicated in South Africa and Brazil in relation to the global poverty debate.

Convergence within International Organizations

The global poverty debate illustrates the crucial role that international organisation plays in bridging the gap between markets and states and more specifically, the dangers accompanying the enormous inequalities which have coincided with globalisation. Putting poverty on the agenda, conceptualising it and popularising the idea of poverty reduction has largely been spearheaded by multilateral organisations. However, reflecting developmental divides, the global poverty debate has only recently showed some signs towards convergence, though differences remain. This section provides a brief historic overview of these divides and—following Jean-Phillipe Therien[10]—is divided according to three periods, the era of Keynesian Consensus from the 1960s to the 1980s; the triumph of neo-liberalism 1980–1995; and a period of relative convergence, since 1995.

The Keynesian Consensus

One of the earliest incarnations of redistribution by the developing world was extrapolated from the founding principles of the United Nations Relief and

---

8. *Ibid.*, p. 62.
9. *Ibid.*, p. 64
10. J.P. Therien, "Multilateral Institutions and the Poverty Debate: Towards a Global Third Way?", *International Journal*, Vol. 57, No. 2 (2002), pp. 233–252.

Rehabilitation Administration (UNRRA) as well as the Marshall Plan.[11] These noted the duty of other states to aid the economic development of every other state regardless of the political and economic disagreements one state might have with another's economic or political policy. Latin American countries in particular, argued that as they had contributed to European reconstruction through UNRAA (in response to US appeals based on the economic rights and duties of states) it was only fair for the richer countries to now contribute to *their* development. These principles as well as Raul Prebisch's observations about the shifting terms of trade biased against the developing world and specifically his preference for trade regulation, constituted the core basis around which the New International Economic Order (NIEO) was formed.[12] Yet the trade proposals developed by the South in 1964 with the creation of the United Nations Conference on Trade and Development (UNCTAD) involved a series of initiatives (regional economic development schemes, producers' alliances) in order to enhance the third world's influence over economic relations and which the North rejected. Essentially the third world wanted more power over international economic regimes:

> ... that coordinated, rather than abolished, economic interventions at the national level. They wanted all the advantages of trade-induced growth that they could get, and that mostly meant that they wanted the North to reduce barriers to Southern industrial exports... The ideology that informed the NIEO was *reformist*, not revolutionary. It grew on the same roots—Moynihan called them "Fabian", more accurately, they were "Keynesian"—as the ideology that informed the postwar international order in the first place.[13]

Although the advanced industrialised world read the NIEO as a proposal for a fundamentally revised international order, one more reformist response may well have been the crucial role the World Bank played in placing poverty on the agenda, conceptualising it and developing means to address it as a distinct issue. Until 1968, poverty alleviation was never an articulated and institutionalised goal of states and multilateral development agencies. Rather development equalled industrialisation and states were supposed to become accumulators of capital and planners of infrastructure investment, not guarantors of welfare. The World Bank and Robert McNamara in particular, were instrumental in popularising this shift. To cite Martha Finnemore, "[B]efore McNamara, 'being developed' meant having dams, bridges and a (relatively) high GNP per capita. After McNamara, being developed also required the guarantee of a certain level of welfare to one's population".[14] McNamara for example, intended the Bank to lend nearly as much in the 1969–1973 period as it had in its entire 22-year history.[15] Besides the World Bank, numerous other measures were initiated by Bretton Woods institutions such as the International

---

11. Fourty four nations created the UNRAA on 9 November 1943 and it was disbanded in 1946. Its primary function was to administer relief for victims of war. Its functions were transferred to several UN agencies, notably the International Refugee Organization.
12. Murphy, *Global Institutions, op.cit.*, p. 111.
13. *Ibid.*, p. 114–115, emphasis added.
14. M. Finnemore, *National Interests in International Society* (Ithaca, NY: Cornell University Press, 1996), p. 92.
15. *Ibid.*, p. 108

Development Association in 1960, the IMF's Compensatory Financing Facility in 1963 and the addition of Part IV of GATT in 1985 that prepared the groundwork for launching the generalised system of preferences and the creation of the Joint IMF-World Bank Development Committee in 1974.[16]

The Rise of Neo-Liberalism

The decision by the US Federal Reserve to increase interest rates to avoid the declining value of the dollar not only deflated the world economy but plunged the South into unmanageable debt and thus deepened the North's capacity to impose neo-liberal policies on the developing world. Northern policy-makers somewhat more sympathetic to Southern demands sought to sustain the North-South dialogue in the form of the Brandt Commission. With its emphasis on poverty reduction through a kind of Keynesian "new deal"—the Brandt Commission drew on the "mutual interest argument": that the prosperity of the rich is linked to the progress of the poor. It also made a number of proposals. These included the obligation on wealthy countries to allocate at least 0.7 percent of GDP to development aid (set to rise to 1 percent by 2000); a tax on arms exports and the exploration of seabed minerals; a World Development Fund; the use of Special Drawing Rights; a greater role for developing countries in the decision-making procedures of the IMF; stabilising export prices of raw material exports; the roll back of protectionist policies by Northern governments; and an international code of conduct for transnational corporations.[17] Cancún proved to be a defining moment in the history of the twentieth century and symbolised the transition from global Keynesianism to the unchallenged hegemony of neo-liberalism. However, some of these concerns would be repeated in the many Commissions to follow—Palme (1982), Brundtland (1987), the South Commission (1987–1990), the Commission on Global Governance (1995)—keeping global redistribution on the agenda, even as these were overshadowed by global security and other interests.

The confrontational posturing of the 1970s aside, why was the aspiration for a global neo-Keynesian project—initially based on accepted post-war principles of autonomous development drawn from the UNRAA—seen as a fundamental affront to the very basis of world order by Northern policy-makers? Notions of redistribution and large scale transfers were seen by many as simply serving the interests of the ruling and rent-seeking elite, condemning the North-South debate to the circular arguments that beset the development discourse (i.e. between varieties of modernisation theory on the one hand and dependency on the other). In short, the dividing lines in the debate centred over the *cause* for underdevelopment. Was it due to external factors (the international system) or internal conditions (domestic inefficiencies)? Policy-makers in the North saw the NIEO as blaming the system rather than dealing with domestic economic and governance challenges with little regard for the continued viability of the liberal international system. Krasner cited international organisations as the

---

16. Therien *op.cit*. p. 239.
17. J.P. Therien, "The Brandt Commission: The End of an Era in North-South Politics", in R. Thakur, A.F. Cooper and J. English (eds.), *International Commissions and the Power of Ideas* (Tokyo: United Nations University Press, 2005), p. 33–34.

means whereby weak, small developing governments sought to bolster their impact on decisions, yet as Craig Murphy suggests, it was some of the large developing countries, who would later become known as "BRIC" countries, like India and Brazil, who also supported the NIEO.[18]

Nevertheless, by the early 1980s the basic premise of the Bretton Woods institutions was that "the primary responsibility for fighting poverty lay with the governments and people of developing countries themselves", clearly abrogating debates about systemic change as the World Bank Report *Poverty Reduction and the World Bank* made plain.[19] Yet, structural adjustment policies aimed at opening markets, sought to undo old style statist policies whilst the conclusion of the Uruguay Round of GATT and the creation of the WTO would boost developing country exports. However, contrary to supposed "trickle down" effects, the UNDP revealed that global inequality was increasing. The ratio between the share of world income of the richest 20 per cent and that of the poorest 20 per cent went from 30:1 in 1960, to 60:1 in 1990 and to 78:1 in 1994.[20] The impact of structural adjustment policies in terms of prospects for the poor and the sustainability of social services triggered considerable criticism beginning with the UNICEF report, *Adjustment with a Human Face*.[21] In subsequent policy incarnations the World Bank, the IMF and other institutions on the right sought to help the poor, but without sacrificing the economic requirements of adjustment. Governments were urged to protect the poor whilst resisting demands from labour movements and popular urban classes. The result was a social safety net approach to poverty alleviation through which the Bank wanted the poor to compel the powerful to address their needs "rather than across to other social groups to create a stronger social movement for radical social change".[22] By the early 1990s, the left and UN agencies argued that with all the economic and technological progress of globalisation, the liberalisation of trade and opening of financial markets tended to increase inequality and reduce governments' capacity to address social concerns. The devastating effects of the Asian crisis exposed the limitations of the neo-liberal model and helped create the conditions for greater consensus between the left (and UN agencies) and the Bretton Woods institutions on the right.[23]

Towards Convergence through a "Global Third Way"? 1995-

The increasing salience of the anti-globalisation movement, coinciding with the Asian Crisis and the questioning of the neo-liberal model, as well as electoral victories of the social democrats in Europe[24] added to what Anton Hemerijck and

---

18. Murphy, *Global Institutions, op.cit.*, p. 106.
19. cf. Therien, "Multilateral Institutions", *op.cit.*, p. 240.
20. *Ibid.*, p. 241.
21. Giovanni Andrea Cornia, Richard Jolly and Frances Stewart (eds.) *Adjustment with a Human Face* (Oxford: Clarendon Press, 1987).
22. B. Deacon, *Global Social Policy and Governance* (London: Sage, 2007) pp. 28–30.
23. Therien, "Multilateral Institutions", *op.cit.*, p. 241.
24. In Europe, the challenges of German unification and the overall increase in unemployment and poverty following adoption of the 1992 Maastricht Treaty compelling member states to comply with a budget deficit below three per cent of GDP gave impetus to the drift towards the centre-left. A. Noel, "The New Politics of Global Poverty", Paper prepared for the Social Justice in a Changing World Conference, Graduate School of Social Sciences (GSSS), University of Bremen, Germany 10-12 March 2005, available: <www.gsss.uni-bremen.de/socialjustice>, p.15 (accessed 15 July 2011).

Martin Schludi call a "system-wide search for a new, economically viable, politically feasible and socially acceptable profile of social and economic regulation".[25] In the world of the multilateral institutions, despite their differences, greater cooperation and dialogue between UN agencies and Bretton Woods institutions became apparent.[26] In 2000 the IMF, the World Bank, the United Nations and the OECD jointly signed the document, *A Better World for All*, agreeing on a number of specific developmental targets, as well as a timetable geared towards the reduction of world poverty.[27] Reflecting the tensions of the early 1990s, many NGOs and social movements, however, saw this as a betrayal:

> To communicate a coherent international agenda, which could be accepted by these fractious groups, required a message that would finesse the "market is best...market is worst" positions of the IFIs and the anti-globalisation NGOs. The Millennium Development Goals (MGD)'s achieved this through focussing on people and the ends of development—something around which a common vision could be established—rather than the means to get there, which was contested.[28]

It was this consensus that lay the foundation for the objectives contained in the UN's Millennium Declaration and the Millennium Development Goals. Central to this consensus is the acknowledgement on the side of the Bretton Woods institutions, regarding the risk of rising inequality and the recognition amongst the left and the UN agencies, that globalisation also offers opportunities from opened and enlarged markets, suggesting something of a softening of the old developmental divide between systemic and domestic causes of poverty and inequality.[29] In short, the renewed focus on poverty alleviation enabled the right to claim that globalisation and market-based policies were unfavourable to the poor, while the left could make redistribution and social justice central political concerns.[30]

Whether this convergence at the level of global governance coincided or preempted similar dynamics at the domestic/state level is uncertain, what is clear is that leaders in both Brazil and South Africa capitalised on this global *zeitgeist* to galvanise their countries' esteem and seek to *reform* rather than transform processes of global governance. Before briefly examining these efforts, some historic contextualisation is called for in order to highlight the conditions that enhanced a centre-left orientation in both Brazil and South Africa.

---

25. *Ibid.*, p.24
26. While the 1995 Copenhagen Summit on Social Development was significant, it was a 1998 meeting of high-level officials from the Bretton Woods institutions and the ECOSOC in preparation for the Financing for Development Conference (FFD) in Mexico, that illustrated that a new rapprochement was on the cards. Thérien contends that the FFD conference "was widely regarded as the most significant breakthrough in North-South politics since the 1970s". Thérien, "Multilateral Institutions", *op cit.*, p. 240.
27. OECD, *A Better World for All: Progress Towards the International Development Goals* (Paris: OECD, 2000).
28. D. Hulme and S. Fukudu-Parr, "International Norm Dynamics and the "End of Poverty": Understanding the Millennium Development Goals (MDGs)", *Brooks World Poverty Institute Working Paper*, 96 (Manchester: University of Manchester, 2009), p. 16.
29. Thérien, "Multilateral Institutions", *op cit.*, p. 242.
30. Noel, *op.cit.*, p. 30.

Domestic Policy Convergence: South Africa and Brazil

Briefly examining how the ANC in South Africa and the PSDB and thereafter the PT in Brazil moderated and adopted policies consistent with the emerging centre-left consensus at the global level is instructive given these countries' rank position as amongst the most unequal societies on earth.[31] Unsurprisingly, shortly before the ANC and the PT came to power, expectations that both may be tempted to impose considerable redistribution demands and a strong state-led developmental programme, were rife. However, once in power, Cardoso in Brazil and Mbeki in South Africa "were accused of moving rapidly to the right whilst using leftist discourse to justify conservative policies. Both seen as intellectuals, they co-opted powerful figures behind their economic reforms, whilst marginalising opponents both in and outside of government".[32]

Admittedly, the PT is much more solidly grounded in the social democratic tradition than the ANC whose liberation movement identity is a much more salient feature. Yet some social democratic orientations cannot be denied. First, although there may not be much of a historical legacy of social democracy in the ANC—despite extensive assistance from Nordic countries—one could argue that the ANC has been transformed into a social democratic party in recent years "due to the absorption of ideas that were not previously assimilable" as Raymond Suttner suggests.[33] Second, the previous president, Thabo Mbeki may well have drawn upon the remaking of "New Labour" in Britain as a model for the ANC's makeover from liberation movement to political party. For example, Stanley Greenberg, Bill Clinton's political marketer, was used for both the 1994 and 1999 elections. Moreover, Mbeki is known to have aligned himself ideologically with Tony Blair, Gerard Schroeder and the Swedish Social Democratic leader, Goran Persson. (In his late teens and twenties Mbeki supported the British Labour leader, Harold Wilson.)[34] Finally and probably most significantly, is relative similarity in policy terms. For example education—especially at primary and secondary level—has earned a growing share of the national budget, while access to higher education has been broadened considerably. Major reforms have been made in the public health care sector with a growing emphasis on access to primary health care clinics and regulating the private health care sector, so as to also make it more accessible, whilst expanding the number of recipients to qualify for social grants. As De Beus and Koeble note, while there are differences between European third way social democrats and the ANC in terms of levels of economic development and the size and scope of the welfare state, there is also considerable overlap.[35] The ANC's 2007 National

---

31. Since 1995 however, inequality in Brazil has declined significantly. In 2006, the Gini Inequality Index ranked Brazil .55 and South Africa .63, available: <http://www.epi.org/economic_snapshots/entry/webfeatures_snapshots_20060419/> (accessed: 12 July 2011).

32. W.M. Gumede, "Modernising the African National Congress: The Legacy of President Thabo Mbeki", in *State of the Nation 2008* (Pretoria: HSRC Press, 2008).

33. Raymond Suttner, Review of Dubow, Saul, *The African National Congress*, H-S Africa, H-Net Reviews, January 2003, available: <http://www.h-net.org/reviews/showrev.php?id=7123> (accessed 28 May 2011).

34. W.M. Gumede, *Thabo Mbeki and the Battle for the Soul of the ANC* (Cape Town: Zebra Press, 2005), p.127.

35. J. De Beus and T. Koelble, "The Third Way Diffusion of Social Democracy: Western Europe and South Africa Compared", *Politikon*, Vol. 28, No. 2 (2001), p. 181. See also G. Prevost, "The Evolution of

Conference also reconfirmed the party's commitment to social democracy within the context of a "developmental state" and couched within a discourse which clearly echoed "third way" modes of thinking.[36]

In Brazil, although centre-left thinking is associated with the presidency of Lula, its legacy can be traced to the PSDB of former president Cardoso. As Cardoso has stated "What is the difference between my government and the Lula government? We have differences, but not in terms of liberalism".[37] Emerging as a breakaway faction of the broad opposition party to the military regime of 1964–1985, the PMDB—the PSDB pronounced parliamentarism to be superior to presidentialism. Benefiting immensely from the temporary success of the Cruzado Plan in 1986, the PMDB grew spectacularly, occupying near hegemonic political power. However, with size came a multitude of opportunistic conservatives—one in five members elected in 1986 had previously been a member of the official party of the military regime—and the emergence of new intraparty fault lines (notably the defeat of parliamentarism and the shutting out of a number of *autênticos* from Sao Paulo state politics). The *Partido da Social Democratica Brasileira* (PSDB) was from the outset an explicitly social democratic party and drew heavily on European models. However, unlike their European counterparts the party was created from the top down, via a parliamentary faction and—in contrast to the ANC and the PT—was more middle class-based than constructed bottom-up via a mass-based labour party.[38]

What prompted these shifts and how does one account for these transformation processes? Drawing on *power*, four analytical lines—with reference to both Cardoso's PSDB and the Worker's Party, the PT in Brazil, and the ANC in South Africa—are discernable: first, the constraints of the international system; second, shifting domestic coalitions; third institutional factors; and finally, ideational factors.[39]

Constraints of the International System

In both South Africa and Brazil these parties sought to realise their social democratic dreams at probably the worst possible time: at the height of globalisation and the ideological hegemony of neo-liberalism. Moreover, specific domestic conditions meant that the capacity for agency—whether in Pretoria or Brasilia—was very limited. For Cardoso, Brazil's historic battle with hyperinflation superceded all other demands and quite simply dampened the prospects for major redistributive projects. By the late 1990s, the PT also conceded increasingly to adapt to

---

the African National Congress in Power: From Revolutionaries to Social Democrats?", *Politikon*, Vol. 33, No. 2 (August 2006), pp. 163–181.

36. Conference documentation notes for example that, "the NDR [National Democratic Revolution] seeks to ensure that every South African, especially the poor, experiences an improving quality of life. It seeks to build a developmental state shaped by the history and socio-economic dynamics of South African society... The ANC therefore seeks to build a democracy with social content. Informed by our own concrete conditions and experiences, this will, in some respects reflect elements of the best traditions of social democracy...". "Building a National Democratic Society: Strategy and Tactics of the ANC", ANC 52nd National Conference, 2007, Revised Draft, pp. 5-6.

37. S. Burges, *Brazilian Foreign Policy After the Cold War* (Gainesville, FL: University Press of Florida, 2009), p. 159.

38. T.J. Power, "Blairism Brazilian Style? Cardoso and the 'Third Way' in Brazil", *Political Science Quarterly*, Vol. 116, No. 4 (2001), p. 620.

39. *Ibid.*

international market trends, beginning with Lula's third run at the presidency in 1998 to the complete omission of the term "socialism" from the party's programme and the promise that the PT would adhere to all existing agreements with the IMF and other arrangements with the financial community by 2002. In short, market conforming policies would be pursued while targeting welfare to the very poor through job creation and a minimum income provision. Remarkably, the PT-led government even surpassed the fiscal-surplus target agreed upon between the IMF and the Cardoso government, and whereas Cardoso's attempt to reduce the deficit by introducing a pension reform bill was defeated—due to PT obstructionism—under Lula's watch it was passed raising the effective minimum retirement age, reducing survivor benefits and taxes on the pensions and benefits of the most affluent.[40]

South Africa faced similar constraints—the new government had to win the confidence of both local white and international capital and rebuild an economy devastated by years of international isolation. Yet in contrast to Brazil, South Africa's relative isolation from international capital markets meant that by 1993 the country had relatively little debt compared to other middle-income developing countries.[41] As Mitchie and Padayachee[42] have noted, "few countries would have been able to command as much international goodwill and such a groundswell of local popular support".[43] Yet—as in Brazil—a currency crisis in 1996 and increased debt strengthened calls for a much more fiscally conservative approach and thus the rapid abandonment of the Reconstruction and Development Programme (RDP), a programme of macro-economic state intervention modelled on the South Korean developmental project. In both countries, currency crises exacerbated processes whereby international norms regarding macro-economic "discipline" became more easily diffused and legitimated into the domestic policy-making process. In both countries, the left, once in government, were even more constrained "by the need to shift policies even further to the right than the Right would itself, so as to convince investors of its credibility".[44] In short, these two cases suggest that the coincidence of left leaning governments and economic crisis prompt a greater degree of macroeconomic policy conformity.

---

40. W. Hunter, "The *Partido dos Trabalhadores*: Still a Party of the Left?", in P.R. Kingstone and T.J. Power (eds.), *Democratic Brazil Revisited* (Pittsburgh, PA: University of Pittsburgh Press, 2008), pp. 26–27.

41. South Africa's foreign debt to GDP ratio stood at just 14.8 per cent at the end of 1993 compared to an average ratio of 45.8 per cent for severely indebted middle income countries and 35.2 per cent for moderately indebted middle income countries. Cf. J. Van der Westhuizen, *Adapting to Globalization: Malaysia, South Africa and the Challenges to Ethnic Redistribution with Growth* (Westport, CT: Praeger, 2002), p. 116.

42. J. Michie and V. Padayachee, "South Africa's Transition: The Policy Agenda", in J. Michie and V. Padayachee (eds.), *The Political Economy of South Africa's Transition: Policy Perspectives in the Late 1990s* (Fort Worth, TX: Dryden Press, 1997), pp. 15–16.

43. For a fascinating account detailing why South Africa need *not* have embarked on a series of privatization drives, see J. Hentz, "The Two Faces of Privatisation: Political and Economic Logics in Transitional South Africa", *Journal of Modern African Studies*, Vol. 38, No. 2 (2000) pp. 203–233.

44. A.D. Amaral, P.R. Kingstone and J. Krieckhaus, "The Limits of Economic Reform in Brazil", in P.R. Kingstone and T.J. Power (eds.), *Democratic Brazil Revisited* (Pittsburgh, PA: University of Pittsburgh Press, 2008), p. 147.

Shifting Domestic Coalitions

The PSDB known for its political articulators rather than its economic managers, rapidly became more infused with a technocratic political outlook with the incorporation of a number of economists who had developed the *Plano Real*. The success of the *Plano Real* meant that Cardoso and others built political support for the programme, leaving its content to the technocrats. The effect of this division of labour meant that the tables had turned. The PSDB political heavyweights aspiring that their coming to power would mean the introduction of a parliamentary system and European style social democracy, found themselves "working essentially as marketing managers for faceless bureaucrats who propounded controversial and often unpopular macroeconomic reforms".[45] Second, given the nature of Brazil's presidential system and the need for coalition government, Cardoso formed a coalition with the most unlikely of allies, the conservative and clientelistic PFL known to be dominated by veterans of the 1964–1985 military regime—suggesting that PSDB's transformation was well under way by 1994. The PFL controlled the political machinery of the Northeast and within less than a month after the introduction of the *Plano Real*, Cardoso overtook the PT's Lula in the polls, winning the election outright with 54 per cent of the popular vote.[46]

Despite a very different political process, in South Africa similar dynamics prevailed. Three conditions facilitated the rise of the technocrats. First, the relative absence of a tradition of vigorous economic debate within the ANC itself, coupled with progressive intellectuals being ill-prepared to offer alternative development models in the early 1990s. Second, both local big business as well as officials of the IMF and World Bank proselytised the new incumbents into realising the need for limited state intervention, increasingly couching debate within technocratic discourse and with more distance from grassroots activists.[47] Although unlike the PSDB or later the PT, the need for a coalition with another party was obviated for the powerful ANC. Moreover, the terms of the democratic transition included the formation of a government of national unity and with it, retention of a vast civil service in which bureaucrats from the *ancien regime* still occupied important positions, notably in the Treasury. Finally, under Mbeki modernisation of the ANC as well as of governance structures involved a vast programme of centralisation of control—not only of the party—but nearly the entire public administration process (ranging from provincial premiers to directors-general and even mayors) centred within the presidency. Here policy was developed within presidential working groups and subsequently presented to parliament and the public as *faits accomplis*.[48] Since the PSDB lacked strong linkages to the Brazilian labour movement, it lacked the brake that is often applied to the most controversial policies in European social democracies.[49] However, in South Africa and despite the ANC's initial dependence upon its alliance with labour, the decision by both labour and the South African Communist Party to

---

45. Power, "Blairism Brazilian Style", *op cit.*, pp. 628–629.
46. *Ibid.*, pp. 623–624.
47. For example the idea of creating Development Research Centres for local intellectuals and activists to meet and strategise on ideas about transformation at the local level, thereby helping to demobilise forces in the shanty towns, was never implemented. Prevost *op cit.*, p. 170.
48. Gumede, "Modernising the African National Congress", *op cit.*, p. 45.
49. Power, "Blairism Brazilian Style", *op cit.*, p. 629.

subsume their economic policy to that of the ANC, in combination with corporatism, effectively overrode much of these "braking" effects. Yet even within the PT—the trade unions and social movements that had played such a crucial role in the rise of the Workers Party—there was limited capacity to provide "braking effects", although the PT retained its commitment to redistribution and the incorporation of popular participation in decision-making (such as the well-known participatory budgeting process). As in South Africa, civil society organisations initially supported the PT's historic agenda, but later disillusioned and cut off from the policy-making process, formed the Coordination of Social Movements to counter growing corporatist pressures expressed through such initiatives as the Economic and Social Development Council (CDES).[50]

Institutional Factors

Another factor accounting for the PSDB's rightward shift was the effect of Brazil's permissive electoral system promoting party switching—the tendency to migrate from party to party in the hope of improved electoral prospects. The post-1994 PSDB having captured not only the presidency, but doubling its parliamentary representation and having captured six governorships, prompted opportunistic bandwagoning by politicians, particularly by the infusion of new party recruits from the North, Northeast and Centre West region renowned for a more clientelistic and conservative form of politics. In addition many had served in the PFL and PDS parties and had supported the pre-1985 military regime.[51]

Yet when the PT ultimately won, it also had to create coalitions with parties that some in the PT would have preferred to keep at arms length, most notably an alliance with the Liberal Party in 2002 that proved to be highly controversial. An alliance with the PL—known to be supported by evangelical pastors and wealthy businessmen—would not only enhance the PT's support in the state with the second largest electorate, Minas Gerais (with many impoverished rural areas where the PT had not been able to make inroads), but links between the leader of the PL and businessmen would subside populist fears about a Lula-led government.[52]

In contrast, very little fragmentation marks South Africa's parliamentary system. In fact, with the ANC commanding nearly 66 per cent of the parliamentary vote (after 2009 elections), a culture of strong party discipline (reinforced by a party list system in which the support of party mandarins rather than voter constituencies prevail), the institutional factors in the South African case approximate the complete opposite of the Brazilian system.[53] Moreover, Mbeki's modernisation of the ANC also entailed growing centralisation and control of the party, discouraging contestation for posts and the use of a party deployment committee to ensure that members toed the line. In short, as little internal dissent as possible was allowed to emerge. The effect was that the entire

---

50. K. Hochstetler, "Organized Civil Society in Lula's Brazil", in P.R. Kingstone and T.J. Power (eds.), *Democratic Brazil Revisited* (Pittsburgh, PA: University of Pittsburgh Press, 2008), p. 33.

51. Power, "Blairism Brazilian Style", *op. cit.*, p. 630.

52. Hunter, *op cit.*, p. 24.

53. Although the ANC attained 66 per cent of the vote in the 2009 elections—within a whisker of a two-thirds majority—the patterns of a *de facto* one party dominant system remain.

governance structure was "locked in" to whatever new policy shift was undertaken, even if this included a clear conservative shift to the centre.

Ideational Factors

Networks play a significant ideational role in terms of agenda-setting, consensus building, the coordination of policy, knowledge exchange and production and finally, norm setting and diffusion. Networks also often emerge due to shortcomings within existing formal institutions and offer the prospect of influencing policy as much as running the risk of becoming an instrument whereby weaker members of the network can be co-opted.[54] For our purposes three networks are of particular significance, the Progressive Governance Movement, the World Economic Forum (WEF), and the G20.

Both the ANC and the PSDB drew heavily on their international connections with other sister social democratic parties. For both, the experience of exile and foreign support strengthened such links. In the case of the PSDB this was especially the case with those in Spain and Portugal, and in particular the prime minister and later president of Portugal, Mario Soares and the Spanish Prime Minister Felipe Gonzalez who rebuilt the PSOE, the Spanish Socialist Workers Party. The experience of parliamentarism in the transition to democracy in these cases, as well as the fact that the more Marxist variant of social democracy was in terminal decline, underscored the need for a more market-friendly orientation. The global attraction of this approach was greatly enhanced by the coming to power of "New Labour" in 1994, intellectual support for Giddens' notion of a "third way" and its acclamation in Germany, Italy and elsewhere in Europe.[55]

These conditions also affected the ANC and Thabo Mbeki in particular as he sought to modernise the ANC. For example, at the 1997 National Conference ANC MPs demanded that the parliamentary wing be given a formal constitutional role as had been the practice with other social democratic parties (a proposal that never came to pass). Since 2000 the ANC has debated the possibility of establishing a policy institute where policies can be developed along the lines of the German Social Democratic Party think-tank, the Frederich Ebert Foundation, and creating a permanent Electoral Commission akin to the Swedish Democratic Party to oversee all internal elections in the party and selected from party elders and neutrals.[56]

That "meeting of the minds" between socially reformist statesmen and women of the advanced industrial world and the rising powers in the developing world—also came to be to diffused through the so-called "Progressive Governance" network and its secretariat, the Policy Network (as the subsequent, more low-key incarnation of "third way" advocates). Launched in 1999 and 2000 respectively, it was initiated, by the then heads of government, Bill Clinton, Tony Blair, Gerhard Schröder, Wim Kok and Massimo D'Alema, in order to enhance cooperation and links between key "progressive" policy-makers and academics

---

54. L. Martinez-Diaz and N. Woods (eds.), *Networks of Influence? Developing Countries in a Networked Global Order* (Oxford: Oxford University Press, 2009), pp. 6, 10.
55. Power, "Blairism Brazilian Style", *op cit.*, p. 632–633.
56. Gumede, "Modernising the African National Congress", *op. cit.*, pp. 39, 48, 50.

as well as to provide a meeting place for exchanging concrete policies and practices. India, South Africa and Brazil play a significant role in this network. In 1999 Fernando Henrique Cardoso from Brazil was the only leader from the developing world to be invited to its annual conference; in February 2006, when the Progressive Governance Summit was hosted for the first time in a developing country, it was held in South Africa upon invitation from Thabo Mbeki, and in 2005 India was invited to join. These efforts to be seen as acknowledged "voices of the South" and enhance Brazil, South Africa and India's claims to membership of a reformed UN Security Council are also aimed at feeding into domestic discourse. For all three governments stand accused by leftist critics of having "sold out" to the neo-liberal project—for South Africa especially since its adoption of a liberalisation and privatisation programme, GEAR in the mid-1990s, and Brazil even after the election of a PT-led government in 2003. New initiatives aimed at reforming institutions of global governance on the one hand and varied attempts to infuse more socially egalitarian outcomes from the process of globalisation at home on the other, serve to illustrate to leftist critics at home that engaging globalisation is a prerequisite for transforming it and that development does not involve abandoning the social democratic dream by disengaging from globalisation, but actively trying to transform it. The debate between these state leaders and their leftist opponents is whether the institutions of global governance can be reformed "from the inside" or not at all. State elites in Brasilia, and Pretoria believe more can be accomplished by being inside and that liberal internationalism can be reformed—however modestly—to reflect the interests of the developing world.

The WEF is of particular significance given its role as a multi-stakeholder in global governance, facilitating the kind of diplomacy between firms and states Susan Strange often wrote about,[57] and in recent years, also included non-governmental organisations at the WEF.[58] In fact, a quick survey of the agenda of the major World Economic Forum conferences during the end of the 1990s and early 2000s reveals the extent to which more attention was being given to global social concerns such as poverty and the subsequent proliferation of public-private partnerships (including the UN's "Global Compact") and the rise of public health issues like HIV/AIDS, malaria and tuberculosis.[59] For example, at the Davos 2005 meeting the French president, Jacques Chirac, proposed a new global tax on aviation fuel and financial transactions or capital flows to finance development aid. South Africa's Thabo Mbeki—supported by Bill Clinton and Bill Gates—however argued that such a tax would be too difficult and time consuming to implement and would fail to garner sufficient global political backing to be enacted.[60] South African and Brazilian leaders not only regularly attend the annual Davos meetings, but often host the regional WEF

---

57. J. Stopford, S. Strange and J.S. Henley, *Rival States, Rival Firms: Competition for World Market Shares* (Cambridge: Cambridge University Press, 1991).

58. Partly the decision to invite some NGOs to attend WEF meetings was also to co-opt potential massive protest in the wake of the December 1999 Seattle World Trade Organization ministerial meeting, which was marred by violent protest. G.A. Pigman, *The World Economic Forum: A Multi-Stakeholder Approach to Global Governance* (London: Routledge, 2007), p. 71.

59. "The History of the World Economic Forum on Scribd", <http://www.scribd.com/fullscreen/45780093?access_key=key-fz6n72jb90ac9bacj27> (accessed 3 July 2011).

60. Pigman *op cit.*, p. 18.

conferences. One of the first meetings outside the country between ex-South African president F.W de Klerk, then Zulu leader Mangosuthu Buthelezi and Nelson Mandela, occurred at the 1992 WEF Davos meeting and the WEF has been an instrumental platform for Thabo Mbeki to launch the NEPAD. President Lula probably best exemplified Brazil's intermediating role by being one of very few world leaders who participated in both the meetings of the World Economic Forum in Davos as well as its counter, the World Social Forum in Porto Allegre in 2005.[61] Indeed, medium-sized countries are generally over-represented at the WEF, and the Forum invests heavily in the emerging markets (in 2007 the WEF launched the "New Champions" an annual meeting in China of stake-holders from 1,500 "Global Growth Companies" in the emerging markets).[62]

South Africa and Brazil have played critical roles in the G20, with South Africa accepting invitations to every one of the G8 summits since the Okinawa Summit in 2000 and Brazil having participated in the G20 since its first summit in Berlin in 1999. (Both were also part of the Outreach 5 Heiligendamm Process that preceded the formalisation of the G20.)[63]

It is instructive that as the *zeitgeist* in favour of a reform of global capitalism, eroded following the events of 9 September 2001, both Lula and Mbeki seized the initiative to argue that poverty bred violence. Lula reiterated this point at the UN General Assembly in September 2006, whilst Mbeki argued the same even more forcefully earlier at the G8's Kananaskis Summit in 2002, while seeking support for his more ambitious developmental blueprint, the New Partnership for Africa's Development (NEPAD):

> Somebody [who] is mobilising for terrorism... can use the fact of poverty, the fact of large disparities of wealth, the fact of a process of globalization, which produces great success at one end of the globe and great disasters at the other end... [They] can exploit that to say these are the devils, let's carry out a terrorist campaign against them.[64]

Within the G20 both Brasilia and Pretoria seek to prevent protectionism, enhance conditions for greater financial market regulation and special assistance arising from the collapse of financial flows in the emerging economies and support limited fiscal stimulation measures. However, for both, complications also arise due to multiple roles as partners of emerging economies, spokesmen for their respective continents and as advocates for the global South.[65] Yet

---

61. During his second term and having moved considerably to the right, he did not receive the same kind of response in Porto Allegre.
62. J. Graz, "How Powerful are Transnational Elite Clubs? The Social Myth of the World Economic Forum", *New Political Economy*, Vol. 8, No. 3 (2003), p. 331.
63. B. Vickers, "South Africa: Global Reformism, Global Apartheid and the Heiligendamm Process", in A.F. Cooper and A. Antkiewicz (eds.) *Emerging Powers in Global Governance: Lessons from the Heiligendamm Process* (Waterloo: Wilfred Laurier Press, 2008), p. 165; J. Kirton, "Brazil's Contribution to G20 and Global Governance", available: <http://www.g20.utoronto.ca/biblio/kirton-eneri-110518.html> (accessed 6 July 2011).
64. *Business Day*, "Mbeki Urges Action on Africa", 19 July 2002, p.5.
65. B. Vickers, "Country Fact Sheet: South Africa", in Reichert S. Pohlmann, H.R. Schillinger (eds.), *The G-20 "A Global Economic Government" in the Making?"* (Berlin: International Policy Analysis, Friedrich Ebert Stiftung, 2010), p. 55; D. Schäfer, J. Steinhilber, "Country Fact Sheet: Brazil", in Reichert S. Pohlmann and H.R. Schillinger (eds.), *The G-20 "A Global Economic Government' in the Making?"*

both see the G20 as a platform whereby the international financial institutions could be reformed to become more representative of the emerging powers' growing economic and political significance. As deputy president Mbeki had already floated the idea of a countervailing "G-8 of the South" as early as 1998, whereas Brazil saw the need for a coalition to oppose a joint US-EU agricultural proposal for the 2003 Cancún WTO ministerial meeting that ultimately enabled Brasilia to "push its own agenda in a seemingly disinterested manner that created a space between Brazilian desires and attributions of ownership for a particular policy proposal".[66] The severity of the global financial crisis of 2007–2008 prompted more than simply the immediate management of the crisis, but the need for a fundamental restructuring of the global financial architecture, with Brazil coordinating the BRIC position at the G20 2008 Sao Paulo finance ministers meeting against the maintenance of the veto powers of the major countries. South Africa's then finance minister, Trevor Manuel, who had had been asked to chair the Committee of Eminent Persons on IMF Governance Reform, recommended amongst others, that in terms of the size and composition of the Board, the process of raising and rebalancing shares set in motion in October 2007, "is much too gradual" and needs to be brought forward to 2010.[67] And yet, for all the frustration at the foot-dragging over such reforms—prompting Lula to famously remark that the crisis "was fostered and boosted by irrational behaviour of some people that are white, blue eyed"[68]—little came of demands for the appointment of a new IMF managing director based on merit and not from Europe as convention dictated, with the appointment of the French finance minister, Christine Lagard.[69] Whilst the World Bank approved a slight shift of voting shares in favour of developing countries (a 4.59 per cent shift to developing and transition countries since 2008), in the case of the IMF, China became the third largest stake-holder, with what the Fund calls "emerging dynamic economies" Brazil, China, Russia and India gaining a further 6 per cent of shares.[70] The G20 ambition of increasing the quota shares of developing countries has been only partially met without altering the dominance of the US or the OECD.

Effects of the Global-Domestic Interface

Social grants to alleviate poverty provide one of the most interesting illustrations of the outcomes of this interface at the level of international organisation, the domestic policy context and subsequently to some extent, also in the realm of foreign policy. While both Brazil and South Africa embarked upon far-reaching market

---

(Berlin: International Policy Analysis, Friedrich Ebert Stiftung, 2010), p. 17, available: <http://library.fes.de/pdf-files/id/ipa/07284.pdf> (accessed 5 July 2011).

66. Burges, *op cit.*, p. 167; B. Vickers, *op cit.*, p. 174.

67. T. Manuel, *Report of the Committee of Eminent Persons on IMF Governance Reform*, (Pretoria: Ministry of Finance, Republic of South Africa, 24 March 2009).

68. R. Roett, *The New Brazil* (Washington: Brookings Institution, 2010), p. 141.

69. The hypocrisy of European contentions that only one of their own can understand European complexities was well-pointed to by *The Economist* in the article "The IMF: Time for a Change" (26 May 2011, p. 16), as being akin to similar arguments made in favour of appointing Argentina's finance minister in the 1980s or Thailand's in 1997 to the IMF.

70. IMF Fact Sheet, "IMF Quotas", March 2011, available: <www.imf.org/external/np/exr/facts/quotas.htm> (accessed 7 July 2011); C. Jakobeit, "IBSA and the G-20: Scope for Change?", Paper presented at the 4th Regional Powers Network Conference, Stellenbosch, 6-7 September 2010.

liberalisation, this has also coincided with notable initiatives in terms of social policy.

Both under Cardoso and especially Lula conditional cash transfer programmes have become part of mainstream social policy. Under Cardoso social assistance spending increased to 5.6 per cent of total social spending; by 2004 it increased to 0.9 per cent of GDP.[71] Under Lula, the *bolsa-escola* and *bolsa-alimentacao* programmes were merged into a single programme, named *bolsa-familia*, increasing spending from 1.1 per cent to 2.5 per cent of total government expenditure, increasing from 0.2 to 0.5 per cent of GDP. The *bolsa escola*, the flagship of these programmes provides mothers with a monthly stipend of US $7 per child if their child attends school for at least 85 per cent of the time. Originating in Brasilia in 1995 the programme was adopted nationally in 2001 and by the end of 2003 had been adopted by more than 5,561 municipalities which had distributed nearly US $500 million in grants to over five million families.[72] In three years the number of beneficiaries has doubled to over 30 million, nearly three quarters of those living below the poverty line. Moreover according to official estimates the average level of benefit paid per family has almost tripled and by the end of 2005 nearly 8.7 million families had been included. It is reported that rural poverty levels declined from 39.5 per cent in 2003 to 35.4 per cent in 2004.[73] By 2006 an IMF expert cited the *bolsa-familia* as a successful strategy for reducing poverty.[74]

In South Africa, between 2003 and 2007 social assistance grants increased from ZAR 37 billion to ZAR 62 billion. The 2010/2011 allowance of ZAR 89 billion represents a 12 per cent increase year-on-year and covers state pensions, disability allowances, child support, foster care, care dependency grants, war veterans and grant-in-aid. From 2.4 million beneficiaries in 1996, the number of social grant beneficiaries had expanded six-fold to 12.3 million in 2007. For three out of ten African households their single largest source of income comes from the state, while nearly 25 per cent of all South Africans (or 14,608,008) receive some form of social welfare.[75] Among developing countries South Africa and Brazil have the largest non-contributory pension programmes, reaching 5.3 million in Brazil and 1.9 million in South Africa (at 2003 figures), at a relatively low cost of 1 per cent of GDP in Brazil and 1.4 per cent in South Africa with significant impacts on poverty, given that such benefits are shared within households.[76]

That the World Bank supports such programmes and is fond of citing their success, especially of the Brazilian model, underscores the extent to which South Africa and Brazil seek to project poverty alleviation in the domestic

---

71. A. Hall, "From 'Fome Zero' to 'Bolsa Familia': Social Policies and Poverty Alleviation under Lula", *Journal of Latin American Studies*, Vol. 38, No. 4 (2006), p. 693.

72. *Ibid.* p. 695.

73. *Ibid.* p. 699.

74. R. Bourne, *Lula of Brazil: The Story So Far* (Berkeley, CA: University of California Press, 2008), p. 160.

75. The child support grant, reflective of the HIV/AIDS impact, constitutes the largest grant with 9,895,053 recipients (given to their caretakers). *South Africa Survey 2008/9* (Johannesburg: South African Institute of Race Relations, 2009), p. 529.

76. A. Barrientos (ed.), *Non-Contributory Pensions and Poverty Prevention: A Comparative Study of Brazil and South Africa* (London: Institute for Development and Policy Management & HelpAge International, 2003) p. 5.

sphere as an enduring concern at the global level.[77] In 2004 the International Action against Hunger and Poverty was launched with Lula and the presidents of France, Chile and Spain and the support of Kofi Annan, the UN Secretary-General as part of the MDG targets for 2015. Lula made the call for a global campaign against hunger to parallel the project operating at home during meetings of the World Social Forum in Porto Allegre and shortly thereafter at the World Economic Forum in Davos, Switzerland. Unlike Brazil, South Africa has not drawn on its social grants as a form of "soft power" partly because it has not succeeded in alleviating poverty nearly as dramatically as Brazil (which reduced income inequality between 1995 and 2004 by almost 4.6 per cent). Moreover, Pretoria does not wish to attract even more economic migrants from the region and thus face yet further xenophobic attacks. Rather, the concern with poverty alleviation, especially in the African context, is sought in more institutional terms as part of "good governance" criteria as set-out in the NEPAD for example, or in seeking debt cancellation on behalf of the continent and other initiatives. Whereas the NEPAD project seems to have lost its political prominence under Mbeki's successor, Jacob Zuma, in discursive terms, the NEPAD remains interesting. For example, consistent with the attempt to *not* be associated with those social forces that may be held responsible by the privileged for the collapse of the previous era of prosperity (i.e. the more radical demands for restitution in the latter part of the NIEO era), the NEPAD refrains from blaming Western imperialism/neo-colonialism for African underdevelopment, rather emphasising ideas such as "partnership" and "good governance". The idea of partnership was used by Kofi Annan in his Millennium UN Summit Heads of Government Report in which he endorsed the idea of partnership between the North and South. Specifically, his plea was to reduce the proportion of people living in extreme poverty and to improve the lives of more than one billion by 2015. The partnership idea had also long been underwritten in Western developmental policy papers by Clinton in the US, Schroeder in Germany and Blair in the UK.

Finally, the most obvious institutional expression of these initiatives is of course, the India-Brazil-South Africa Forum (IBSA) with its strong focus on development cooperation, more specifically the IBSA Facility for Poverty Alleviation. Although the Fund is comparatively small, since each of the three countries only contributes about US $1 million for developmental projects across the South, its real significance is probably symbolic.[78] Despite its insignificant size, the Fund has been given a Millennium Development Goal Award by the UNDP's Millennium Campaign and the Office for Partnerships, with the IBSA Fund considered a "breakthrough model of South-South Technical Cooperation" in September 2010. Equally symbolic is the fact that the Global Poverty Summit—with emphatic calls for the WTO's Doha Round to tie trade talks with the reduction of poverty—was hosted in Johannesburg in January 2011.

---

77. World Bank, "Bolsa Familia: Changing the Lives of Millions in Brazil", available: <http://web.worldbank.org/WBSITE/EXTERNAL/NEWS/0,print:Y~isCURL:Y~conte> (accessed 8 July 2011).

78. The Fund's contributions include waste removal and sanitation in Haiti; agricultural training techniques for women, literacy programmes and water pumps in Guinea-Bissau; the rehabilitation of two health centres in Cape Verde; capacity building workshops on HIV/AIDS in Burundi; construction of a sports centre in Palestine; and medical care for special needs children in Cambodia. Department of International Relations and Cooperation, Republic of South Africa, Daily Email Update (20 September 2010).

Certainly, one of the consequences of the "Great Recession" is that the historiography of North-South relations and movements such as the NIEO are less likely to appear as radical as they were at the time. We may yet find that the old principle that had inspired leaders of the developing world about the economic rights and duties of states as embodied in UNRAA supporting more autonomous developments paths, resurrected with renewed vigour. Whatever the developmental model, what is certain is that the magnitude of global inequality is likely to deter adopting "one-size-fits-all" models, especially if democracy consolidates in the emerging powers.

Conclusion

Leading powers in the developing world are taking on more responsibilities and clamouring for more recognition in global governance consistent with their rising economic significance and importance as vast new markets in terms of consumption, production and investment. As these emerging powers draw on their collective heft to influence the global agenda, redistribution is clearly set to once again constitute a significant part of these negotiations.

Drawing on a Gramscian perspective, this article has argued that the privileged powers are more likely to consider such demands provided these proposals help reform deficiencies in the existing liberal international order and do not fundamentally transform it. Accordingly, the global poverty debate provides an illustration of the way in which global crises enhance conditions for rising powers such as South Africa and Brazil to influence the agenda of global governance. That considerable policy convergence at both the level of international organisation and the state has occurred—however moderate or insignificant these may seem to those on the left—makes a significant contribution toward generating the required global sentiment, *within* which emerging powers' redistributive demands are more likely to receive a sympathetic hearing.

Strategies and Tactics for Global Change: Democratic Brazil in Comparative Perspective

SEAN W. BURGES

Brazil has consistently been seeking a more influential place at global decision-making tables in order to preserve its sovereignty and protect its national policy autonomy. The challenge for Brazilian diplomats is that their country lacks the economic or military muscle to force a way onto these tables. Subtler avenues for inclusion are thus needed. Seven of the main tactics employed in Brazilian foreign policy are outlined here, and range from the defensive/passive (avoiding mindless opposition, collectivisation) through the neutral (consensus creation, technocratic speak) to the assertive (building new organisations, propagating new thinking) and finally to the aggressive (principled presidential righteousness).

Ask any Brazilian diplomat about José Maria da Silva Paranhos Junior, the Baron of Rio Branco, and they will likely wax lyrical about their 'patron saint', the muse of contemporary Brazilian foreign policy practices. It was Rio Branco who most effectively floated the idea that Brazil should be actively engaged in the international system, pushing hard for Brazil to host the 1906 Rio de Janeiro Pan American Summit and participate in the 1907 Hague Conference. This initiative from Rio Branco laid the internationalist foundation stone that saw Brazil participating in the Versailles Treaty negotiations and take a position on the Executive Council of the League of Nations. Similar ambitions were repeated in San Francisco when the United Nations was formed, with Brazil working very hard to get the organisation off the ground.[1] The San Francisco conference also emerges as symptomatic of the problem that senior diplomats often see afflicting their country's engagement with global governance: Brazil actively contributes to the formation of workable international institutions, but as often as not receives little thanks for its efforts and is subsequently left at the margins. In the case of the UN, Brazil received the consolation prize of making the first speech at each year's General Assembly rather than the still-coveted permanent seat on the Security Council.

---

*This paper was first presented at the German Institute of Global and Area Studies' 4th Regional Powers Network Conference, *Emerging Regional Powers and Global Redistribution*, held at the Stellenbsoch Institute for Advanced Studies in 2010. The paper has benefited greatly from suggestions made by the other conference participants as well as the comments of the two anonymous referees for this journal.

1. E. Bradford Burns, *The Unwritten Alliance: Rio Branco and Brazilian-American Relations* (New York: Colombia University Press, 1966); Joseph Smith, *Unequal Giants: Relations Between the United States and Brazil, 1889-1930* (Pittsburgh: University of Pittsburgh Press, 1991).

Brazil has consistently been one of the actors involved in the creation and management of key institutions in global governance such as the UN and the GATT/WTO. The traditions established by Rio Branco created a proclivity within the foreign ministry, known as *Itamaraty*, to identify Brazil with the Western tradition, to seek inclusion in the halls of decision-making dominated by the Western powers.[2] While there are definite ups and downs in Brazil's adherence to the dictates of the power centres guiding the international system, the abiding reality that has continued strongly since the end of the Cold War is one of adhering to the core precepts of global hegemony, which in this article is taken to mean the dominant liberal economic and political ideology that underpins global governance institutions,[3] without accepting that this requires adoption of a subordinate position within the global hegemony.[4] This led to the sort of contradictions seen during the Cardoso years when Brazilian foreign and economic policy appeared supine before the US when it was in reality taking an approach that accepted the core ideological propositions, but asked questions about their practical implementation.[5] Some of these tendencies continued as a persistent theme during the Lula's administration, most notably the absence of outright opposition to the core precepts of the existing global hegemony.[6]

Brazil has nevertheless remained unwilling to blindly suffer the current application of the hegemony, pushing persistently for a voice in global affairs and more equitable distribution of decision-making across the North-South divide. During the Cardoso era (1995–2002) the underpinning logic was not articulated particularly forcefully, largely because Brazil remained in a very tenuous economic situation. The Lula era (2003–2010) marked a shift that saw an increasingly vocal and forceful presentation of Brazil's position on the international distribution of power, which was neatly summarised at the start of the Dilma Rousseff presidency by newly appointed foreign minister Antonio Patriota: "Brazil, with its tradition of peace and tolerance, is uniquely positioned as an actor to promote more inclusive models of development and to strengthen cooperation between countries through mechanisms that are more representative and legitimate".[7] To emphasise the redistributive nature of Brazil's Southern-oriented,

---

2. Celso Lafer, "Brazilian International Identity and Foreign Policy: Past, Present, and Future", *Daedalus*, Vol. 129, No. 2 (2000), pp. 207–238.

3. The understanding of hegemony used in this paper can be reduced to a melding of the Gramscian interpretation of Robert W. Cox and the structuralist approach to IPE of Susan Strange. This has been set out in the context of Brazilian foreign policy in Sean W. Burges, "Consensual Hegemony: Theorizing the Practice of Brazilian Foreign Policy", *International Relations*, Vol. 22, No. 1 (2008), pp. 65–84. See also Robert W. Cox, "Gramsci, Hegemony, and International Relations: An Essay in Methdon", in Robert W. Cox and Timothy Sinclair (eds.), *Approaches to World Order* (Cambridge: Cambridge University Press, 1996); and Susan Strange, *States and Markets* (London: Pinter Books, 1994), pp. 124–144.

4. Tullo Vigevani and Marcello Fernandes de Oliveira, "Brazilian Foreign Policy in the Cardoso Era: The Search for Autonomy Through Integration", *Latin American Perspecitves*, Vol. 34, No. 58 (2007): pp. 61–62.

5. Luiz Alberto Moniz Bandeira, "Política Exterior do Brasil – De FHC a Lula", *Plenarium*, Vol. 2, No. 2 (2005), pp. 64–82.

6. Jean Daudelin, "Joining the Club: Lula and the End of the Periphery for Brazil", in Peter Birle, Sérgio Costa and Horst Nitschack (eds.), *Brazil and the Americas: Convergences and Perspectives* (Madrid: Iberoamericana, 2008), pp. 43–65.

7. Antonio Patriota, "Discurso do Ministro Antonio de Aguiar Patriota na cerimônia de transmissão do cardo de Ministro de Estado das Relações Exteriores", Brasília (2 January 2011), available: <www.itamaraty.gov.br> (accessed 22 July 2011).

developmentalist priorities in global governance reform, Patriota continued on with a warning, noting that "the G-20 and other restricted groupings will only succeed in consolidating their authority if they remain sensitive to the ambitions and interests of the over 150 countries who are not present at the meetings".[8] The focus is consequently on fundamentally shifting the tone and set of priorities addressed at global governance forums to reflect the developmental challenges that Brazil faces, and fortunately for its foreign policy approach shares with a large number of other countries. It also quietly entrenches Brazil's new position of global importance as the 'voice' of the South.

Patriota's remarks pointed to the myriad on-going negotiations about what form global governance structures should take in the twenty-first century, which raises the question of what Brazil's strategic approach might be in these bilateral and multilateral talks. Here the work of John S. Odell is useful for making a broad statement about overarching Brazilian strategy. Odell sets out a continuum that runs from a distributive strategy through to an integrative strategy, with mixed approaches lying in the middle.[9] Simplifying for the sake of brevity, negotiators following a distributive strategy view issues in value-claiming terms, meaning that there is a limited pool of gain available and the negotiators' job is to maximise the share of the pie claimed for their side. In contrast, an integrative strategy views negotiations as an opportunity to create value, meaning that both sides will be able to secure gains through any eventual agreement by making the pie larger. By looking at past behaviour, this article interprets Brazil as a largely distributive negotiator, viewing most issues in zero-sum terms that reflect a well-entrenched realpolitik approach to international affairs within *Itamaraty*.

The quirk with the larger pattern of the Brazilian negotiating strategy that forms a theme in this paper is that its diplomats consistently seek to present their position as integrative, that is as value-creating, positive and solution seeking, not conflictive or negative. Odell's observations about negotiating objectives are particularly important in explaining this. Beyond the obvious economic dimensions of trade talks, Odell also points out that there are important relational considerations about what impact negotiations will have on future bilateral relations, as well as domestic political ramifications for the contemporary government.[10] For Brazilian negotiators the most important element largely remains the potential impact on bilateral foreign relations; the domestic is much less important because foreign policy still has a very limited political audience within Brazil. In other words, how does Brazilian diplomacy work with a distributive negotiating strategy to fashion and morph the global hegemony to reflect Brazil's view of an appropriate North-South decision dialogue? More importantly, what tactics are used? How is this done without leaving Brazil open to the charges of stubborn and destructive resistance that would allow the North to summarily reject Brazilian input in favour of a more malleable spokesperson from the South? Expressed very simply, Brazil's goal is not to enter into 'wars' in order to reform international political and economic regimes and power realities, but to engage plethora small, seemingly insignificant skirmishes that in their

---

8. *Ibid*.
9. John S. Odell, *Negotiating the World Economy* (Ithaca, NY: Cornell University Press, 2000), chapter 2.
10. *Ibid*.

totality can quietly shift the sands beneath the feet of the putative 'powers'. If executed perfectly, a 'war' would become unnecessary because nobody would realise a battle had taken place.

The question at the core of this article thus is not what is Brazil's overarching strategic approach to negotiations, but rather what set of tactical devices are employed by Brazilian diplomats within their distributive negotiating outlook to maintain a quasi-integrative veneer? How does Brazil take a forceful zero-sum approach while still retaining the confidence of both the North and South that it needs if it is to retain a front-row seat at international negotiating tables?[11] The central proposition in this article is that Brazil has found a substantive place at international decision-making tables because it employs a set of tactics that possess an outwardly constructive and supportive approach to pursuing the reform of global governance institutions and practices. In Odell's formulation, these are tactics that at first blush appear consistent with an integrative, value-creating negotiating strategy. Rather than seeking to destroy, overturn, or abolish processes and regimes seen as broadly inimical to Brazilian interests, the diplomats working in *Itamaraty* have adopted a more measured approach that accepts the legitimacy of the global liberal economic hegemony, but asks questions about the efficiency and equity of its application. More significantly, a core element of the Brazilian tactical approach is to collectivise its position on a particular international issue, allowing its diplomats to claim with reasonable legitimacy that they are bringing a larger agglomeration of interests to the table and acting as a positive international policy entrepreneur.[12] This puts Brazil in the middle between the North and the South. The North gives Brazil of the South a nod of inclusion because the country brings a sense of global inclusiveness and implicit redistribution to discussions and thus added legitimacy to existing institutions and process. For its part, the South is, on balance, positively disposed towards Brazil, although not entirely trusting, because the coordination activities of Brazilian diplomats offer an avenue for including Southern points of view and priorities in the evolution of global governance institutions.

The discussion in this article will revolve around seven tactics utilised by the Brazilian foreign policy establishment under a distributive strategy to advance their country's place in the global order. While not devised as or organised into a rigorous continuum, they can loosely be grouped as ranging from the defensive/passive (avoiding mindless opposition, collectivisation) through the neutral (consensus creation, technocratic speak) to the assertive (building new organisations, propagating new thinking) and finally, for *Itamaraty*, to the aggressive (principled presidential righteousness). The cataloguing and description of these Brazilian foreign policy tactics is intended to provide insight to the non-expert on the main foreign policy approaches employed by Brazil, something that still remains absent from the literature. On a theoretical level the seven tactics presented here may provide a starting point for exploring how the new band of supposed middle powers interact with major powers to support the shape of the international system without resorting to the policies of near-automatic alignment

---

11. Leonard J. Schoppa, "The Social Context of International Bargaining", *International Organization*, Vol. 53, No. 2 (1999), pp. 307–342.

12. Andrew Moravcsik, "A New Statecraft? Supranational Entrepreneurs and International Cooperation", *International Organization*, Vol. 53, No. 2 (1999), pp. 267–306.

and support of the US seen in traditional middle powers such as Australia and Canada.[13] While the emphasis in this article will be on foreign economic policy, aspects of political and security relations will enter into the discussion. The article will close with a discussion of the successes and limitations of Brazil's efforts at achieving some self-benefiting redistribution of global decision-making powers.

Tactic #1: Avoid Mindless Opposition (Defensive/Passive)

The 2003 Cancún WTO ministerial meeting closed with a thunderous denunciation from US Trade Representative Robert Zoellick that the whole Doha development round was in danger because obstreperous countries like Brazil were mindlessly opposing a good deal. In his memoirs Richard Feinberg, a key member of the Clinton presidency's Latin American team, points to a similar level of dissatisfaction and frustration with *Itamaraty* during the early stages of the Free Trade of the Americas negotiating process.[14] At first blush such charges seemed to make sense. After all, the strong tradition of flat resistance from the New International Economic Order of the 1970s had apparently been revived at the 1998 Seattle WTO ministerial meeting. But, as officials in the US and EU came to recognise, the situation in Miami and Cancún was considerably more complicated.

While it is doubtful that policy-makers in *Itamaraty* ever had any intention of recommending to their president that Brazil sign on to the FTAA,[15] public governmental criticisms of a free trade deal with the US were few and far between. One of the most vocal critics of the possible deal was Samuel Pinheiro Guimarães, a career diplomat who was to become Lula's Secretary General of Foreign Affairs in 2003. Prior to being appointed the number two diplomat in 2003, Guimarães was placed in a kind of internal administrative exile by then-Foreign Minister Celso Lafer in 2001, during a moment of sensitivity in the bilateral US-Brazilian relationship. Other diplomats of the period opted for a more moderate language of opposition. *Itamaraty* Secretary General Osmar Chohfi noted that Brazil and other regional countries were interested in the idea of an FTAA, but not simply as an extension of NAFTA.[16] Chohfi's comments simply mirrored a more elaborate speech given by Celso Lafer in 2001, where Brazil's trading commitment was forcefully reasserted before he implicitly side lined the entire FTAA process as simply one option that could be pursued on the way to a larger global trade deal through the WTO. Lafer concluded by noting that simply rejecting the FTAA idea was overly risky, but this did not mean that Brazil should simply accept what was put on offer. Careful analysis was necessary.[17]

---

13. Andrew F. Cooper, Richard A. Higgott and Kim Richard Nossal, *Relocating Middle Powers: Australia and Canada in a Changing World Order* (Vancouver: UBC Press, 1993); Carsten Holbraad, *Middle Powers in International Politics* (London: Macmillan, 1984).

14. Richard Feinberg, *Summitry in the Americas: A Progress Report* (Washington DC: Institute for International Economics, 1997).

15. Lampreia, Luiz Felipe Lampreia, *Luiz Felipe Lampreia – depoimento, 2008* (Rio de Janeiro: FGV-CPDOC, 2010), pp. 255–256.

16. Interview with Oscar Vladimir Chohfi, Brasília, 8 October 2002.

17. Celso Lafer, "ALCA: Futuro", Discurso do Senhor Ministro de Relações Exteriories, Embaixador Celso Lafer, ao o Seminário "O Continente Americano e o Futureo das Integrações REgionais", São Paulo, Memorial da América Latina, 4 April 2001.

Such careful analysis lay at the heart of the position that Celso Amorim advanced as Brazil's foreign minister at the 2003 Cancún and 2005 Hong Kong WTO ministerial negotiating sessions. While Brazil said no to the agreement that the US and EU trade negotiators presented as a *fait accompli* in Cancún, it was a qualified no. The trans-Atlantic position was instead taken as an opening position for negotiations to which Brazil, through the G20, presented alternative language and interpretations. Zoellick's attempts to marginalise Brazil as simply objectionist pointed to an effort to resurrect the sort of strong-arm tactics that had traditionally been used to keep developing countries in line at global trade talks.[18] The effort failed in part because the principles and ambitions of global trade liberalisation were embraced by the Brazilian position, which pointed at a valid alternative way to a greatly liberalised world trading system.[19]

A subset of this tactic is to stretch out an issue until all parties lose interest or decide that the opportunity costs of continuing talks is not worth the effort. Clinton's original intent with the FTAA was to sign the deal at the 1994 Miami Summit of the Americas.[20] A decade later officials around the hemisphere effectively gave up when they came to realise that the US as much as Brazil was elaborating irreconcilable lines in the sand. Nevertheless, the negotiations have yet to be declared formally dead. The negotiating groups just do not meet anymore and officials rarely talk about it. The WTO is not quite in the same state, but there are also clear indications that Brazil is much more positively inclined to a successful conclusion of the Doha round, not least due to the tremendous personal energy put into the talks by Amorim.

In effect, the guiding principle underlying this tactic is for *Itamaraty* negotiators to concentrate their attention and criticism on the micro-level details with a macro-level rhetoric that tells their counterparts that if they could just iron out these pesky wrinkles then this much needed and wanted agreement could be signed. The message broadcast by Brazil through this defensive tactic is particularly effective because it gives off an implicit signal that Brazil wants things to 'progress', that Brazil is a positive and constructive player uninterested in zero-sum games. More importantly, the explicit signals and demonstrated effort of Brazilian diplomats in the form of alternative language and proposals, positions Brazil as an actor committed to a successful resolution of talks, which in turn creates a strong logic for including Brazil as a mediating voice in the small 'executive councils' that generally hammer out the nuts and bolts of international agreements.

Tactic #2: Collectivise (Defensive/Passive)

One of the interesting characteristics of Brazilian efforts to shape international negotiations and regimes is the extent to which their position is presented as a

---

18. Fatoumata Jawara and Aileen Kwa, *Behind the Scenes at the WTO: The Real World of International Negotiations* (London: Zed Books, 2003).

19. Amrita Narlikar and Diana Tussie, "The G20 at the Cancun Ministerial: Developing Countries and Their Evolving Coalitions in the WTO", *The World Economy*, Vol. 27, No. 7 (2004), pp. 947–966; Amrita Narlikar and Rorden Wilkinson, "Collapse at the WTO: A Cancun Post-Mortem", *Third World Quarterly*, Vol. 25, No. 3 (2004), pp. 447–460; Andrew Hurrell and Amrita Narlikar, "A New Politics of Confrontation? Brazil and India in Multilateral Trade Negotiations", *Global Society*, Vol. 20, No. 4 (2008), pp. 415–433.

20. Magalhães, Fernando Simas, *Cúpula das Américas de 1994: Papel Negociador do Brasil, em busca de uma agenda hemisférica* (Brasília: IRBr/FUNAG/Centro de Estudos Estratégicos, 1999).

shared approach or articulated by another country or institution as the shared view. The tactic at play here is to collectivise what Brazil wants to do or say. This brings three important factors into play. First, it deflects direct attention and accountability for the position away from Brazil. For example, the US was advancing an aggressive interpretation of the OAS's Democratic Charter at the 2005 OAS General Assembly that would have effectively turned the organisation into a sort of political policeman for the Americas. The debate carried immediate resonance because the Bolivian government of Carlos Mesa fell halfway through the meeting while hemispheric leaders were still sorting through their reaction to the toppling of Jean Bertrand Aristide in Haiti. In keeping with a long tradition of opposing such efforts, Brazil organised behind the scenes to quash Washington's proposal.[21] Negotiations over the language for the OAS General Assembly's final declaration were tied up over grammatical minutiae while Brazilian diplomats rallied like-minded Latin American nations around an alternative proposed text for the final declaration. In a rather bizarre turn of events, the dormant Latin American trade grouping ALADI was awakened in order to release a completely political document that tied the OAS General Assembly up to the point that there was no agreed final declaration when the majority of participants left after the scheduled conclusion of the Assembly.

A second aspect of the collectivisation approach is that it introduces an element of plausible deniability. Brazilian negotiators can express sympathy with the position of their interlocutors, but still disagree by claiming that their hands are tied by the agreed position of the collective. Brazil is consequently able to follow a strong distributive strategy and flatly reject positions it does not like without appearing unduly obstructionist, or buy its Brazilian negotiators time to continue working behind the scenes to shape a stronger coalition in support of their position. This is one of the characteristics that marked Brazil's management of the Doha Round of WTO talks. By working very hard to keep the WTO G20 coalition of developing nations together Brazil was able to consistently advance ideas that pushed the boundaries of what the EU and US would have liked to see. It also allowed Brazil to stall and ensure that there was ample time to refine negotiating positions and work on recalcitrant members of its own coalition.[22] While the Doha deal remained moribund at the start of 2011, the extent to which the US and the EU have been moved from their initial positions of outright rejection of trade G20/G90 demands could not have been expected in 2003. More to the point for the denizens of *Itamaraty*, the incitement of this substantial position change from the US and EU did not result in damage to bilateral relations, which in some respects strengthened during Lula's second term in office.

A final and critical aspect is that collectivisation greatly expands Brazil's international gravitas. Irrespective of the vaunted technical expertise of Brazilian negotiators and their consultants in São Paulo, the mere ability to construct negotiating positions with intricate econometric models would not have been sufficient to earn Brazil a position as one of the 'new quad' of core countries in the WTO negotiating process. A significant part of the reason that the US and EU chose Brazil and India as critical negotiating partners after Cancún

---

21. Sean W. Burges, *Brazilian Foreign Policy after the Cold War* (Gainnesville, FL: University Press of Florida, 2009), chapter 5.
22. "International: US Meets 20 for WTO Talks in Geneva," *Oxford Analytica Daily Brief* (22 March 2004); "International: G-20 Sets Agenda for Hong Kong," *Oxford Analytica Daily Brief* (5 April 2005).

was that these two countries were seen as representing – and able to deliver – the global South that had proven so difficult in Seattle in 1998 and Cancún in 2003. Brazil thus gained credibility due to its role as a representative for a larger group of nations. The status was amplified by the strenuous efforts of Brazilian diplomats in preaching patience to the global South and encouraging the continued engagement of groups such as the G90 in WTO negotiations through the trade G20 rather than as an independent voice in trade talks.[23] Indeed, the role of spokesman for the global South came to mark Brazilian diplomacy during the Lula presidency, with its bevy of summits linking Brazil and South America with Africa, Asia and the Arab world. Whether it was Lula's very symbolic decision to donate his Prince of Asturias prize to a new UN anti-hunger fund, his active acceptance of the global role as a friendly face of the left and thus trusted interlocutor for the global capitalist elite gathered in Davos, or the unremitting use of a rhetoric of Southern solidarity in nearly all foreign policy statements, the sense of Brazil as a collectivised voice and embodiment of the sentiments of a vast swathe of humanity has been used to amplify the country's importance in international efforts to reach implementable and sustainable consensus decisions in a wide-range of global governance areas.

Tactic #3: Consensus Creation (Neutral)

One phrase frequently used by Brazilian diplomats is "we work to create consensus". The nuance of this phrase is important because they speak of 'creating', not 'reaching' consensus, suggesting that there is a preferred Brazilian option which *Itamaraty* is patiently working to explain as being common to all. Within the context of the FTAA negotiations, one Brazilian negotiator explained that *Itamaraty* reasoned that if Brazil was dubious about the prospect of a sudden launch of a hemispheric free trade zone, then it was likely others were as well. As he explained, Brazil was one of the countries best prepared to deal with the US, but still at a point where *Itamaraty* considered Brazil weak. The trick, therefore, was to bring other countries around to Brazil's point of view, which was achieved through a detailed and patient process of discussions seeking to bring others to commonalities and shared positions.[24]

The same tactic was repeated within the WTO in the lead up to and after the 2003 Cancún ministerial meeting. Comparative economic analyses were undertaken by *Itamaraty* in cooperation with consultants from São Paulo-based trade groups such as the São Paulo Federation of Industrial Enterprises (FIESP) and the Institute for International Trade Negotiations (ICONE) to identify countries facing the same challenges as Brazil in the face of the *fait accompli* which the US and EU were planning to announce. Again, detailed and lengthy discussions were undertaken to establish a consensus position and to create strength around this consensus in Cancún. Significantly, efforts to build and strengthen this consensus continued as the Doha round dragged on, with weekly strategy and analysis sessions being hosted at the Brazilian mission in Geneva. The process was, as one participating trade G20 diplomat observed in 2007 with

---

23. Celso Amorim, "Statement by Minister Celso Amorim at the G-90 Meeting", Georgetown, Guyana (3 June 2004).

24. Interview with Brazilian diplomat, 3 October 2002.

more than a bit of ennui, very comprehensive, lengthy, consultative, and ultimately constructed around a Brazilian-led vision of where the talks should go. That aside, it also allowed Brazil to ensure that all members of the trade G20 had ample opportunity to participate in reviewing the joint position even if they lacked the technocratic capacity to comprehensively address the totality of the trade negotiations.

For *Itamaraty* the pay off has been to position Brazil as a good faith negotiator that can bring disparate interests to the table whilst ensuring that Brazil's central ambitions are included by all as core considerations. Diplomats in Brazil partly attribute this to the vicissitudes of trying to reconcile the myriad internal interests of a country as complex as Brazil in order to present a national position to an international audience. At regional and global meetings this does not translate into instant trust that Brazil is acting in a disinterested, munificent manner – indeed, the other South American countries are wary of the distributive tendency in Brazil's negotiating strategy – but it does create confidence that Brazilian diplomats will continue patiently talking rather than attempting the sort of strongarm tactics sometimes deployed by the traditional major powers. This gives Brazil a great deal of traction at international negotiating tables because it becomes a country that can prevent collapse and get some clarity on where resolution might eventually lie.

Tactic #4: Technocratic-Speak (Neutral)

Another cultural aspect often highlighted by Brazilian diplomats is their country's fascination with juridical procedure. In the modern policy context this translates into a willingness to dive into the technocratic arcana of an issue, something that is most especially evident in the economic realm. In itself this gives Brazil quite bit of influence and power because it is one of a limited number of countries that can attack a question with the at times exclusionary language of econometric modelling and economic theory.[25] Nowhere has the Brazilian mastery of technocratic language been more evident than at the WTO, with Celso Amorim perhaps being one of a handful of people in the world who fully understands the Doha round talks. The ability to stymie the US/EU Cancún deal in large part came down to *Itamaraty*'s ability to attack the technocratic merit of the proposal, not the morality of the proposition on the table. The great difficulty for European and US trade negotiators is that the Brazilian diplomats sometimes take a more orthodox approach to questions such as free trade than its erstwhile proponents, asking question about the full gamut of trade distorting measures such as subsidies and export supports, not just tariffs. In broad strokes this is precisely what has taken place with the dispute over trade-affecting agricultural supports, which Brazil is attacking on the basis of market imperfections that fail to serve the greater good of expanding global trade.

Again within the WTO, Brazil has made ample use of the technocratic possibilities of that institution to incrementally dismantle barriers affecting the country's export earnings. Of the 411 cases that had been brought before the WTO Dispute Settlement Body by mid-2010, Brazil was the complainant in 25 and a third party

---

25. Teivo Teivaninen, *Enter Economism, Exit Politics: Experts, Economic Policy and the Damage to Democracy* (New York: Zed Books, 2002).

in an additional 60. In addition to an infamous series of regional jet export credit complaints against Canada, Brazil targeted such things as US agricultural export subsidies, cotton subsidies, patent codes, anti-dumping laws, and steel protection measures. The EU was targeted for its practices with respect to agricultural commodities such as sugar, chicken and coffee. While the US and EU have certainly not enthusiastically embraced Brazil's WTO actions, there is a reluctant recognition that the very systems these countries sought to construct are being proven effective by Brazilian action. The corollary of this is that the defendants in the cases often exhaust appeals processes and push delaying tactics to their limits, minimising the real world efficacy of the WTO tribunal decisions. The quirk is that this type of action by a Southern-based actor was something relatively new when Brazil launched the first of its series of cases, but has now become more commonplace, although still hampered by the costs of retaining the necessary legal and technical advice.

The critical aspect of Brazil's WTO success is that it demonstrates that there is space to shift the orientation of the global governance rules while playing the game by the established rules and ensuring that they are applied. A similar example can be found in the Brazilian response to the HIV/AIDS crisis that confronted the country in the 1980s and 1990s. Rather than discarding global norms on patents, Brazil actually signed into law strong pharmaceutical patent protection rules that closely reflected the language found in the international agreements on trade related intellectual property rights. The Cardoso government's response to the public health crisis of HIV/AIDS was thus to invoke these measures, specifically the "national emergency" clause to compel the major pharmaceutical companies to deliver a massive reduction in the costs of the needed drug cocktail. Similar measures were subsequently pursued or discussed in 31 other countries, including South Africa, Namibia, Uganda and Ethiopia.[26] Brazil has also incorporated the provision of affordable antiretroviral drugs in its African South-South engagement programme.

Brazilian technocratic expertise also helped to shift thinking in global financial governance ideas at the IMF. One of the complaints that Cardoso had about the IMF and economic policy during his tenure as finance minister and president was that the Fund consistently questioned the workability of Brazil's approach to financial crisis, quietly working to subvert international confidence in the Brazil-grown policies.[27] In part the problem was that officials at the IMF were far from convinced that a developing country such as Brazil possessed the technocratic capacity necessary to independently formulate successful economic policies. The successes of Cardoso's economic policies in preventing a series of complete fiscal collapses in the 1990s laid the groundwork for 2004 proposals during the Lula presidency that the rules for calculating the primary fiscal surplus be altered to exclude capital investment on critical infrastructure and profit-making state enterprises.[28] While both of these developments did not result in a fundamental reshaping of how the IMF operates, they did drive a substantial wedge into the hegemony of Northern economic policy dictates and gave

---

26. Jillian Clare Cohen and Kristina M. Lybecker, "AIDS Policy and Pharmaceutical Patents: Brazil's Strategy to Safeguard Public Health", *The World Economy*, Vol. 28, No. 2 (2005), pp. 211–230.

27. Interview with Fernando Henrique Cardoso, São Paulo, 30 August 2007.

28. Paulo Sotero, "Brasil vai testar novo modelo de investimento", *O Estado de São Paulo* (26 April 2004).

demonstrable substance to the idea that Southern countries were in fact capable of indigenously managing their own economic affairs. This combined with the dramatic economic improvements under the Lula presidency – which saw Brazil go from owing the IMF US $50 billion in 2002 to loaning it US $10 billion in 2009 – opened the space for Brazil's legitimate inclusion in key economic governance institutions such as the G20 Finance and the quieter, but possibly more significant Financial Stability Forum.

Tactic #5: Build New Organisations (Assertive)

On one level this article is concerned about how an emerging country has worked to shift global governance structures to suit its own ambitions and thus shift benefits to itself. Implicit in this subject is the reality that the existing system does not already adequately advance these interests and that the space for Brazil to pursue its own interests within existing structures is limited. The response from *Itamaraty* and the Planalto Presidential Palace has been to create new organisations. This has either been done to prepare for coming changes, protect existing positions, or construct parallel orders that can easily slot into a revised version of the existing hegemony that redistributes power and benefits to Brazil.

Perhaps the most notable example of a structure being created by Brazil to prepare for coming changes in the world order is the Southern Cone trade bloc Mercosul. While there are certainly democracy-protecting and regional security imperatives to the bloc, its seed was planted in the mid-1980s during a time when scholars and analysts were talking about the possibility of three 'fortress blocs': Europe, North America, and Japan-dominated ASEAN.[29] Paralleling this strategic concern in the early 1990s was the decision by the Collor presidency to liberalise the Brazilian economy and the subsequent international identity shift to one of 'global trader'.[30] As leading *Itamaraty* figures explained after the 2002 Argentine economic crisis, a crucial precept behind Mercosul was that the bloc be used as an incubator to prepare Brazilian business for the global market place. The intent was not to position the bloc as the sort of permanent protectionist institutional approach that evolved around ALALC and ALADI. Rather, the intention was to bring Brazilian economic actors up to speed so that they could be full and competitive members of the global political economy. On the policy side, government officials in all departments benefited from the opportunity to 'practice' the negotiating and inter-governmental relations techniques that are at the heart of global governance regulatory work.

Perceived failures in existing systems also prompted attempts to advance new organisational opportunities. As suggested above, *Itamaraty* was never particularly enthused about the FTAA. The preferred option was a phased expansion of Mercosul into some sort of South American Free Trade Area, which might then be used to leverage a more equitable negotiating environment in hemispheric trade talks.[31] By the end of the 1990s it became increasingly apparent to Cardoso

---

29. Robert Gilpin, *The Political Economy of International Relations* (Princeton: Princeton University Press, 1987).

30. Rubens Antonio Barbosa and Luís Panelli César, "O Brasil como 'Global Trader'", in Gélson Fonseca Júnior and Sérgio Henrique Nabuco de Castro (eds.), *Temas de Política Externa Brasileira II*, (São Paulo: Editora Paz e Terra, 1994), pp. 37–52; Ney Canani, *Política Externa no Governo Itamar Franco, 1992-1994* (Porto Alegre: Editora do UFRGS, 2004).

that Argentina was greeting the Mercosul expansion plans with the same scepticism that Brazil was directing towards the US. The problem was that any attempt to expand and deepen Mercosul would require unanimity of the four full members. Cardoso's response was to direct a recalcitrant *Itamaraty* to organise the 2000 South American Presidents Summit in Brasília. Two important things came out of the meeting. First, invited leaders accepted South America as a distinct geopolitical entity that had its own internal potentials and challenges, which ultimately lead to the launch of the South American Union (Unasur) in 2008. Second, in order to address the challenges and realise the possibilities, the collected leaders agreed to an ambitious physical infrastructure integration plan, an initiative which in and of itself put the idea of 'road-building' back on the global development programming radar.

The 2000 agreement to pursue IIRSA (*Integração de la Infraestrutura Regional na América do Sul* – Regional Infrastructure Integration in South America) has two implications for the argument being made in this paper. Although not articulated as such or explicitly claimed at the time, Brazil established a clear leadership role for itself in South America and provided concrete reasons for the other states to follow the lead from Brasília. Acceptance of this leadership, in some cases tacit and grudging, arose from a vision that framed Brazil's goals and ambitions in terms amenable to the other countries in the continent – tactics two and three articulated with the dryness of tactic four. Critically, there was no discussion of turning to South America *instead* of the US. Rather, the focus was on building the transportation, energy and telecommunications infrastructure necessary to develop nationally and trade regionally, with the US, and with the wider international economy. While there was certainly an element of building a 'look to Brazil first' attitude in South America, it was dressed in an underlying liberal logic. It focused on creating the conditions to more equitably attract foreign direct investment and take advantage of the sort of regionalist logic long-advocated for, but never achieved in the Americas. As policy-makers such as Darc Costa noted and subsequent trade and investment patterns have demonstrated, this would also likely have the benefit of entrenching Brazil at the centre of a dense continental economic web with a corresponding greater share of the market and investment opportunities.[32] The integrative mask to Brazil's overarching distributive strategy began to be felt towards the end of the Lula years and the start of the Dilma years when regional countries started to voice concerns about trade imbalances, with the mini trade war launched by Argentina within Mercosul being the highest profile example.[33]

The idea that existing patterns of international relations were not necessarily framed in a manner conducive to Brazilian developmental ambitions is one of the many themes carried through from the Cardoso to the Lula and then Dilma presidency. Brazilian diplomats are not shy about opining that the existing talk shops such as the OECD and the World Economic Forum dominating international discussions between industrialised countries do not offer a country such as Brazil the space for inclusion of the policy questions it wants to

---

31. Celso Luiz Nunes, *Celso Amorim (depoimento, 1997)* (Rio de Janeiro: CPDOC, 2003).

32. Darc Costa, *Estratégia Nacional: A Cooperação Sul-Americana como Caminho para a Inserção Internacional do Brasil* (Rio de Janeiro: Aristeu Souza, 2003).

33. Marina Guimarães, "Ministra da Argentina faz críticas em carta a Pimentel", *O Estado de São Paulo* (13 May 2011); "Os 20 anos do Mercosul," Editorial, *O Estado de São Paulo* (29 March 2011).

address. One analysis within *Itamaraty* was that India, Brazil and South Africa appeared to have remarkably similar voting behaviours in a number of different international institutions as well as a shared series of national development challenges. More to the point, each country had successes in different areas, offering opportunities for mutual learning and cooperation. The launch of the India, Brazil, South Africa (IBSA) Dialogue Forum in 2003 erupted with a flurry of interest in policy and business circles that quickly collapsed into apathy as the triumvirate failed to launch the sort of bold, global transformative initiatives that industrialised-country analysts expected from hyper-active Southern countries. But, as in the case of Brazil's larger foreign policy agenda, revolution was never the guiding premise behind IBSA. Rather, finding a stronger insertion into the global system to gain a greater share of the spoils was the dominant external aim of the grouping.[34]

As one Brazilian diplomat explained about IBSA in 2010, multilateral diplomatic gain was a secondary goal that would naturally fall from the main goal. The real ambition was to start and entrench substantive and sustained cross-bureaucracy interaction with a view to greatly expanding all levels of bilateral and trilateral interaction on both a government and private level. None of this, the diplomat pointed out, happens quickly, emerging more as a process of slow accretion than the dramatic surge sought by Western observers. Tellingly, IBSA is also positioned as a more sustainable and useful device than the disposable Goldman Sachs-created BRIC concept because the trilateral initiative is now growing organically through work in areas that are of pressing concern to the three countries, but of marginal interest to the OECD members interested in exploring North-South relations. What IBSA explicitly does not attempt to do is to disengage any of its members from the existing global order. Quite the reverse. It is explicitly designed to use the norms and rules of the international order and through intra-South cooperation and collective action carve away some of the power and privilege of the North for Brazil, India and South Africa.

Tactic #6: Propagate New Thinking (Assertive)

Tactic six parallels the fifth, but focuses more on the conceptual and ideational than action. Cardoso's intellectual output during his years as president demonstrated a clear understanding that global governance structures were in need of reform because they codified a fundamentally unequal distribution of power and potential that did not reflect emerging realities. In a sense he was refining the basic argument he scripted with Enzo Faletto,[35] namely that the international system was not so much one of exclusion as marginalisation. The challenge was to find a way to take advantage of the structure to improve its relative position.

---

34. Chris Alden and Marco Antonio Vieira, "The New Diplomacy of the South: South Africa, Brazil, India and Trilateralism", *Third World Quarterly*, Vol. 26, No. 7 (2005), pp. 1077–1095.

35. Fernando Henrique Cardoso and Enzo Faletto, *Dependency and Development in Latin Ameirca* (Berkely, CA: University of California Press, 1979); Susan M. Cunningham, "Made in Brazil: Cardoso's Critical Path from Dependency via Neoliberal Options and the Third Way in the 1990s", *European Review of Latin American and Caribbean Studies*, No. 67 (1999), pp. 75–86; Theotônio dos Santos and Laura Randall, "The Theoretical Foundations of the Cardoso Government: A New Stage of the Dependency Theory Debate", *Latin American Perspectives*, Vol. 25, No. 1 (1998), pp. 53–70.

While Cardoso was able to get the ball rolling with ideas such as the Community of Portuguese Speaking Nations,[36] in substantive terms he could offer little more than inspiring speeches and interesting analyses because of the restraints imposed on his presidency by rolling financial crises and the challenges of establishing Brazil as a serious country. A different situation greeted the Lula presidency, with the business community's calm reaction to the election of the leftist leader working to quickly position Brazil as a positive model of left-leaning governance in the face of rather more radical alternatives in countries such as Venezuela.

Lula's foreign policy crew also asked a series of rather provocative questions, chief of which was why Southern countries had to use Northern intermediaries for their bilateral exchange? Why should we expect improvements in South-South trade and interaction if most exchanges involved trans-shipment through a Northern port or airport? In response to these questions they floated the idea of a new international economic geography. Distinct from the New International Economic Order of the 1970s, the idea of a new economic geography held more in common with the Cardoso era IIRSA project in that the focus was on laying down the physical and emotional infrastructure needed to facilitate direct bilateral commerce and travel. New air routes and shipping lanes opened up the idea that cargo and people could travel in straight lines between Southern destinations. Bolstering this proposition was a revivification of earlier Brazilian ideas of the strategic import substitution model that was used to bolster Mercosul and regional trade through the purchase of Argentine wheat and Bolivian gas. An added push came from the series of Brazil/South America and 'X' summits that married political meetings with business and civil society forums designed to bring peoples closer together, all of which worked to redistribute some existing and future economic opportunities in Brazil's direction.

Work to create a realisation within the South that there were ample opportunities for direct bilateral interaction was supported by the technocratic demonstration effect from places such as the WTO. In a sense Brazil helped to shine a light into the dark recesses of the global political economy and demonstrate how to effectively deal with the dragons hiding in the corners. The result was a 'Southernisation' of the *auto-estima,* or self-confidence that allowed Brazil not only to elect a street-smart, formally uneducated president, but also to retreat from the precipice of economic disaster and lift over 30 million people from poverty in half a decade and create realistic ambitions of abolishing extreme poverty by 2016.[37] Knock-on effects of this can be seen internationally and regionally, fed further by the global commodities boom. One example was the emergence of coalitions such as the Small and Landlocked Group of States within the WTO as a technocratically serious grouping.[38] In a South-South context, where African countries were at one point delighted to except Chinese investments and assistance as an attractive alternative to the strictures of OECD-DAC, many countries have begun to actively question the terms and conditions proposed by their

---

36. Fernando Henrique Cardoso and Mário Soares, *O Mundo em Português: Um Diálogo* (São Paulo: Paz e Terra, 1998).
37. IPEA, "Dimensão, evolução e projeção da pobreza por região e por estado no Brasil", *Comunicados do IPEA*, No. 58 (2010).
38. "Limited Traction for Landlocked Group", *Oxford Analytica Daily Brief* (23 August 2005).

new patron, showing instead a more hard-edged approach to international negotiation rather than what at times has appeared to be simple gratitude.[39]

The concept is simple, but the suggestion here is that, in part prodded by Brazilian ideas and examples, the South is rapidly developing the confidence to express itself in global governance forums and in bilateral relations, taking more than just a defensive attitude to their foreign relations and the evolution of international regimes. Keep in mind that Brazil is also busy engaging these newly active states in rolling policy discussions to marshal them behind the Brazilian vision. Irrespective of what this might mean in terms of more aggressive positioning from smaller Southern countries and coalitions in talks about global governance reform, the mere fact of inciting an increase in the density of South-South interaction that in turn boosts the South-South share of things such as global trade and investment flows is enough to cause a shifting of the priorities that need to be considered in the global reform agenda and increase Brazil's relative power at the bargaining table.

Tactic #7: Principled Presidential Righteousness (Aggressive)

The more aggressive stances in Brazilian foreign policy have found their greatest success in the political realm and have been most tightly linked to traditional concepts of sovereignty and the new ideal of defending democracy and human rights. The interesting aspect of the transition from the centre-right Cardoso administration to the centre-left Lula presidency is that in areas where we might have expected the left to be stronger, it appears to have proven weaker.[40] Two examples stand out strongest in this respect. First is the defence of democracy. Cardoso took a hard, but nuanced line to democracy in the Americas, which amounted to a position that a country could arrange and rearrange its democracy any way it chose, provided that it stuck to its own duly constituted mechanisms for change. Under Cardoso this at times involved taking a very pointed stance against Canada and the US at the OAS, particularly with respect to the 2000 presidential election in Peru and the 2002 attempted coup against Hugo Chavez in Venezuela. Lula proved somewhat more pragmatic and interest-centred. While Brazil was central in blocking the US democratic police force proposal for the OAS discussed above, this was arguably more an issue of sovereignty protection than a forward-looking approach to democracy. Indeed, Lula's *Itamaraty* was willing to turn a blind eye to the Franco-American-backed deposition of Jean Bertrand Aristide in Haiti. Intervention during the 2009 Honduran crisis was even more direct, with Brazil at times being seen to actively block the operation of domestic institutions to the frustration of other major regional players.[41] On a personal level Lula was far from averse to expressing his preference for particular presidential

---

39. Ngaire Woods, "Whose Aid? Whose Influence? China, Emerging Donors and the Silent Revolution in Development Assistance", *International Affairs*, Vol. 84, No. 6 (2008), pp. 1205–1221; Deborah Brautigam, *The Dragon's Gift: The Real Story of China in Africa* (Oxford: Oxford University Press, 2009); Julia C. Strauss and Martha Saavedra (eds.), *China and Africa: Emerging Patterns in Globalization and Development* (Cambridge: Cambridge University Press, 2009).

40. Sean W. Burges and Jean Daudelin, "Brazil: How Realists Defend Democracy", in Thomas Legler, Sharon F. Lean and Dexter S. Boniface (eds.), *Promoting Democracy in the Americas* (Baltimore, MD: Johns Hopkins University Press, 2007), pp. 107–132.

41. Marcus V. Freitas, "Honduras and the Emergence of a New Latin America", *Latin American Policy*, Vol. 1, No. 1 (2010), pp. 157–161.

candidates in the various contests throughout the region if he felt it would advance his agenda.

On the human rights file the distinction appears to be even starker. While Cardoso's foreign policy never went as far as severing relations or pursuing other punitive reprisals in support of human rights, it did not shy away from speaking plain truths with individuals such as Cuba's Fidel Castro. In contrast, the last few years of Lula's presidency were marked by a succession of incidents fiercely criticised by the international human rights community, including a refusal to address the hunger strike death of a Cuban dissident during a state visit to the island and an unwillingness to criticise the Iranian regime for allowing a woman to be sentenced to death by stoning for adultery.[42] Lula's foreign policy crew provided some justification for this stance by explaining that their public silence allowed them to retain access and influence events from behind the scenes.[43] The concerns expressed by commentators was that while this may have been the case, there were limits to this approach and Lula had exceeded them, which partly explains Dilma's decision to reverse her patron's policy and take a much harder line on human rights with Iran and in the UNHCR.[44]

A critique of Lula's human rights and democracy positions highlights one of the real challenges of the principled righteousness approach. When Lula rejected the G8 Hellingendam outreach process as demeaning or called on the international community to take global hunger seriously he gained a great deal of international traction because of the inherent 'rightness' of the stance. The difficulty comes when the line between national interest and state position is blurred with the desire to secure an historical legacy, or drifts into a nakedly distributive negotiating agenda. Again, the contrast is with Cardoso, who managed to reject participation in the coalition invading Afghanistan without crippling US-Brazil bilateral relations because of the larger threat he felt it raised for international stability, not to mention the sustainability of the policy. Complaints about US post-2001 anti-terror policies were put in technocratic terms, and largely ignored in Washington. Similarly, Cardoso's decision to sign the NPT treaty but not the additional protocol was grounded in the solid legal logic that additional measures were unnecessary because democratic Brazil's constitution explicitly forbids development of nuclear weapons. When disputes arose over Brazil's refusal to allow IAEA inspections per the additional protocol, word eventually came from Washington that all was okay because Brazil was manifestly different from a North Korea or Iran and thus not a threat to global peace and security. The challenge for diplomats, and a key reason why this tactic is rarely seen, is that it becomes very difficult to keep the personal political prerogative separate from the national interests. Moreover, overuse erodes the effectiveness of the tactic, as evinced by reactions to the sometimes-perceptive, continuous stream of commentaries from leaders such as Hugo Chavez and Fidel Castro.

---

42. "Lula rejeita intervir por condenada a apedrejamento," *O Estado de São Paulo* (29 July 2010).

43. Celso Amorim, Thomas Friedman and David Rothkof, "The New Geopolitics: Emerging Powers and the Challenges of a Multipolar World", transcript of a Foreign Policy public forum, Carnegie Endowment for International Peace, 30 November 2010.

44. Lisandra Paraguassu, "Dilma atrela diplomacia a direitos humanos", *O Estado de São Paulo* (20 April 2011).

Conclusions

As was suggested in the introduction, one future direction for research is to examine how the menu of tactics commonly used by Brazil to advance its distributive agenda might offer a potential starting point for exploring how the new generation of 'middle' powers engages the international system. Just as Brazil was not accepted as a legitimate middle power before 2008 because it was unwilling to provide the systemic support services seen in the foreign policies of countries such as Australia and Canada, Brazil itself rejected the expected role of middle power as illegitimate and unethical because of the barriers it would raise to development in Brazil and the South. Instead, Brazil turned to a distributive approach to international negotiations masked in an integrative façade, wrapping itself in a blanket South-South solidarity that Argentine, Bolivian and Paraguayan officials might protest was at times too thin to offer much comfort to others. Moreover, this rebellious middle power approach strengthened as Brazil gained increased international recognition after the global financial crisis. Amorim closed off his term as foreign minister with some telling comments: "I think there is no way in which the United States can impose its will", he continued on to note that "there is no way that you can change things without the participation of the United States. So, I think the big challenge is not to replace one leadership with another... [it] is to develop partnerships in which the United States can have the humility to see that they can learn from us, and we can learn from you".[45] This points to a shift in the role of the new crop of middle or emerging powers in the international system. While the so-called middle powers such as Brazil lack the power or proclivity to impose their vision, they not only have a soft veto that undercuts the legitimacy of imposed decisions to which they do not consent, but also have and will use a varying set of tactics that can be used to quietly achieve distributive aims in the reform of global governance institutions and the creation of new trade regimes.

The material presented here paints a picture of how an organised, technically capable state can seek to push the global hegemony in a more amenable direction, claiming a greater share of power and influence for itself. The key points that run as consistent themes throughout this article are that mindless opposition simply results in arguments being ignored, and that use of exclusionary, technocratic language effectively depoliticises potentially difficult ideas to the point where they have to be considered. Ability to have ideas considered and co-opted grows if you not only Brazilian Foreign Policy are able to mobilise a larger group behind your idea, but are also able to have this group take public ownership of the ideas. To do so does not preclude the possibility that the successful proposer is working in an entirely self-interested fashion. In the Brazilian case, the obvious subsequent question is to what ends are these tactics being utilised. The apparent answer only serves to strengthen the initial proposition that Brazil is taking a distributive approach to negotiations: a stronger voice in international talks and an ability to reap greater benefits appear to be pursued for their own sake. This bolsters the claims of existing research that the main goal of Brazilian foreign policy is protection of national sovereignty and autonomy.[46]

---

45. Amorim, Friedman and Rothkof, *op.cit.*
46. Burges, *Brazilian Foreign Policy After the Cold War, op. cit.*; Tullo Vigevani and Gabriel Cepaluni, *Brazilian Foreign Policy in Changing Times: The Quest for Autonomy from Sarney to Lula* (New York: Lexington,

An interesting aspect in the Brazilian case is the shift from national to personal political that crept in towards the end of the Lula presidency, with Lula beginning to introduce Odell's element of domestic political concerns to negotiations by using foreign policy ventures to boost his own domestic popularity. Where *Itamaraty* has historically tended to seek a voice as a defensive mechanism, Lula and his presidential foreign policy advisors began to do so offensively, particularly on a regional level and as a device to build domestic political support. Over the last three years of Lula's rule a steady sense of pride in Brazil as a global player began to emerge within the Brazilian polity, but more as a passing fad than as a serious driver of political careers and decisions.[47] Again, the absent factor for many was the sense of why and what for, a sentiment that appeared to be shared by Lula's successor, Dilma Rousseff. As of the completion of this article the initial signs were that Dilma was taking a disengaged approach to foreign policy issues, resulting in a shift in control back towards *Itamaraty*. What remained largely unchanged was use of the set of tactics outlined here to present a wider distributive negotiating strategy to others as a value-creating, integrative ambition.

2009); Denis Rolland and Antônio Carlos Lessa (eds.), *Relations Internationales du Brésil* (Paris: L'Harmattan, 2010).

47. Larry Rohter, *Brazil on the Rise* (New York: Palgrave Macmillan, 2010); Riordan Roett, *The New Brazil* (Washington DC: Brookings, 2010).

India's Identity and its Global Aspirations

KAREN SMITH

This article engages with the question whether India's identity predisposes it to playing a specific international role, in particular one which promotes the redistribution of power and wealth in the international system. This is done by exploring emerging and competing identity constructions and perspectives on the role that India should play in the world. It is argued that the liberal or pragmatic view, which advocates working within the prevailing global order and integration with the global economy in order to advance India's economic performance, is currently dominant. At the same time, however, it is contended that India has numerous identities that are not necessarily mutually exclusive, and which lead to what has been called India's foreign policy ambiguity. Four possible explanations for this ambiguity are proposed, namely: mimicry versus differentiation; reluctant radicalism; strategic moral posturing; and differentiation across issue areas. The article concludes that the Indian state is predominantly concerned about its own position in the global order, and less so about the plight of the developing world, but that global redistribution may well be a by-product of India's foreign policy.

Recent years have witnessed a proliferation of studies exploring the rise of the emerging powers and their amplified role in international affairs. Most of these studies, however, focus on material considerations such as these powers' increased share of the global economy, with issues of identity usually taking a back seat. In addition, the historical context is often left out of the equation. In an attempt to address some of these shortcomings, this paper seeks to advance an exploration of India's identity within a broader historical framework.[1]

In particular, the underlying question this paper seeks to engage with is the following: Does India's historically constructed identity predispose it to playing a particular international role, in particular one which promotes the redistribution

---

*This article was first presented as a paper at the GIGA Regional Powers Network Workshop on Emerging Regional Powers and Global Redistribution, Stellenbosch, 6–7 September 2010. The author, Karen Smith, would like to thank Dirk Nabers, Philip Nel and two anonymous reviewers for their valuable comments. Karen is a senior lecturer in the Department of Political Studies at the University of Cape Town.

1. For an overview of India's foreign policy, see the following: Sumit Ganguly (ed.), *India's Foreign Policy: Retrospect and Prospect* (New Delhi: Oxford University Press, 2010); V.P. Dutt, *India's Foreign Policy Since Independence* (New Delhi: National Book Trust, 2007); Stephen Philip Cohen, *Emerging Power India* (Washington DC: Brookings Institution Press, 2002). For a fascinating exploration of the changing nature of the identity, or what he calls the "idea of India", by means of a historical perspective, see Sunil Khilnani, *The Idea of India* (New York: Farrar, Strauss and Giroux, 1999).

of power and wealth in the international system? It is based on the assumption that the identity of a state implies its preferences and consequent actions,[2] and that the role that India has played and will play in the world is heavily, but not exclusively, contingent on historical and cultural factors. The paper then looks at emerging and competing identity constructions and perspectives on the role that India should play in the world, and explores the notion that its foreign policy is characterised by ambiguity.

It is assumed for the purposes of this study that state-building and foreign policy are mutually dependent processes. As Krishna[3] emphasises, India's foreign policy cannot be seen simply as a product of the Indian state but is, instead, closely tied up with and to a large extent constitutive of the development of the state. As identities are fluid and constantly evolving, while a state's identity undoubtedly impacts on its foreign policy, the opposite is also true: through formulating foreign policy strategies, existing identities are reinforced or undermined, and new ones created. In short, the nature of India's role in the world can therefore not be separated from the evolving identity of the Indian state.

In the post-Cold War era we have witnessed, to use the words of Lapid and Kratochwil,[4] the return of culture and identity in international relations (IR). In particular, the emergence of constructivism in IR in the 1990s made the identity of states a focal point. Constructivism thus provides a useful starting point for exploring the role identity plays in shaping a state's interests, and hence its impact on foreign policy. It challenges the notion that identities and interests are exogenously given (as rationalist theories would have us believe). In other words, exploring the identity that the Indian state wants to project internationally (articulated by policymakers and other elites) will ultimately give us some insight into its global aspirations, including the redistributive potential of its foreign policy. This ties in with Abdelal et al.'s notion of collective identity being purposive, in that certain goals and outcomes are attached to particular identities.[5] Given the lack of a universally accepted understanding of the term identity, specifically as it applies to IR, it may be useful to briefly outline how it is understood here.[6]

Contrary to the neorealist assumption that state identities are permanent, this paper adopts the constructivist notion that the identities of states are variable, ever-changing, and dependent on the socio-political, cultural and historical context. Weldes emphasises that "threats and the corresponding national interest are fundamentally matters of interpretation".[7] Put differently, how states behave towards their external environment (foreign policy) is closely tied to how they

---

2. Ted Hopf, "The Promise of Constructivism in International Relations Theory", *International Security*, Vol. 23, No. 1 (1998), p. 175.

3. Sankaran Krishna, *Postcolonial Insecurities: India, Sri Lanka, and the Question of Nationhood* (Minneapolis: University of Minneapolis Press, 1999), p. 4.

4. Yosef Lapid and Friedrich Kratochwil (eds.), *The Return of Culture and Identity in IR Theory* (Boulder, CO: Lynne Rienner, 1997).

5. Rawi Abdelal, Yoshiko M. Herrera, Alastair Iain Johnston and Rose McDermott, "Identity as a Variable", *Perspectives on Politics*, Vol. 4, No. 4 (2006), p. 698.

6. For useful discussions of identity and how it is used in the social sciences, see James Fearon, "What is Identity (as we now use the word)?", Unpublished paper (Stanford University, 1999) available: <http://www.stanford.edu/~jfearon/papers/iden1v2.pdf> (accessed 5 December 2010); Abdelal, Herrera, Johnston and McDermott, *op. cit.*, pp. 695–711.

7. Jutta Weldes, *Constructing National Interests: The United States and the Cuban Missile Crisis* (Minneapolis: University Minnesota Press, 1999), p. 7.

view themselves in relation to that environment. Following Katzenstein,[8] it is further assumed that identities are both constructed by the actor itself (in this case the Indian state) but also through the environment and through its interactions with external actors (giving it an inter-subjective or relational element).

It is important to bear in mind that identities by nature are multiple, constructed and constantly evolving. While it is common in the literature to speak of a state's *identity*, it is perhaps more accurate to use the plural form *identities*, for no state has only one identity. Following Hopf,[9] one can argue that defining the self vis-à-vis the other is a process that occurs internally as well as externally. The other can be an external actor, a historical past, or even an idea. This broad notion of identity construction is adopted here, for it allows us to explore not only how contemporary domestic and international factors shape India's identity, but also how its past continues to influence the identity of the state.

While the focus of this article is not on external influences, the discussion needs to be set against the backdrop of significant changes in the international system which have forced Indian policy-makers to reconsider their construction of the Indian state and its role in the world. The dramatic power shifts that have taken place in the wake of the end of the Cold War, together with India's unprecedented economic growth and new-found status as a nuclear power, have provided the Indian state with new opportunities in terms of its global position. Wendt's[10] conceptualisation of social identity, which suggests that the interactions states have with other international actors, in particular other states, can construct 'social' forms of identity that may or may not be compatible with different forms of domestic group identities, provides us with further insight into external impacts on India's identity. Often states take on certain roles (in other words, expected behaviour) in international interactions, in response to dominant global discourses. For example, if the international community perceives India to be an emerging power and even a potential great power, this inevitably affects the way in which the Indian state perceives its own role in the world. International norms and the institutions that promote them also play an important part in shaping states' identities. India's membership of the Non-Aligned Movement (NAM) and G77, as well as more recent groupings such as the G20 and IBSA Forum are relevant in this regard.

With regard to internal influences, various domestic factors shape state identities and how these are expressed in foreign policy. When speaking about India's national or state identity, it must be kept in mind that this exists in tension with India's numerous sub-national identities. Some authors emphasise the fact that India's national identity is particularly precarious and that numerous subnational ethnic, religious and linguistic identities threaten the notion of a united India.[11] It must also be kept in mind that internally, multiple perceptions of identity vie for dominance, and Khilnani's view that "[o[ver the past generation the presumption that a single shared sense of India—a unifying idea and concept—can at once define the facts that need recounting and provide the collective subject for the

---

8. Peter Katzenstein (ed.), *The Culture of National Security: Norms and Identity in World Politics* (New York: Columbia University Press, 1996).

9. Hopf, *op. cit.*

10. Alexander Wendt, *Social Theory of International Politics* (Cambridge: Cambridge University Press, 1999); Alexander Wendt, "Collective Identity Formation and the International State", *American Political Science Review*, Vol. 88, No. 2 (1994), pp. 384–396.

11. Although an important topic, this will not be the focus of this paper.

Indian story has lost all credibility" rings particularly true.[12] This suggests that there are competing domestic conceptions of a state's identity and interests, with the socio-political context and issue at hand often determining which is dominant at any given time.

Elaborating on the contested nature of identity, it is important to note that particular identities become powerful when they are held and promoted by influential segments of society. The role of elites in shaping a state's national identity as well as translating it into policy is unquestionable, and therefore the views about India's identity held by elites (specifically, policy-makers and scholars) will be the focus of this article.

In light of the fact that the identity of any state is complex and multi-dimensional, there are countless factors that could be taken into account in an analysis of identity construction. While acknowledging that that identity in India has been constructed along a number of dimensions, various scholars have chosen to focus on specific aspects of identity and their implications for foreign policy. While Krishna focuses on India's post-colonial identity, Banerjee explores the construction of India as a non-aligned state, and Adeney and Lall[13] present a comparison of the way in which two different ruling parties—the BJP and the Indian National Congress (INC)—have attempted to build an Indian national identity. Commuri[14] focuses on secular and religious-cultural narratives shaping Indian identity and their implications for foreign policy, particularly in respect to Jammu and Kashmir, Pakistan and China.

In line with Commuri's contention that many discourses around identity that centre around things like caste, language, region, and so forth are more relevant to a localised political context, this article focuses on exploring India's foreign policy identity. To this end, this paper chooses to focus predominantly on the way in which history has shaped India's foreign policy identity. Specifically, as an entry point into the foreign policy identity of the Indian state, I have chosen to focus on India's civilizational identity and its colonial legacy.

Indian Civilization and the Impact of Colonialism

> India's 3000 year history has left its imprint on Indian society and its political elite. While this past does not dictate contemporary policy, it does influence it.[15]

This quote by Cohen highlights the notion that, to a large extent, India's identity can be called a civilizational identity, based on what is believed to be India's ancient and morally superior civilization. It forms an important part of India's post-colonial identity and its foreign policy discourse, and is a significant way in which Indian elites distinguish the Indian state from other states.[16] Some authors claim that India has certain civilizational attributes that push it towards playing a particular role in the world. Cohen, for example,

---

12. Khilnani, op. cit., p. 2.
13. Katharine Adeney and Marie Lall, "Institutional Attempts to Build a 'National' Identity in India: Internal and External Dimensions", India Review, Vol. 4, No. 3 (2005), pp. 1–29.
14. Gitika Commuri, Indian Identity Narratives and the Politics of Security (New Delhi: SAGE, 2010).
15. Cohen, op. cit., p. 34.

emphasises the role of India's distinct civilizational identity in creating the notion that "India (and Indians) has something to teach the rest of the world, and that of other major civilizations India is uniquely unassertive towards others".[17] There is thus an underlying notion of India's civilizing mission, despite the construction of Indian civilization as tolerant, peaceful and non-interfering.

On account of India's ancient culture and civilization, its large territory and demographic size, Indians have always felt that their state deserves to play a more significant role on the global stage. Scholars and policy-makers agree that, from the very beginning, the foreign policy of India was driven by a desire to achieve major power status.[18] Cohen, for example, claims, "Since the heady days of Nehru, all Indian leaders have proclaimed a special destiny or mission for India in Asia and the world, based on the greatness of its civilization, its strategic location, and its distinctive view of the world".[19]

The drive to play a greater global role was further underlined by India's colonial experience, which continues to play an important part in the national imaginary. Post-colonial scholars such as Chatterjee, Krishna and Muppidi,[20] emphasise the importance of the way in which the post-colonial state reacted to and dealt with its colonial legacy. India's struggle against colonial oppression, characterised by Mahatma Gandhi's pacifist approach, continued to have a strong influence on India's worldview in the post-independence period, and arguably still today.[21] After independence, those who fought in the freedom struggle, wanted to extend the principle of non-violence or *satyagraha* on which it had been based, into the realm of the international. As Krishna reminds us, "The non-violent nature of the anticolonial movement contributed to the ideas that the new nation, India, represented a vastly different entity in a world dominated by realpolitik".[22] Nehru sought to translate this notion of moral exceptionalism into policy. He subsequently became a champion for the developing world, and founding father of the Non-Aligned Movement (NAM). The policy of non-alignment, which was largely a result of a political culture that developed out of the colonial legacy and privileged autonomy, was essential to the newly independent state's international identity. Sikri notes that, "India's position on world issues was informed by a rare moral clarity and courage which won India many admirers, made India the leader of the developing countries."[23]

---

16. For a detailed analysis of how Indian civilization was constructed both by Western and Indian thinkers, see Priya Chacko, *Indian Foreign Policy and the Ambivalence of Postcolonial Modernity*, unpublished doctoral dissertation, (Adelaide: University of Adelaide, 2007).

17. Cohen, *op. cit.*, p. 8.

18. For an excellent overview of India's aspiration and rise to major power status, see Baldev Raj Nayar and T.V. Paul, *India in the World Order: Searching for Major Power Status* (Cambridge: Cambridge University Press, 2003).

19. Stephen Cohen, "India Rising", *The Wilson Quarterly*, Vol. 24, No. 3 (2000), p. 46.

20. I would like to thank Vineet Thakur for introducing me to the scholars I refer to here.

21. See Rajiv Sikri, "Mahatma Gandhi's Influence on India's Foreign Policy", in I. Ahmed, R. Sikri, D.M. Nachane and P.N. Mukherji (eds.), *The Legacy of Gandhi: A 21st Century Perspective* (Singapore: Institute of South Asian Studies, 2008), available: http://www.isn.ethz.ch/isn/Current-Affairs/Security-Watch/Detail/?ots591=0c54e3b3-1e9c-be1e-2c24-a6a8c7060233&lng=en&id=46805 (accessed 18 June 2010).

22. Krishna, *op. cit.*, p. 14.

23. Sikri, *op. cit.*, p. 11.

While India's aspirations to great power status were initially hampered by a lack of economic and military resources,[24] Indian policymakers used ideological and diplomatic power in its stead. As a result, in the first two decades after independence, India acquired a leadership role in international relations out of proportion to its material power capabilities. This new leadership role was something that many Indians believed was long overdue. Over the past two decades, in light of India's unprecedented economic growth and new status as a (albeit unofficial) nuclear power, the rest of the world is finally catching up with India's own image of itself.

This vision of India as a regional and global power continues to be shared by many Indians, who however differ with regard to what *kind* of role India should be playing globally. As Ollapally[25] notes, the lack of transparency of the Indian state makes it difficult to identify dominant perspectives within government. There are also different conceptions of the debates in Indian foreign policy. Some analysts simply distinguish between an idealist and realist or pragmatic strand,[26] while others diffentiate between a number of different strands. Bajpai,[27] for example, describes the three streams of Indian strategic culture as being Nehruvian, neoliberal and hyperrealist, while Cohen[28] identifies them as Nehruvian (which he further divides into classical Nehruvian and militant Nehruvian), conservative realism, and Hindu revitalism. More recently, Ollapally[29] identifies four strands, namely: traditionalist, nationalist, regionalist and new globalist. While there are minor variations between the various authors, Sagar's[30] framework provides a useful summary of the main differences. He claims that there are four main competing visions that Indians have of the role that their state should play in the world, namely: moralist, Hindu nationalist, strategic and liberal.

The moralist strand is characterised by moral exceptionalism and the Nehruvian vision is that India should serve as a model of principled action, shy away from using force in its international relations, and respect international law and institutions. The Hindu nationalist strand is an ideologically-driven approach, based on the belief that India should pursue a muscular foreign policy and act as a defender of Hindu civilization.[31] It draws heavily on the notion of India as a great and ancient civilization, and is partly based on the notion that Hindu civilization was dealt a blow by the non-violent influences of the Buddhists and Jains which made it vulnerable to invaders, and that a revival of Hindu nationalism and military prowess is necessary to restore India's greatness.

---

24. Nayar and Paul, *op. cit.*, also identify various non-material constraints on India's aspiration to achieve great power status, including the legacy of non-violence and resistance to becoming involved in power politics, as well as the perceptions of India held by the West and based in orientalist cultural stereotypes.
25. Deepa Ollapally, "New Discourses on India as an Economic Power", Paper presented at the Institute of Peace and Conflict Studies, New Delhi, India, 4 January 2010.
26. See, for example, Nayar and Paul, *op. cit.*
27. *Future Strategic Balances and Alliances* (Carlisle, PA: Strategic Studies Institute, 2002), pp. 245–303.
28. Cohen, *Emerging Power India, op. cit.*
29. Ollapally, *op. cit.*
30. Rahul Sagar, "State of Mind: What Kind of Power Will India Become?", *International Affairs*, Vol. 85, No. 4 (2009), pp. 801–816.
31. See the BJP's website for a treatise on "Hindutva: The Great Nationalist Ideology", <http://www.bjp.org/index.php?option=com_content&view=article&id=369:hindutva-the-greatnationalist-ideology&catid=92&Itemid=501>.

While the basis of the Hindutva movement appears to be religious, this form of Hindu nationalism is in fact predominantly political. What Sagar calls the strategist approach is similar to Bajpai's hyperrealist and Cohen's militant Nehruvian strands. It advocates cultivating state power by developing strategic—and specifically military—capabilities. The argument is that India will not be able project its great power identity on a regional and global scale without significant military power. Finally, the liberal strand's emphasis is on seeking prosperity and peace through increasing trade and interdependence. It calls for a much more pragmatic foreign policy, and criticises morally or ideologically-based foreign policy decisions.

These strands are of course ideal types and are not meant to imply that such 'pure' strands of thought exist in reality or even in individuals. Paraphrasing Bajpai,[32] there are few pure moralists, strategists, Hindu nationalists or liberals, with Indian elite views instead being a complex mix of all these tendencies.

Finally, none of the authors identify what might be called a radical strand which is critical of existing global inequalities, problematises the prevailing order, is concerned with social justice and redistribution, and promotes solidarity with the South. This has important implications for one of the underlying questions of this article, however, namely whether India's historically constructed identity predisposes it to playing a specific international role, in particular one which promotes the redistribution of power and wealth in the international system. As this strand has the same colonial roots as the moralist or Nehruvian strand, it could arguably be subsumed under it.

Sagar[33] holds that none of these visions is likely to dominate the worldview of Indians in the twenty-first century, because they represent ideas that change with the political climate. However, it does appear as though the liberal view is currently dominant and will continue to be so for the foreseeable future. It corresponds to what has also been called a pragmatic strand, which advocates working within the prevailing global order, integration with the global economy, and cooperation with Western states in order to advance India's economic performance. It is evidenced through statements such as the following excerpt from a speech by Prime Minister Singh to Foreign Service probationary offers, in which he promotes a clearly pragmatic approach to foreign policy, and dismisses a foreign policy based on Nehruvian principles outright: "The world is not a morality play. The world's political and economic system is a power play and those who have greater power use it to their advantage".[34]

Similarly, in a statement to the Rajya Sabha, External Affairs Minister Krishna outlines what he regards as one of the main aims of Indian foreign policy:

> One of the main challenges of our foreign policy lies in creating and maintaining a regional and international environment which would enable us to sustain a high rate of economic growth, create more opportunities for Indian entrepreneurship and enable India to realize her vast, latent potential. The pursuit of enhanced trade, investment inflows, technology

---

32. Quoted in Cohen, *Emerging Power India, op. cit.*, p. 50.
33. Sagar, *op. cit.*, p. 802.
34. Manmohan Singh, "Address by Prime Minister Dr. Manmohan Singh to Indian Foreign Service Probationary Officers, New Delhi, June 11, 2008", in Bhasin, Avtar Singh (ed.), *India's Foreign Relations—2008 Documents (New Delhi: Geetika Publishers, 2009)*, pp. 169–175.

transfers, energy security and other economic imperatives has become an overarching imperative of our foreign policy.[35]

'This approach is a direct response to what many Indians felt were the shortcomings of the Nehruvian policy of principled action. According to Sagar, many felt that India's policies of non-alignment and solidarity with the South resulted in "little material benefit", "lost opportunities for profitable benefit", and a confrontational attitude towards the West.[36] The shift in emphasis thus seems to be in favour of material outcomes rather than strict adherence to moral principles. From this worldview, cooperation with western powers is promoted, in order to further advance India's economic performance. In the words of Prime Minister Manmohan Singh, "The challenge before us is to create an external environment that is conducive to our long-term and sustained economic development. We want mutually beneficial relations with all our neighbours, with all major powers and with all our economic partners".[37] Similarly, in the following statement, former External Affairs Minister Pranab Mukherjee makes it clear that there is no room for distinction between trading partners on the basis of ideology or other value-based criteria:

> In all of India's bilateral relationships and in all her multilateral engagement, the focus is on the facilitation of trade and investment flows, the modernization of infrastructure, the assuring of predictable and affordable energy supplies and the widest possible access to technologies. India is strengthening her relationships with all the major powers—US, Russia, EU, China and Japan—as well as with emerging economies in Asia, Latin America and Africa, with an eye on all these critical ingredients of economic success.[38]

This liberal or pragmatic view was also underlined by contributors to a volume entitled *Indian Foreign Policy Agenda for the 21st Century* (Vol. 1), published by the Indian Foreign Service Institute in 1997.[39] Not one of the contributing leading scholars and foreign policy specialists explicitly promoted the idea that Indian foreign policy should be aimed at advancing the interests of the world's poorest nations and promoting global equity and redistribution. Instead, all of the authors focus on what India should be doing to promote its own national interest, with many explicitly stating that India should stop identifying with the developing world as this may compromise its economic development. Bhattacharyya, for example, notes that in the current international context where states belong to different groupings depending on their national interest, "an uncritical

---

35. S.M. Krishna, "EAM's statement in Rajya Sabha on working of MEA", Ministry of External Affairs, 31 July 2009, available: <http://www.mea.gov.in/mystart.php?id=530115072> (accessed 5 August 2011).

36. Sagar, *op. cit.*, p. 813.

37. Manmohan Singh, Statement by Prime Minister at Asian-African Conference, 23 April 2005, available: <http://www.mea.gov.in/mystart.php?id=53019413> (accessed 5 September 2011).

38. Pranab Mukherjee, "Shaping India's Foreign Policy to its Rightful Place in the Comity of Nations", Address at the Defence Services Staff College, Wellington, 22 January 2008, in Bhasin, Avtar Singh (ed.), *India's Foreign Relations—2008 Documents* (New Delhi: Geetika Publishers, 2009), pp. 47–52.

39. L. Mansingh, D. Lahiri, J.N. Dixit, B.S. Gupta, S. Singh and A. Sajjanhar (eds.), *Indian Foreign Policy Agenda for the 21st Century*, Vol. 1 (New Delhi: Foreign Service Institute, 1997).

identification with the South is no longer possible nor desirable".[40] Instead, he suggests that "India will have to continually seek allies in a specific context, independent of their development status. Flexible roles will have to become the norm in economic diplomacy rather than an unquestioning commitment to G-77".[41] Malik agrees that, "It is no longer a tenable position for India to appear as the leader of the lowest common denominator that the NAM and the G-77 denote. It should be developing its economic strength and utilizing this to develop a stance based on its interests with like-minded countries".[42] These sentiments were shared unanimously by numerous informal discussions I had with scholars, diplomats, business people, politicians and ordinary Indians.[43]

This ties in with the assessment many commentators have made that while, in the post-colonial period, Indian foreign policy focused on promoting idealism and anti-Western sentiment, this has been replaced with a more pragmatic, self-interested approach.

Not all scholars view this development as a positive one. Some are troubled by what they regard as a "narrow and exclusive" vision. Parekh, for example, argues that:

> ... the idea that India's overarching aim should be to become an economic and military superpower then is deeply flawed. We need an alternative vision of the kind of country we wish to be, and of our place in the world. That vision must have a moral core, and should embody the principles of individual liberty, social justice, equal opportunity, and fraternity or a sense of community...[44]

Despite the apparent dominance of the liberal strand, one could argue that the moralist strand of principled action that Parekh calls for remains a strong undercurrent of India's identity. This strand is consistent with the ideals upheld by the freedom struggle and entails a respect for human rights and democracy and a striving towards global justice. Although statements such as "striving for an equitable global system for socio-economic development was and continues to be one of the priorities of India's foreign policy"[45] appear to be increasingly absent from most recent MEA annual reports and foreign policy speeches, the moralist strand in India's foreign policy is still emphasised in statements to audiences from the developing world. For example, in his opening speech at the India—Least Developed Countries Ministerial Conference, External Affairs Minister Krishna recalls the words of Nehru, which he claims "encapsulate India's commitment from

---

40. B. Bhattacharyya, "India's Foreign Economic Policy: Evolving Context and Tasks", in Mansingh *et al*, (eds.), *Indian Foreign Policy Agenda, op. cit.*, p. 218.

41. *Ibid.*

42. P.M.S. Malik, "The Changing Face of India's Economic Diplomacy: The Role of the Ministry of External Affairs", in Mansingh *et al*. (eds.), *Indian Foreign Policy Agenda, op. cit.*

43. These discussions took place in December 2010 in Delhi. I would especially like to thank Siddharth Mallavarapu, Vineet Thakur, Samir Saran, and Chris Miller for their valuable inputs.

44. Bhikhu Parekh, "Defining India's Identity: An Alternate Vision", *Mainstream*, Vol. XLV, No. 39, (2007), available: <http://www.mainstreamweekly.net/article320.html> (accessed 10 June 2010).

45. Nirupama Rao, "Key Priorities for India's Foreign Policy", Address at the International Institute for Strategic Studies, 27 June 2011, available: <http://meaindia.nic.in/mystart.php?id=530115731> (accessed 5 August, 2011).

the earliest days after its independence to sharing its development experience with fellow developing countries".[46]

This dovetails with Hurrell's claim that India continues to identify itself as a developing country and to understand its foreign policy through the lens of North-South relations. However, he asks:

> But is the language of Third Worldism and southern solidarity simply a hangover from the past? Or is it an interest-driven strategy that reflects a particular set of contingent interests (as on trade issues within the WTO)? Or is it reflective of a deeper set of beliefs, interests and commitments? If so, what happens if that "developing country identity" comes into conflict with the "aspiring great power identity"?[47]

These questions point to dilemmas and what some have referred to as ambiguities or contradictions in India's foreign policy.

Ambiguous Policy and Competing Identity Constructions

Various explanations could be put forward for what appears to be India's ambiguous foreign policy stance. I will limit my discussion to four: mimicry versus differentiation; reluctant radicalism; strategic moral posturing; and differentiation across issue areas.

Mimicry versus Differentiation

The roots of what can be regarded as India's foreign policy ambiguity lie in what post-colonial scholars refer to as the tension between developing an alternative form of government and nationhood to Western powers (in other words, carving out an identity which differentiates it from the West) and a desire to mimic the colonial structures and policies. Chatterjee[48] makes a distinction between the material and spiritual aspects of post-colonial nationalism, claiming that in the material domain the colonised mimic the coloniser, but in the moral domain, the colonised declares it superiority. In particular, there was recognition that "a certain level of mimicry of the West was unavoidable if it were to survive in the modern world as a sovereign nation-state".[49]

A case in point is India's decision to develop nuclear power. Nuclear technology was arguably seen as a vehicle to international status and prestige, and as a symbol of modernity, which India was aspiring to in mimicking the West. The decision to develop nuclear power also speaks to India's conception of itself and its role in the world, as discussed earlier. It also served to juxtapose the colonial image of

---

46. S.M. Krishna, Inaugural Address by the External Affairs Minister at the *India—Least Developed Countries Ministerial Conference*, New Dehli, 18 February 2011, available: <http://www.mea.gov.in/mystart.php?id=530117194> (accessed 28 July 2010).
47. Andrew Hurrell, "Hegemony, Liberalism and Global Order: What Space for would-be Great Powers?", *International Affairs*, Vol. 82, No. 1 (2006), p. 19.
48. Partha Chatterjee, *Nationalist Thought and the Colonial World—A Derivative Discourse* (London: Zed Books, 1986).
49. Chacko, *op. cit.*, p. 10.

India as a feminine state with a powerful image of masculinity.[50] This is illustrated by leader of the militant Hindu nationalist Shiv Sena Party, Bal Thackeray's, statement in support of the 1998 nuclear tests when he said, "we have to prove that we are not eunuchs".[51] India's 1998 nuclear tests proved to have the desired effect on India's position in the international community. Despite initial condemnation, the major powers, lead by the US, soon took on a more conciliatory approach, and started seeing India as a serious candidate for major power status.

At the same time, the issue of India's ambiguous nuclear policy (developing nuclear technology and at the same time promoting a policy of disarmament) clearly illustrates this dilemma between mimicking the West and at the same time enacting difference. Chacko suggests that:

> India's inability to develop a scientific outlook and modern technology was seen as a civilizational 'lack' that led to its failure to reach the standard of civilization set by Europe and, eventually, its subjugation by Britain. In this context, nuclear technology took on a special significance as an explicit example of both the promise and the violence of Western modernity. Yet, because the nationalist critique of the dehumanizing nature of Western modernity constitutes a vital part of India's postcolonial identity, the outright adoption of a technology which had the capacity to unleash an unprecedented level of destruction was untenable. The discourse of disarmament is an attempt to resolve this dilemma by recourse to India's moral strength, which is seen as the innate attribute of an Indian civilization gendered as feminine and the basis of its postcolonial difference.[52]

While India's colonial legacy lingers, the country has undergone significant changes since independence, and in particular over the past decade. This has forced the government to rethink old alliances and ideological positions, leading to further accusations of ambiguity.

Reluctant Radicalism

In the post-independence decades, caught up in its new-found freedom, India, like most of the newly-independent, ideologically-driven African and Asian states seemed keen to form bonds with its counterparts in the global South and to pursue activist foreign policies aimed at changing the world. Subsequently, India went on to play leading roles in what developed into the NAM and the G77, and was driven by the intellectual framework of the New International Economic Order (NIEO).

As mentioned above, however, despite proclamations of the continued importance of normative change in the international system, this once strong aim seems to have given way to more pragmatic and self-interested considerations among states in the global South. Palat[53] argues that, despite states

---

50. See Ashis Nandy, The Intimate Enemy: Loss and Recovery of Self under Colonialism (Delhi: Oxford University Press, 1983).
51. *Ibid.*, p. 127.
52. *Ibid.*, pp. 125–126.
53. Ravi Arvind Palat, "A New Bandung? Economic Growth vs. Distributive Justice among Emerging Powers", *Futures*, Vol. 40 (2008), pp. 721–734.

like China, India and Brazil's increased economic clout, their leaders do not challenge the current world order in the way that states like Iran or Venezuela do. He argues that their reluctance to question the status quo as well as the widening inequalities within their borders suggests that they are increasingly complicit in this new world order. Ironically, given the increased collective economic power of these states, their ability to subvert the existing US-Europe dominated world order has never been greater. The effects of neoliberal globalisation are, of course, to a large extent to blame for the shift in the foreign policy emphasis of states in the global South. As a result of the demands that accompany participation in the global economy, states' ability to pursue independent economic policies that challenge global norms has been severely undermined. It would appear that developing states that have advanced economically seem more interested in joining the club of powerful states than in promoting the cause of global redistribution. Depending on which worldview one subscribes to, this is of course not surprising. The realist view of international relations suggests that all states ultimately act out of self-interest and to increase their power. It is this view that many see as increasingly guiding the actions of those in the foreign policy circles of India and the new emerging powers in the global South.

Another way to view the current situation is to assume that states tend to become less idealistic and more conservative with regard to ensuring their development and prosperity as they mature. As a state becomes entangled in global affairs, and increasingly co-opted into the structures of global power, the stakes of promoting radical reform become too high and—in the pursuit of national interest—a state starts to side-line its idealist impulses in exchange for maintaining the status quo. In India's case, the rhetoric of solidarity with the oppressed and poor of the world may not have disappeared, but actions speak louder than words, and its actions of states like India seem to suggest that solidarity with the South is not always a national priority. Brar holds that this ambivalence "seems to result from what might be called 'reluctant radicalism'; a deeply felt desire to see the world fundamentally transformed, but a desire that is held constantly in check by the urge to ensure success even in the world such as it is".[54] Once a state reaches the level of middle power or emerging great power, theory[55] and practice show that they tend to behave in a way which maintains the status quo—calling for incremental reform or within-change at times, but shying away from systemic or transformational change which may ultimately be detrimental to themselves. Part of this, as Narlikar points out, has to do with the fact that as India is increasingly recognised as an emerging great power and important player in all spheres of global governance, it arguably

---

54. Bhupinder Brar, "State, Civil Society, Nation, Nonalignment: Discourses of Freedom and Foreign Policy in India", in K. Bajpai and S. Mallavarapu (eds.), *International Relations in India – Theorising the Region and Nation* (New Delhi: Orient Longman, 2005), p. 207.

55. See, for example, Robert Cox, "Middlepowermanship: Japan and the Future of World Order", in R. Cox and T. Sinclair (eds.), *Approaches to World Order* (Cambridge: Cambridge University Press, 1996), pp. 241–275; Eduard Jordaan, "The Concept of a Middle Power in International Relations: Distinguishing between Emerging and Traditional Middle Powers", *Politikon*, Vol. 30, No. 2 (2003), pp.165–181; and Janis van der Westhuizen, "South Africa's Emergence as a Middle Power", *Third World Quarterly*, Vol. 19, No. 3 (1998), pp. 435–455.

no longer needs the comfort of third world solidarity, making "the old radicalism...unnecessary".[56]

At the same time, however, these radical, anti-western tendencies are so entrenched in the Indian state's identity, as well as in the ruling Congress Party, that it is difficult to simply cast off an identity that was constructed over decades. This parallels the dilemma of the African National Congress (ANC) in South Africa, which Black and Wilson argue is "struggling with the demands of an historical identity forged in struggle and bound to a commitment to human rights and social justice for the poor and oppressed".[57] As India continues to grow economically, there will be increasing pressure to take on a new identity and shed its old radical, anti-Western, developing world identity.

An important development in this regard and one which may have a crucial impact on India's perception of its role in the world in the coming years is the emergence of a younger generation of politicians—with 79 members of parliament in the 15th Lok Sabha under 40 years of age, together with (and most likely linked to) an increase in the number of young voters.[58] Cohen agrees that "a new generation of Indians is coming to power, and their experiences, memories and possibly their policies could differ markedly from those of their predecessors".[59] As 39-year-old minister of state for commerce and industry, Jyotiraditya Scindia notes, "Every 25 years there is a generational shift in politics".[60] He adds, "But what's different this time around is the huge demographic dividend in India. It's a unique opportunity". The new generation of emerging leaders includes 39-year-old Rahul Gandhi, grandson of Indira Gandhi and great-grandson of Jawaharlal Nehru. Many of these young politicians have significant international experience, having studied and worked abroad. In addition, they seem to share an interest in promoting India's global integration and economic rise, in other words, they subscribe to Sagar's liberalist worldview. While this generation is not yet well represented in government, things are changing. Sachin Pilot, the 33-year-old minister of state in the Ministry of Communications and Technology, contends, "We are going to see a civil society accepting a leadership that doesn't have to have an experience of 40 years",[61] referring to the tendency in Indian government and society at large to privilege age over youth. What needs to be further investigated is what worldview this younger generation of the ruling elite subscribe to, and what role they see India playing.

---

56. Amrita Narlikar, "Peculiar Chauvinism or Strategic Calculation? Explaining the Negotiating Strategy of a Rising India", *International Affairs*, Vol. 82, No. 1 (2006), p. 60.

57. David Black and Zoe Wilson, "Rights, region, and identity: Interpreting the Ambiguities of South Africa's Regional Human Rights Role", *Politikon*, Vol. 31, No. 1 (2004), p. 33.

58. Currently, two-thirds of India's population is under 35, see Nivedita Mukherjee "Raring to Grow", *India Today* (23 August 2010), available: <http://indiatoday.intoday.in/site/Story/113791/Top> (accessed 2 September 2010).

59. Cohen, *Emerging Power India*, op. cit., p. 37.

60. Quoted in James Lamont, "India: The Loom of Youth", *Financial Times* (10 May 2010), available: <http://www.ft.com/cms/s/0/8aefdf1e-5c68-11df-93f6-00144feab49a,s01=1.html> (accessed 30 July 2010).

61. Ibid.

Strategic Moralist Posturing

In trying to making sense of India's continued commitment to southern solidarity, which has resulted in significant material costs and losses to the country, Narlikar[62] argues that it cannot all be ascribed to entrenched identities. Instead, she points out that the costs must be weighed up against the "less quantifiable" wins. Referring to India's hard-line position in the World Trade Organisation (WTO), she claims that this has contributed to India being viewed as leader of the developing world, and points out that this is in line with the choice India made to use its existing leadership position in the NAM and the developing world as a whole as its vehicle to global power. Relatedly, India's reputation as a tough and principled negotiator is based on the position it has built over half a century as the leader of the developing world. Narlikar notes that "[a]ccomplished Indian negotiators recognized...that Third Worldism can be as pragmatic as idealist".[63] Former Indian diplomat Rajiv Sikri underlines this when he warns:

> India should not forget its old friends. For it is from among the developing countries that India will get both the resources to fuel India's economic growth and the political support to fulfill its aspirations to become a permanent member of the United Nations Security Council. India's unique strength lies in its reputation as the leader of the developing countries...[64]

As Robert Cox and others have pointed out, recognition by other states, especially in its region, is an important factor in any state's aspiration to be a global power. This is no different in the Indian case.

Of course, this is not the only strategic reason why India continues to (at least rhetorically) advance the interests of the global South. By positioning itself as part of the developing world, it can also continue to benefit from trade and other concessions. A case in point is India's role in the on-going climate change talks in which it has taken a strong position based on the argument that developed countries must shoulder a heavier burden of the costs of reducing environmental degradation on account of benefiting from environmental exploitation historically. Here it is clearly in India's advantage to align itself with the developing world.

India may therefore continue to rhetorically promote the global redistribution of power and resources to the poorest nations while in practice focusing on achieving its own national interests. Sagar, for example, claims that India often "deploys the language of morality instrumentally, asserting the principle of equality when it wants to combat its exclusion, and the principle of proportionality when it wants to maintain its privileges."[65] However, when India's interests and those of the poorest nations coincide, this can lead to positive spin-offs in terms of global redistribution. One such development has been a higher demand and subsequent increase in the price of commodities as a result of the continued economic growth and increased demand for raw materials of India and China. This can have a positive impact on the terms of trade of exporters of predominantly

---

62. Narlikar, "Peculiar Chauvinism", *op. cit.*, p. 75.
63. Amrita Narlikar, "All That Glitters is Not Gold: India's Rise to Power", *Third World Quarterly*, Vol. 28, No. 5 (2007), p. 989.
64. Sikri, *op. cit.*
65. Sagar, *op. cit.*, pp. 805–806.

primary products, many of which are developing world countries. It also reduces many third world states' dependence on the North as trading partners. It is questionable how sustainable this is in the long run, however. It must also be pointed out that these benefits have not been widespread and have arguably benefited mostly the government and business elite, while widening inequalities in the broader society. Palat[66] claims that one of the reasons why elites from emerging powers like India have been reluctant to push too hard for global justice and redistribution of wealth is their own inability to address deepening inequalities in their own societies. There has thus been a certain amount of redistribution of global wealth, but mainly from one group of elites to another.

Another case in point refers to the fact that through providing development assistance—including initiatives under the Indian Technical Cooperation (ITEC) programme and the provision of concessional lines of credit—to African and other developing countries, India is enhancing its reputation as a great power. This was underlined by Foreign Secretary Rao in 2010 when she stated, "India's global role is also being articulated as it becomes an increasingly effective development and technical cooperation source for a number of countries in regions like Africa",[67] and again in 2011, "I think India's global profile has transformed itself. You see it for yourself the role that we are seeking to play in Africa, in our profile as a country that is able to deliver on development cooperation and assistance to the developing world, and also in our immediate neighbourhood".[68]

Finally, the issue of India's ambiguous foreign policy can be approached by considering specific foreign policy issues and context, in other words by examining India's foreign polic*ies*rather than its foreign polic*y*.

Differentiation across Issue Areas

This is the approach taken by Narlikar[69] who, instead of evaluating India's foreign policy in totality, differentiates between different foreign policy issue areas. She identifies the perceived tensions in India's foreign policy as occurring in the security (specifically nuclear) versus economic (specifically trade) arenas. In her analysis of India's negotiating strategy in the WTO, Narlikar argues that despite the fact that India's position in the world has changed, "It still acts as a leader of coalitions involving developing countries, makes concessions to smaller members, tolerates free-riding, and fights for causes of global justice and fairness".[70] These tactics of speaking on behalf of the developing world of course hark back to India's role as a founding member of the NAM and leading member of the G77. She insists, "That this support goes beyond just rhetoric is suggested by some concrete actions that India has taken". In interviews she did with Indian negotiators, she notes they claim that, "irrespective of costs to country, India's long-standing position as a

---

66. Palat, *op. cit.*, p. 729.
67. Nirupama Rao, "India's Global Role", Address by Foreign Secretary at Harvard, 20 September 2010, available: <http://meaindia.nic.in/mystart.php?id=530116512> (accessed 5 August 2011).
68. Nirupama Rao, "Key Priorities for India's Foreign Policy" Address at the International Institute for Strategic Studies, 27 June 2011, available: <http://meaindia.nic.in/mystart.php?id=530115731> (accessed 5 August 2011).
69. Amrita Narlikar, "India and the World Trade Organisation", in S. Smith, A. Hadfield and T. Dunne (eds.) *Foreign Policy* (Oxford: Oxford University Press, 2008), pp. 269–284.
70. *Ibid.*, p. 271.

leader of the developing world makes it impossible for them to present any opposition to such proposals".[71] It would therefore seem that, even today, India's identity of being a voice for the developed world is so strong that, in some cases, it is followed even when this undermines India's material national interest.

On the other hand, if one looks at India's position with regard to the proliferation of nuclear weapons, it becomes clear that there is another side to the state's foreign policy: a more pragmatic approach, far removed from the third worldist position India has become associated with. Narlikar explains these apparent contradictions partly on the basis of bureaucratic politics, noting that India's trade relations and role in the WTO fall under the mandate of the Ministry of Commerce, while the nuclear issue and closer relations with the US has been driven by the Ministry of External Affairs. Another reason she mentions is that while India's rise in the WTO has largely been based on its claim to leadership of the developing world, India's nuclear programme has been developed indigenously, and its nuclear diplomacy has not enjoyed much support from other developing state.[72]

The conclusion one can draw from this analysis is that India draws on different identities and different interests in relation to different foreign policy issues. The accusation of ambiguity may be misplaced, for it assumes that a state with as complex a history, as varied a 1.3 billion strong population and as vibrant a democracy as India has only one homogenous identity. This inconsistency or ambiguity is reflected in analysts' views of its future trajectory. While Narlikar claims, "it would be premature to see India's improving relations with the North as a radical restructuring of its foreign policy"[73] and that, "So far, there is little in the history of that relationship to encourage India to completely abandon its old Third Worldist diplomacy, its civilizational rhetoric or its distributive strategy in favour of conformity with the developed world",[74] Ganguly claims that, "given the internal shifts in political power, its rapid rate of economic growth and its emerging position in the global order, it is doubtful that the country will lapse into its past posture as a revisionist critic of the global order".[75] Despite these apparent ambiguities, some scholars insist that, while India's official doctrine appears to be characterised by ambiguity, in practice it is possible to identify much clearer action with the potential to become a coherent doctrine.[76]

Conclusion

If one assumes that interests are the product of identity, then particular identities will lead to pursuing particular interests. What this paper has thus tried to show is that India has numerous identities that are not necessarily mutually exclusive.

---

71. *Ibid.*
72. *Ibid.*, p. 281.
73. Narlikar, "Peculiar Chauvinism", *op. cit.*, p. 74.
74. Ibid.
75. Sumit Ganguly, "India's Foreign Policy: Retrospect and Prospect" (n.d.), available: <http://www.ufmg.br/cei/wpcontent/uploads/indianforeignpolicy_ganguly.doc> (accessed 12 June 2010).
76. Subrata K. Mitra and Jivanta Schöttli, "The New Dynamics of Indian Foreign Policy and Its Ambiguities", *Irish Studies in International Affairs*, Vol. 18 (2007), p. 20.

As Cohen points out, "Indian thought is both idealist and realist, Gandhian and Machiavellian, and individuals who hold such views can be found across the spectrum. Indeed, many hold such seemingly incompatible views simultaneously".[77] In fact, all of these at times contradictory identities compete within public and foreign policy forums to shape the contours of policy outcomes. India's changing identity (both in terms of how it sees itself, as well as how it is seen by other states) has affected how Indian policy-makers perceive their state's interests. Labels such as 'emerging great power' imply a set of interests different from those implied by the identity 'leader of the developing world' or 'member of the Non-Aligned Movement'. These multiple identities thus vie with each other with regard to affecting the state's interests and foreign policy. Ultimately, it is the role of policy-makers to navigate these complex identity issues and try to balance or at least reconcile the varied, and often inconsistent, identities.

While India's foreign policy continues to be influenced by various identities, the notion of India as a great civilization remains a powerful motivating factor for India's ever increasing global role. This civilizational identity plays out in new ways, however, and is no longer as strongly linked to the post-colonial Nehruvian legacy of moral leadership and non-alignment. Today, India's aspiration to great power status is much more pragmatic and based on economic strength, with the liberal or pragmatic view in foreign policy-making coming to dominate over the past decade. Relatedly, while India still professes to have an independent, non-aligned foreign policy, it is no longer based on ideological convictions but on pragmatism, with New Delhi basing its sometimes controversial foreign relations and alliances on what is believed to be in the national interest.

Ultimately, it would seem as though India, like the other emerging powers, is predominantly concerned about its own position in the global order, and less so about the plight of the developing world. In theory, this does not bode well for India playing an active role in advocating global redistribution, beyond rhetorical support. Having said that, global redistribution may well be a by-product of India's foreign policy, despite its focus primarily being the advancement of its own interests.

---

77. Cohen, *Emerging Power India*, op. cit., p. 63.

India and the Redistribution of Power and Resources

JOACHIM BETZ

India's spectacular growth in the last 15 years and its increasing integration into the world economy should have influenced the country's foreign policy goals away from the isolationist stance of former times. The government should also have become more interested in the distributional effects of global integration, become more assertive in demanding influence within global governance institutions and more sensitive to the demands of domestic interest groups affected by the actions of other countries. This is indeed the case, as we aim to show in this article. The government is still insulated to a certain but declining degree against the influence of specific interest groups on foreign policy strategies, however. Redistribution at the domestic, regional and international levels is a concern of the political elite, but activities at the domestic level target those important as voter groups more than those affected by globalisation. Regional activities are only partly proactive, while those at the global level do not challenge the existing international economic order but mostly intend only to carve out a better position for India itself.

India as a Global Economic Giant

India's economic growth after liberalisation, which commenced in 1991, has been quite spectacular in comparison to its era of import-substituting industrialisation. Growth accelerated after a short stabilisation dip and has reached rates of eight per cent and above in the last few years; an acceleration in growth that was only moderately affected by the global financial crisis, from which India recovered faster than most other developing countries. Post-reform growth was driven more by productivity improvement than by factor accumulation; it was financed predominantly by India's own resources, but was also complemented by a growing inflow of foreign direct investment. The external sector – which before the reforms was the Achilles' heel of India's development – did not pose any serious threat; balance-of-payments deficits remained tractable, external debt declined in relative terms and foreign exchange reserves became plentiful.

Growth has been driven mostly by internal demand, although exports have increased by 20 per cent or more per annum; sector wise growth was fastest in services. The share of industry in GDP has increased only slowly and the most dynamic sectors are also rather capital- and skill-intensive. The employment effects of accelerating growth have therefore been rather modest; poverty reduction has occurred at the same speed as before the reforms, whereas income disparities between states and socio-economic groups has markedly increased.[1] This growth pattern also implies a rapidly mounting energy demand, as well as greenhouse gas emissions, although per capita emissions are still far behind those of developed countries, and even China.[2] Nevertheless, India's energy hunger and increasing contribution to global warming has caused conflicts with other emerging powers (most notably China) and India has been put under a great amount of international pressure (not least, by the United States).

The pattern of economic growth after 1991, especially with the growing integration of the Indian economy into world markets, should have influenced and modified India's foreign policy goals and strategies and should have also blurred, to a certain extent, the boundaries between domestic and international politics in India. We might assume that the Indian government should have: (a) developed a less isolationist (or more precisely 'non-aligned') outlook; (b) become more interested in developing good relations with all of its major economic partners; (c) been prepared to shoulder new responsibilities in global governance issues; (d) simultaneously become more interested in the distributional effects of global integration; (e) become more assertive in demanding greater influence in global governance institutions; and (f) become more sensitive to the demands of local interest groups being affected by their more intense integration into the world community. India's approach to regional integration should have also been affected, depending on the potential pay-off from the respective schemes.

In the following sections I will outline the aforementioned shift in declared foreign policy aims and preferences, analyse the preconditions and causes of this shift, and how far it is supported by important social groups, and compare rhetoric and actions. The thematic focus will be on whether pronouncements and actions imply that there are any endeavours underway to alter and improve the national, regional and global distribution of power and wealth. This has to be done by taking into consideration the preferences and actions of the Indian government, against the backdrop of internal exigencies and the influence of the changing international environment,[3] while bearing in mind that: (a) the international environment was in turn influenced by India's rapid rise, (b) shifting policy preferences only followed, with a certain time-lag, the dramatic upheaval of the global political and economic scene, and (c) the influence of domestic factors on foreign policy was filtered and mediated by the political elite more than it was in developed countries (see below).

Starting with the last two points, it can easily be shown that the country's traditional foreign policy roadmap was used by the Indian government well into the 1990s – long after the end of the Cold War and the onset of economic

---

1. World Bank, *Country Strategy: India* (Washington DC: World Bank, 2004); World Bank, *India: Inclusive Growth and Service Delivery: Building on India's Success* (Washington DC: World Bank, 2006); Catriona Purfield and Jerald Schiff (eds.), *India Goes Global: Its Expanding Role in the World Economy* (Washington DC: IMF, 2006); OECD, *India, Economic Surveys* (Paris: OECD, 2007); Group Centennial, *India 2039: An Affluent Society in One Generation* (Manila: Asian Development Bank, 2009); Anne O. Krueger, "The Missing Middle", *Working Paper*, No. 230 (New Delhi: ICRIER, 2009).

2. Brookings Institution, *India, Energy Security Series* (Washington DC: Brookings Institution, 2006); International Energy Agency, *World Energy Outlook 2007* (Paris: IEA, 2007).

3. Cf. Jeffrey W. Legro, and Andrew Moravcsik, "Is Anybody Still a Realist?", *International Security*, Vol. 24, No. 2 (1999), pp. 5–55; Gerry C. Alons, "Predicting a State's Foreign Policy: State Preferences between Domestic and International Constraints", *Foreign Policy Analysis*, Vol. 3, No. 3 (2007), pp. 211–232.

reforms in India.[4] The relative insulation of the foreign policy elite in India from the public in general, and from interest groups in particular, was also partly maintained – albeit to an increasingly diminishing degree – during the growing integration of India into the world economy, which – according to academic critics – became the only foreign policy game in town.[5] The necessity, as a consequence of this integration, to cultivate better relations with all major economic powers and South Asian neighbours was still dependent on the overall political climate existing between India and these respective states. In relation to questions of global governance, India still vacillates between posing as the vanguard of third world solidarity on the one hand, and claiming a more prominent role for itself in rather oligarchic forums on the other. This vacillation demonstrates India's internal struggle between Nehruvian ('idealistic') and realist positionings.[6] This ambivalence also applies to taking over of responsibilities for global public goods, with India seeking better representation in international agencies and negotiations on the one hand while at the same time trying to minimise its own material contributions. This is most pronounced in issue-areas where concessions would have negative repercussions on powerful domestic interest groups and decisive vote banks, or would pose a risk to economic growth and to exercising undivided sovereignty (see below).[7] India is, however, not a special case in this regard, as other current or prospective regional powers have also pursued more or less the same strategic path.

The New Foreign Policy Agenda

In outlining India's new foreign policy approach, as well as its motivational foundations, we will base our assessment on (1) official statements of the prime minister and the leading representatives of the Ministry of Foreign Affairs, (2) complemented, if necessary, by publications of individual ministries, official commissions and state-affiliated think-tanks, and (3) analytical classifications and explanations that have been made by academic experts. This methodology should also give initial indications of whether the new approach is, at least verbally, intended to serve as a blueprint for the national, regional and global redistribution of wealth and power.

The new approach, which has been propagated hesitantly since the mid-1990s and more forcefully from 2004 onwards, addresses the absolute primacy of economic development; proactive integration into both the global economy and the international knowledge society; a closer strategic engagement with the United States; the cultivation of economic and political links with Southeast Asian states ('Look East Policy'); selective cooperation with the international community on climate change, trade and energy; and, more so than ever before, the

---

4. Sumit Ganguly, "India's Foreign Policy Grows Up", *World Policy Journal*, Vol. 20, No. 4 (Winter 2003/04), pp. 41–47.

5. Harsh V. Pant, "A Rising India's Search for a Foreign Policy", *Orbis*, Vol. 53, No. 2 (2009), pp. 250–264.

6. *Ibid.*; Sumit Ganguly, "Explaining Realignment", *Insights*, No. 115, (Singapore: Institute of South Asian Studies, 2010).

7. Aaditya Mattoo and Arvind Subramanian, "India and Bretton Woods II", *Economic and Political Weekly*, Vol. 8 (2008), pp. 62–70; Rahul Sagar, "State of Mind: What Kind of Power Will India Become?", *International Affairs*, Vol. 85, No. 4 (2009), pp. 801–816.

preparedness to make unilateral concessions in order to build up a genuine economic union of South Asian states and to improve bilateral relations with all of its neighbours.[8] These statements mark a remarkable shift when compared to the once-cherished positions of self-reliance, non-alignment, third world solidarity, keeping utmost sovereignty, intending to bring South Asia under the more or less benevolent hegemony of India and keeping a distance from the United States and its formal and informal allies in Asia.[9]

Consequently, the new policy direction has often been characterised as a withdrawal from idealist and outlived concepts towards a more pragmatic/realist – and at the same time compromising – regional and international stance.[10] This argument can be easily overstretched, however: the former policy of non-alignment and self-reliance was not bereft of a self-interested perspective – in the sense that this policy reflected India's still moderate power resources – but was intended to safeguard the country's chances of growing into a respected global power,[11] or was a mere cover for military weakness.[12] At the same time, the 'pragmatic' policy of today is not free of traditional security concerns (especially with regard to the neighbours) and the desire to keep interference by international regulations to a minimum.

We will now turn to a closer inspection of individual foreign policy goals, their possible motivational basis and the question of how far they are shared by important social groups and by the informed public:

---

8. For an analytical summary see Stephen P. Cohen, *Emerging Power India* (New Delhi: Oxford University Press, 2002); Raja Mohan, *Crossing the Rubicon: The Shaping of India's New Foreign Policy* (Basingstoke: Palgrave, 2003); Pratap Bhanu Mehta, "Still under Nehru's Shadow? The Absence of Foreign Policy Frameworks in India", *India Review*, Vol. 8, No. 3 (2009), pp. 209–233; Rohan Mukherjee and David M. Malone, "Indian Foreign Policy and Contemporary Security Challenges", *International Affairs*, Vol. 87, No. 1 (2009), pp. 87–104; for the official view, see Manmohan Singh, "India and the US: Towards a New Partnership", Presented at the Council on Foreign Relations, New York, 2004, available: <www.meaindia.nic.in/speech/2004/09/24ss02.htm> (accessed 7 August 2008); Natwar Singh, "Regional Cooperation for Growth and Prosperity", Address at the Hindustan Times Leadership Initiative, Ministry of External Affairs, 2004, available: <www.meaindia.nic.in/speech/2004/11/06ss01.htm> (accessed 7 August 2008); Shyam Saran, "Present Dimensions of the Indian Foreign Policy", Address at Shanghai Institute of International Studies, Ministry of External Affairs, 2006, available: <www.meaindia.nic.in/speech/2006/01/11ss01.htm> (accessed 16 July 2008); Svivshankar Menon, "2007: India-Pakistan: Understanding the Conflict Dynamics", Speech at Jamia Millia Islamia, Ministry of External Affairs, 2009, available: <www.meaindia.nic.in/speech/2009/01/19ss03.htm> (accessed 11 March 2009); Pranab Mukherjee, "India's Creditable role in world affairs, while ensuring high economic growth, democratic values and social justice", Speech at the 107th Annual General Meeting of the Merchants Chamber of Commerce, Kolkata, Ministry of External Affairs, 2008, available: <www.meaindia.nic.in/speech/2004/09/24ss02.htm> (accessed 7 August 2008); Ministry of External Affairs, "The United States and India: Chartering the future course", Foreign Secretary's Keynote address at the India Initiative of the Centre for a New American Security and the ASPEN Institute India, 2010, available: <www.meaindia.nic.in/speech/2010/01/13ss01.htm> (accessed 9 July 2010).

9. Cf. Cohen, *op. cit.*; Mohan, *op. cit.*; Mukherjee and Malone, *op. cit.*

10. Cohen, *op. cit.*; Mohan, *op. cit.*; Ganguly, "India's Foreign Policy Grows Up", *op. cit.*; Ummu Salva Bava, "New Powers for Global Change? India's Role in the Emerging World Order", *Dialogue on Globalization*, Briefing Paper (Berlin: Friedrich-Ebert-Stiftung, 2010).

11. Cf. Baldev Raj Nayar and T.V. Paul, *India in the World Order. Searching for Major-Power Status* (Cambridge: Cambridge University Press, 2003); David M. Malone, *Does the Elephant Dance? Contemporary Indian Foreign Policy* (Oxford: Oxford University Press, 2011).

12. Mehta, *op. cit.*

1. The first and foremost goal of the Indian government is the country's development – more precisely, high, stable and continued economic growth of eight or even 10 per cent, per annum.[13] The preeminent position of economic growth and transformation (into a developed economy) in the conduct of foreign policy is justified by (1) the necessity to improve the lot of India's masses,[14] and (2) the need to safeguard social stability, which might be endangered by the alienation of India's impoverished masses.[15] Last but not least India has to grow, because power in the twenty-first century stems "from the pores of a well-run economy",[16] as economic interests drive international relations today more than ever before.[17] This argument is made even more explicit by Indian think-tanks, which are already portraying the emergence of a 'tripolar' world composed of the United States, China and India, provided that India is able to bridge the technological gap with the frontier states.[18] There are hardly any national or international experts who deny the capability of the country to reach the aforementioned goals, provided that the necessary reforms are tackled. There are also practically no important interest groups who are calling into question the government's growth aspirations; some of them, however, rightly point out that the fruits of growth must be shared more equally.

2. Liberalisation and deregulation have – according to official statements – decisively helped India to increase its economy, to broaden its middle class and to become an attractive destination for foreign investment. India's current foreign policy paradigm perceives globalisation as being a positive factor in India's development; it has helped India to become a more efficient and competitive economy. Continued economic reforms are considered necessary in order for India to be able to reap the fruits of globalisation.[19] Globalisation itself is seen as being able to tie national economies together while altering the contours of sovereignty and displacing the centre of gravity of global economic activity towards Asia.[20] These views are shared by experts

---

13. Cf. Manmohan Singh, *op. cit.*; Pranab Mukherjee, "India's Foreign Policy and Future India-US Relations", Remarks at Council on Foreign Relations, New York, Ministry of External Affairs, 2007, available: <www.meaindia.nic.in/speech/2007/10/03ss01.htm> (accessed 16 July 2008); Ministry of External Affairs, *op. cit.*; Ministry of External Affairs, PM's opening remarks at the Full format (Plenary) Session at the first BRIC Summit, 16/06/2009, available: <www.meaindia.nic.in/speech/2009/06/16ss01.htm> (accessed 19 January 2010).

14. *Ibid.*

15. Cf. Manmohan Singh, *IDSA Foundation Day Lecture 2005* (New Delhi: Institute for Defence Studies and Analyses, 2005).

16. Yaswant Sinha, Address at India Today Conclave 2004, Building an Indian Century, Ministry of External Affairs, 2004, available: < www.emaindia.nic.in/speech/2004/03/12ss01.htm> (accessed 7 August 2008).

17. Yaswant Sinha, "Commerce Calling", India's Economic Diplomacy in Ministry of External Affairs, 2004, available: <www.meaindia.nic.in/speech/2004/01/31ss01.htm> (accessed 7 August 2008).

18. Arvind Virmani, "A Tripolar Century: USA, China and India", *Working Paper*, No. 160 (New Delhi: ICRIER, 2005).

19. Manmohan Singh, "India and the US: Towards a New Partnership", *op. cit.*

20. Cf. Natwar Singh, *op. cit.*, Mukherjee, "India's Foreign Policy", *op. cit.*; Pranab Mukherjee, "India and the Global Balance of Power", Address at the National launch of Global India Foundation –Ministry of External Affairs, 2007, available: <www.meaindia.nic.in/speech/2007/01/16ss02.htm> (accessed 16 July 2008).

from international organisations and think-tanks, but much less so by academics within India[21] and abroad. There is a nearly universal consensus that economic integration has exacerbated regional and personal income inequalities within India; it is only the extent of these that is still a matter of debate.[22]

3. Knowledge has become, according to the Indian government, the critical resource for development. India was previously already an important player in the knowledge economy, but now needs continued access to the latest technologies, an important source of which is the United States.[23] This is common sense, but both international and Indian experts sometimes doubt whether India is already, or will become, fit for the knowledge economy, especially with an eye to the nearly defunct public education system.[24]

4. As the Indian economy becomes increasingly dependent on foreign markets, foreign direct investments and technology transfers, an important foreign policy goal is the creation of an environment that continues to promote the fulfilment of India's economic aspirations. The government's intention is to forge well-rounded strategic partnerships with all major powers and it has a vital interest in the preservation of a free, fair and open world trade system. Regarding policies that dealt with the recent global financial crisis, the government expressed its intention to contribute to global economic recovery, warning that it must not be strangled by contractive policies or mounting protectionism, while emphasising a slight shift from reliance on exports towards internal demand.[25] This position is by no means shared by all political parties or interest groups; deregulation of the internal market is no longer seriously opposed domestically, with the exception of full-fledged privatisation, but the complete liberalisation of foreign trade, of foreign investments and of capital movements definitely is.[26]

5. India's growing integration into the world economy has, above all, improved opportunities for cooperation with the United States: American investments are required to finance the massive infrastructure needs of India; the Indian diaspora in the United States is also an important asset for improving bilateral

---

21. There is an extensive debate on these matters in Indian journals, most prominently in *Economic and Political Weekly*.

22. Kalpana Kochhar *et al.*, "India's Pattern of Development: What Happened, What Follows?", *IMF Working Paper*, Vol. 06/22 (Washington DC: IMF, 2006); Prachi Mishra and Utsav Kumar, "Trade Liberalization and Wage Inequality: Evidence From India", *Working Paper*, Vol. 05/20 (Washington DC: IMF, 2005); Purfield and Schiff, *op. cit.*; Petia Topalova, "Trade Liberalization, Poverty and Inequality: Evidence from Indian Districts", *Working Paper*, Vol. 11614 (Cambridge: National Bureau of Economic Research, 2005); Gaurav Datt and Martin Ravallion, "Is India's Economic Growth Leaving the poor Behind?", *Journal of Economic Perspectives*, Vol. 16, No. 3, (2002), pp. 89–108.

23. Manmohan Singh, "India and the US: Towards a New Partnership", *op. cit.*; Natwar Singh, *op. cit.*; Ministry of External Affairs, Address by PM at Khazanah Global Lecture on "India's Development Experience", 27/10/2010, available: <www.meaindia.nic.in/mystart.php?id=5301116604> (accessed 19 Nov. 2010).

24. See for example Basanta K. Pradhan and Shalabh Kumar Singh, *Policy Reforms and Financing of Elementary Education in India: A Study of the Quality of Service and Outcome* (New Delhi: National Council of Applied Economic Research, 2004).

25. Ministry of External Affairs, Address of H.E. the President of India to the nation on the eve of the 61st Republic Day, 2010, available: <www.meaindia.nic.in/speech/2010/01/25ss03.htm> (accessed 12 July 2010); Ministry of External Affairs, Prime Minister's remarks at G 20 Summit, 2010, available: <www.meaindia.nic.in/speech/2010/06/27ss01.htm> (accessed 9 July 2010).

26. Relentless debates in journals such as *Frontline* provide ample evidence of this.

relations.[27] This assumption is, again, not one backed by a unanimous consensus – witness the massive opposition to the US-India civilian nuclear agreement of 2008, less because of its technical clauses, but more because it was seen by the communists, the Hindu nationalist BJP and even segments of the atomic energy establishment as either another instrument to force India into a subordinate alliance partnership with the United States or as a threat to India's strategic autonomy.[28]

6. Sustained growth needs secure energy supplies, which will be met through the diversification of sources and partners, the expansion of nuclear facilities and by equity investments overseas.[29] In several respects, closer cooperation with the United States and energy exporters will be necessary to meet domestic demand. The necessity for increased energy supply is disputed nowhere in India, but greater reliance on the United States in this domain is.

7. A major shift has occurred in India's position towards other South Asian countries. The new politics of neighbourliness are based on several arguments, such as "a major power has hardly ever emerged – or sustained itself – on the world scene amidst a conflict-ridden and impoverished neighbourhood".[30] India, as the most important state in South Asia, should bear the majority of responsibility for meeting regional challenges. Most prominent among them is the necessity to reassure its neighbours, by developing "a virtuous web of cross-border, economic and commercial linkages".[31] There are a growing number of civil society organisations that share this view; in addition, employers' organisations are – for economic reasons – even more strongly endorsing such a position and asking for more proactive policies.[32]

8. India's foreign policy should be driven not only by economic interests, but also by core values such as the promotion of democracy, human rights, the rule of law and respect and tolerance for diversity. The two greatest democracies in the world strongly converge on the propagation of these values. As a result, partnership with the United States is thought of as being "a natural one".[33] There are few social groups in India who are interested in exporting democracy, and very few who believe that the US would be the right partner for that endeavour.

9. Support for democratic values should be the basis of international relations; global challenges must, therefore, be addressed by collective decision-making and not through processes dominated by the few.[34]

---

27. Manmohan Singh, "India and the US: Towards a New Partnership", *op. cit.*; Saran, "Present Dimensions of the Indian Foreign Policy", *op. cit.*

28. Sumit Ganguly, "India in 2007: A Year of Opportunities and Disappointments", *Asian Survey*, Vol. XLVIII, No. 1 (2008), pp. 165–176.

29. Government of India, *Integrated Energy Policy. Report of the Expert Committee* (New Delhi: Government of India, 2006): Menon, *op. cit.*

30. Pranab Mukherjee, "Defence Minister's Address at the 5th IISS Asia Security Summit", (New Delhi: Institute for Defence Studies and Analyses, 2006).

31. Natwar Singh, *op. cit.*

32. See for example Asian Development Bank/Federation of Indian Chambers of Commerce and Industry (ADB/FICCI), *Key Proposals for Harnessing Business Opportunities in South Asia*, (Manila and New Delhi: ADB/FICCI, 2010).

33. Ministry of External Affairs, Foreign Secretary's Keynote Address to the India Initiative of the Centre for a New American Security, 2010, available: <www.meaindia.nic.in/speech/2010/01/13ss01.htm> (accessed 9 July 2010); Ministry of External Affairs, Address by NSA at the 9th IISS Asia Security Summit, 2010, available: <www.meaindia.nic.in/speech/2010/06/05ss01.httm> (accessed 9 July 2010).

34. Natwar Singh, *op. cit.*

The United States may well remain the preeminent power in the world for some time, but even this power could not bear all the costs for tackling global problems.[35] India and the United States share a common interest in "work[ing] towards an open and liberal regime for transfers of goods, services, investments and technology" in the fight against international terrorism, climate change and nuclear proliferation.[36] The United States may also be supportive of India's rise as a counterweight to China.[37] That the 'democratisation' of international relations is necessary is not disputed within India; there is, however, no consensus about whether partnership with the United States to achieve this is called for or makes sense.

10. To secure global peace and cooperation, true multilateral endeavours are, therefore, now required.[38] The UN Security Council must be made more representative; India's claim to a permanent seat is justified by its extremely large population, its vibrant democracy and its active role in peace-keeping operations. The Bretton Woods institutions, likewise, have to be not only democratised but also strengthened.[39]

11. In spite of globalisation, state sovereignty and territorial integrity continue to be fundamental principles of international relations, although only in the context of rising interdependence. Military power remains an important pillar of security, one that helps to conserve the autonomy of India's foreign and domestic policies. This includes a nuclear arsenal and a strategy of credible minimum deterrence.[40] This position is, again, shared by all national parties (aside from the communists), think-tanks and major interest groups.

This might do to sketch the official rhetoric and their popular acceptance. Every single idea is obviously destined to support the economic and – by implication – the political rise of India to world status. This is happening with only minor attention being given to domestic redistribution, with limited thought being cast on regional prosperity (for the sake of India's security) and, with regard to global redistribution, foremost attention is being given to the betterment of India's position alone. I will not elaborate on every item below, but instead will focus on those that have at least some relation to the domestic, regional and international redistribution of power and influence. Before entering into this debate, some preliminary remarks are necessary.

---

35. Saran, "Present Dimensions of the Indian Foreign Policy", *op. cit.*

36. Ministry of External Affairs, PM's opening remarks at the Full format (Plenary) Session at the first BRIC Summit, 2009, available: <www.meaindia.nic.in/speech/2009/06/16ss01.htm> (accessed 19 Jan. 2010).

37. Virmani, *op. cit.*

38. Natwar Singh, *op. cit.*

39. Ministry of External Affairs, PM's Remarks at the Plenary Session of the G 20 Summit, 2010, available: <www.meaindia.nic.in/mystart.php?id=530116657> (accessed 19 November 2010); Ministry of External Affairs, Address by foreign Secretary at the 3rd MEA-IISS Seminar on 'Perspectives on Foreign Policy for a 21st Century India', 2010, available: <www.meaindia.nic.in/mystart.php?id=530115586> (accessed 19 November. 2010).

40. Yaswant Sinha, "Building and Indian Century", Address at India Today Conclave 2004, Ministry of External Affairs, 2004, available: <www.emaindia.nic.in/speech/2004/03/12ss01.htm> (accessed 7 August 2008); Mukherjee, "Defence Minister's Address", *op. cit.*; Ministry of External Affairs, Address by NSA at the 9th IISS Asia Security Summit 2010, available: <www.meaindia.nic.in/speech/2010/06/05ss01.htm> (accessed 9 July 2010).

Domestic Influences on Foreign Policy

If we compare India's current foreign policy preferences with the former ones, then the priorities of territorial integrity, national sovereignty and third world solidarity have obviously become of secondary importance. The maintenance of strong economic growth has clearly come to the forefront, supported by access to foreign markets, capital and technology, necessitating friendly relations with all major economic powers – most prominently the United States – as well as nurturing a prosperous South Asian region. Institutionally, India's rise has been assisted by the spread of democracy, by a fair and open global trade and finance system and by strong and representative international organisations and regimes. We should also remark that security is now defined more broadly than ever before, so as to also encompass economic strength and security from internal unrest.

It is not easy to explain the shift in India's foreign policy using typical theoretical approaches. A neorealist attempt would suffer from the fact that India's power resources have grown relative to those of its neighbours, other developing countries or the established powers through economic growth and sophistication. Also, India has won powerful quasi-allies (foremost the United States), has no outspoken enemy (apart from Pakistan) and has experienced only moderate economic and territorial conflicts with China, which have been counterbalanced by common global interests. As such, neorealism would form a rather weak basis to explain India's more compromising/pragmatic strategy. An institutional approach would also have limited explanatory power, as India's presence in international organisations has always been strong (but has increased in regional organisations involving Southeast Asian countries). The most suitable candidate would most likely be a liberal approach, as social groups benefiting from the gradual opening up of the economy should have become more powerful and vocal – asking for further liberalisation – after reforms. In addition, spill-over effects from the actions of other countries should have become more intensely felt by diverse social groups domestically, because of the country's progressive integration into the international economy.

The problem with this approach is that it presupposes a relatively open arena of foreign policy discussion, influence and decision-making. We have, however, already noted that the Indian foreign policy elite formerly enjoyed a considerable degree of autonomy from society in decision-making – and still does so – although this varies across policy fields and is also declining sharply (see below). The former existence of insulation had several root causes: political institutions like the parliament played only a limited role in foreign policy, as its consent was not necessary to declare war or ratify treaties.[41] The military apparatus also enjoyed only a modest say (even in regard to arms procurement), and was informed either late in the game or not at all about important decisions – for example, the nuclear tests in 1998.[42] In international trade negotiations even the line ministry was sidelined by the civic bureaucracy.[43] Foreign policy

---

41. Cf. Citha D. Maass, "Indiens Sicherheitskonzept", in Werner Draguhn (ed.), *Indien 2001: Politik, Wirtschaft, Gesellschaft* (Institut für Asienkunde: Hamburg, 2001), pp. 177–215; Cohen, *op. cit.*; Christian Wagner, *Das politische System Indiens: Eine Einführung* (Wiesbaden: VS-Verlag, 2006).

42. Sreeram Chaulia, "India's "Power" Attributes", in David Scott (ed.), *Handbook of India's International Relations* (London: Routledge, 2011), pp. 23–34.

43. Cf. Amrita Narlikar, "Peculiar Chauvinism or Strategic Calculation? Explaining the Negotiating Strategy of a Rising India, *International Affairs*, Vol. 82, No. 1 (2006), pp. 59–76.

strategies and social goals did not figure prominently in the programmes and election manifestos of the political parties. Indeed, there were (and still are) hardly any programmatic differences in their foreign policy outlooks – with the exception of the communists.

Interest groups rarely press the government to take a specific position on foreign policy issues autonomously, because these organisations (for example, unions and employers' federations) are fragmented and/ or associated with national parties. Civil society, although composed of a multitude of outfits, is also rather weak.[44] Finally, despite having a large range of often critical and widely-circulated newspapers, foreign policy decisions are rarely at the centre of discussion in the press. The government could thus act largely only on its own advice, except in those cases where the intensely felt preferences of large voter groups were negatively affected economically (for example, trade liberalisation) or emotionally (such as the abandonment of non-alignment). During the era of state-led and import-substituting development, social groups understandably also took only a limited interest in foreign policies, as they were only marginally affected by developments outside the country.

But the strong constituencies built around the inward-looking development model did indeed hinder a rapid strategic reorientation of foreign (economic and general) policies, as is often noted.[45] The insulation of the foreign policy elite from domestic pressures – not only with regard to the grand design but also to minor questions – has been perceptibly declining since the mid-1990s. The lively debates about joining the WTO, issues of the Doha Round, the US–India nuclear agreement, as well as India's concessions during the latest climate negotiations are all cases in point. This declining insulation is not only due to more assertive interest groups, but even more so or mediated by the rise of regional parties, representing particular groups and making rather unwieldy coalition governments necessary. Is has, as some analysts deplore, led to a near total loss of strategic vision in foreign policies.[46]

India's Foreign Policy and the Redistribution of Power and Resources

If we consider the overall foreign policy priorities of the Indian government, as mentioned above, the country has clearly developed from an aspiring power challenging the global distribution of power and resources to some kind of status quo power demanding a position of influence corresponding to its increased economic and political weight.[47] We will elaborate on this hypothesis on three levels: the domestic, the regional and the global.

---

44. Cf. Pradeep K. Chhibber, *Democracy without Associations: Transformation of the Party System and Social Cleavages in India* (Ann Arbor, MI: The University of Michigan Press, 2001).

45. Cf. Mohan, *op. cit.*; Ganguly, "India's Foreign Policy Grows Up", *op. cit.*

46. Malone, *op. cit.*; Harsh.V. Pant, "Indian Strategic Culture: The Debate and its Consequences", in David Scott (ed.), *Handbook of India's International Relations* (London: Routledge, 2011), pp. 14–22.

47. Yaswant Sinha, address by Sri Yaswant Sinha at the India Today Conclave 2004, "Building an Indian Century", Ministry of External Affairs, 2004, available: <www.emaindia.nic.in/speech/2004/03/12ss01.htm> (accessed 7 August 2008); Chris Ogden, "International "Aspirations" of a Rising Power", in David Scott (ed.), *Handbook of India's International Relations* (London: Routledge, 2011), pp. 3–13

The Domestic Level

As noted, India's foremost foreign policy goal has been to create an internal and external environment propitious for rapid growth, the benefits of which it was anticipated would also trickle down to the poor. However, the acceleration of growth after economic reform only managed to partially meet this challenge. India has become the second-fastest growth economy in the world, but the country's progress in terms of poverty reduction and social indicators has been slow. Poverty is increasingly concentrated geographically (in the so-called 'BIMARU' states as well as in the countryside) and within certain social groups ('untouchables', tribal peoples and Muslims). Most social indicators have improved, but some (infant and maternal mortality, malnutrition, dropout rates) remain stubbornly high.[48] This is not a consequence of globalisation per se, but rather of low overall public expenditure on health and education, deficiencies in infrastructure, the rigid application of labour laws, bad governance in poorer states and the fact that agriculture was nearly completely omitted from reforms.[49]

Growth was also relatively "jobless", especially for the less-qualified workers; job growth was only a half of economic growth and occurred mostly in the modern service and informal sectors. The causes of the rather poor employment record were: 1) that slowly growing and low-productivity agriculture could not absorb more labour, 2) labour productivity increased rapidly, 3) industrial growth was rather skill-intensive, and 4) industrial employment growth was obstructed by rigid labour laws and deficient infrastructure.[50] Again, this was not due to globalisation per se; economic growth was already capital- and skill-intensive prior to the economic reforms, growth thereafter only strengthened this tendency.[51]

In light of these conditions, it is interesting to scrutinise how the Indian government tried to mitigate the shortcomings of the development model in order to make it globalisation-proof. It has to be realised, first, that social expenditure by both the central government and the states are extremely low, even when compared to developing countries at a similar stage of evolution. Second, health and education expenditures have been biased in favour of tertiary services, making their distribution more unequal (in terms of social impact) than in most other developing countries.[52] Rural people, Muslims, caste members and tribes, as well as the poor in general, have been badly served; social insurance has benefited only a privileged few and the formal sector.[53] The quality

---

48. World Bank, *op. cit*; Purfield and Schiff, *op. cit.*

49. Cf. World Bank, *India: Inclusive Growth and Service Delivery: Building on India's Success*, (Washington DC: World Bank, 2006); Bibek Debroy and Laveesh Bhandari, *Exclusive Growth—Inclusive Inequality*, (unpublished paper, 2007); IMF, *India. Selected Issues* (Washington DC:IMF, 2008).

50. Kochhar *et al.*, *op. cit.*; Purfield and Schiff, *op. cit.*; Planning Commission, Government of India, *Towards Faster and More Inclusive Growth* (New Delhi: Planning Commission, 2006); World Bank, *op. cit.*

51. Montek S. Ahluwalia, "Lessons from India's Economic Reforms", in T. Besley and R. Zagha (eds.), *Development Challenges in the 1990s: Leading Policymakers Speak from Experience* (Washington, DC: Oxford University Press, 2005), pp.189–203.

52. Cf. Ajay Mahal *et al.*, "The Poor and Health Service Use in India", *HNP Discussion Paper* (World Bank: Washington DC, 2001); Deon Filmer, *The Incidence of Public Expenditures on Health and Education*, Background Note for World Development Report 2004: Making Services Work for Poor People (Washington DC: World Bank, 2003); Pranab Bardhan, *Awakening Giants: Feet of Clay. Assessing the Economic Rise of China and India* (Princeton, NJ: Princeton University Press, 2010).

53. Cf. Nita Rudra, *Globalization and the Race to the Bottom in Developing Countries: Who Really Gets Hurt?* (Cambridge: Cambridge University Press, 2009).

of public services has been so bad that even poor people have tried to avoid using them. Poverty programmes have been characterised by grave inefficiencies and corruption, as well as massive diffusion effects to wealthier groups, covering only sections of the poor and in reality many non-poor people too.[54] There have been some noteworthy (but insufficient) efforts to improve the situation. Significant impetus came only after the unforeseen electoral defeat of the centre-right coalition in 2004. The new Congress-led government thereafter initiated quite a few reforms aimed at broadening the impact of social services and poverty programmes.

The most important of these reforms were the *Sarva Shiksha Abhiyan* (Education for All), a programme for the reform of the primary education sector. The National Rural Health Mission assembles the various rural health programmes under one steward and the National Rural Employment Guarantee Act, gives the guarantee to the unemployed in rural areas of 100 days of paid labour per family each year, as well as a scheme of public pensions for the rural poor and a group-based scheme that protects people below the poverty line against the gravest health risks. There was also, recently, a debt waiver introduced for loans taken out by poor farmers with formal financial institutions. These are remarkable innovations, introduced under the banner of inclusive growth, although the scope of the new schemes is still limited.[55]

We may remark that these programmes were only partly destined to make India fit for globalisation or to compensate the losers, as they were meant for groups only marginally affected by mounting competitive international pressure on the Indian economy. As such, they were driven more by a domestic political calculus than by external challenges. The outcomes from the old and (less so) the new programmes would have been more significant if they had not been plagued by endemic mismanagement and corruption. But, the Indian public today is no longer willing to tolerate the existing state of affairs; the hunger strike of a civil society activist in April 2011 was backed by large segments of the middle classes and the economic elite and has forced the government to refine its planned legislation.

The Regional Level

India's strategy for the region, as outlined above, is to engage its neighbours in a web of virtual economic linkages, thereby raising the latter's stakes in a bright, common future as well as dampening their interest in instigating unrest, cross-border terrorism and hostile activities towards India. India's main way of doing this is to enhance intraregional trade and 'connectivity'.[56] This is a rather simple blueprint for overcoming unrest and terrorism. The occurrence of these phenomena in India is not necessarily facilitated by the supportive actions of its neighbours because, in any case, prosperity does not always dampen social

---

54. World Bank, *Social Protection for a Changing India* (Washington DC: World Bank, 2011).

55. Gita Sen and D. Rajasekhar, "Social Protection Policies, Experiences, Challenges", in R. Nagaraj (Hrsg.), *Country Study: India* (Geneva: UNRISD, 2010), pp. 79–112; World Bank, *op. cit.*

56. Cf. Natwar Singh, *op. cit.*; Shyam Saran, *India and Its Neighbours* (New Delhi: Institute for Defence Studies and Analyses, 2005); Ministry of External Affairs, Opening Statement by Prime Minister at the 16th SAARC Summit, 2010, available <www.meaindia.nic.in/speech/2010/04/28ss01.htm> (accessed 9 July 2010).

unrest and poor people or countries are more submissive than restive. As a result, one has to also focus in more on some of the other motives behind India's proactive regional stance, as well as ask what the Indian government is really doing to advance regional integration and 'shared prosperity'.[57]

The intended improvement of neighbourly relations is supported by the economic interests of India itself, as the level of intraregional trade is still very low (less than five per cent of total trade among South Asian countries),[58] far lower than intraregional trade in both East and Southeast Asia. So an increase in this sphere would also serve as another mine of growth for India.[59] Second, if India does not offer an attractive project and vision of regional integration then its neighbours might be inclined to ally more closely with China, as can already be seen happening. Last but not least, unrest in its neighbouring states often triggers migration waves towards India, thereby disturbing the ethnic balance (foremost an issue in India's Northeastern states).

Contrary to the promise of shared prosperity in South Asia, India was for a long time not a great supporter of opening its markets to neighbouring countries. This resistance to opening up declined after 1996, when India signed free trade agreements with the smaller countries of the region (Bhutan, Nepal, Sri Lanka) and took – at least verbally – a proactive stance towards making the whole subcontinent a free trade zone. Without denying that this gives more flexibility on India's part, one should nevertheless bear in mind that the South Asian Free Trade Agreement (which came into force in 2010) operates with long negative lists, restrictive rules of origin, safety clauses, and so on.[60] India's tariff rates are still rather high, especially for sensitive products that can be imported from neighbouring countries (for example, textile products from Pakistan). So the Indian government's verbal commitment to free trade within South Asia, backed forcefully by India's business community within the region, is evolving faster than its actual implementation. Last but not least, India has become a sizeable donor of development assistance to its smaller neighbours, most prominently Afghanistan (where India has become one of the largest donors), Bhutan and Nepal. This assistance was also given with the expectation that it would help to contain China's influence in the region, to stabilise a friendly regime (in Afghanistan) and to open markets for India.[61]

The Global Level

The Indian government argues that on the global level 'true multilateralism' is called for as even the resources of the United States are limited, and because

---

57. Cf. Pranab Mukherjee, "India and the Global Balance of Power", Address at National launch of Global India Foundation, Ministry of External Affairs, <www.meaindia.nic.in/speech/2007/01/16ss02.htm> (accessed 16 July 2008).

58. Cf. Nisha Taneja, "India–Pakistan Trade", *ICRIER Working Paper No. 18* (New Delhi: ICRIER, 2006; Sudhir Kumar Singh, "Preface", in Sudhir Kumar Singh. (ed.), *Post 9/11 Indian Foreign Policy. Challenges and Opportunities* (New Delhi: Pentagon Press, 2009), pp. I–XVI.

59. Cf. World Bank, *Can South Asia End Poverty in a Generation?* (Washington DC: World Bank, 2006).

60. Smruti S. Pattanaik, "Making Sense of Regional Cooperation: SAARC at Twenty", *Strategic Analysis*, Vol. 30, No. 2 (2006), pp. 139–160; Mohsin S. Khan, "India-Pakistan Trade: A Roadmap for Enhancing Economic Relations", *Policy Brief*, No. PB09-15 (Washington DC: Peterson Institute for International Economics, 2009).

61. Cf. Oliver Stuenkel, "Responding to Global Development Challenges", *Discussion Paper*, Vol. 11 (Bonn: DIE, 2010).

power is no longer defined by military means alone but also by economic and technological strength.[62] Economic interdependence sets constrictive boundaries to (interstate) conflict escalation; no power can hope to be protected against the vagaries of world markets or to solve global issues (climate change, energy shortages, international terrorism, and so on) by itself, "no matter how powerful it is".[63] Consequently, India should not lean indiscriminately solely upon one power but should rather create issue-related alliances.

Regarding the global redistribution of power and privilege, the government has the intention of claiming a special international role for India. This is most obvious with regard to nuclear policies. Although India was not a signatory to the Non-Proliferation Treaty and exerted the nuclear option in 1998, it has nevertheless – according to the government (as well as to international experts)[64] – acted as a responsible nuclear power, followed a policy of strict non-proliferation of nuclear technologies, done its utmost to advance universal nuclear disarmament and relinquished the first use of nuclear weapons. In short, India has merited its international recognition as a nuclear power.[65] On the other hand, the Indian government is implicitly making it understood that the boat of would-be nuclear powers is now full; additional aspirants should, therefore, be contained. In this context, India backed UN resolutions against Iran (without consenting to the imposition of harsh sanctions).

The official position with regard to global financial governance is extremely similar. The Indian government has taken a very nuanced position in identifying the causes of the last global financial crisis, blaming not only the systemic risks (leverage of subprime credits) and the lax monetary policies of industrialised countries for its occurrence, but also the excessive savings and current account surpluses of Asian economies and the weak control of systemic risks by central banks worldwide. They have not called into question financial globalisation per se but pleaded for better regulatory and supervisory structures, to be orchestrated by the IMF and the Financial Stability Board (where India has recently become a member state); they were, therefore, also backing an increase in the IMF's resources.[66]

In India's view, the IMF must become a truly multilateral institution, meaning that quota distribution should be adjusted to current economic realities – especially the actual weight of China and India. The government has not called into question the functions and operating procedures of the IMF, but believes it should also deal more decisively with imbalances arising from the current practices of developed economies. Better representation for emerging economies is

---

62. Manmohan Singh, "India and the US: Towards a New Partnership", *op. cit.*; Saran, "Present Dimensions of the Indian Foreign Policy", *op. cit.*

63. Menon, *op. cit.*

64. See Ashley J. Tellis, *India as a New Global Power: An Action Agenda for the United States* (Washington DC: Carnegie Endowment for International Peace, 2005); Michael A. Levi and Charles D. Ferguson, *U.S.-India Nuclear cooperation: A Strategy for Moving Forward*, CSR No. 16 (Council on Foreign Relations: New York, 2006); Esther Pan, *The U.S.-India Nuclear Deal, Backgrounder* (Washington DC: Council on Foreign Relations, 2006).

65. Natwar Singh, "50 Years of Panchsheel: Towards a New International Order based on Genuine Multilateralism", Address at the International Seminar Ministry of External Affairs, 2004, available: <www.meaindia.nic.in/speech/2004/11/18ss01.htm> (accessed 7 August 2008).

66. Cf. Reserve Bank of India, *Financial Stability Report* (New Delhi: RBI, 2010); Reserve Bank of India, *Report on Currency and Finance 2008-09. Global Financial Crisis and the Economy* (New Delhi: RBI, 2010).

also recommended within the Bank for International Settlements. Credit supply by the World Bank and the regional development banks should be enhanced in order to maintain support for a liberal economic policy in these states.[67] One can hardly imagine more market-friendly statements from any other emerging country or, for that matter, from earlier Indian governments.

At the heart of India's UN policy is the reform of the Security Council. The government is demanding a permanent seat for India so as to make the Council more representative. In 2005, India joined the G4 (together with Brazil, Germany and Japan) in order to advance the common goal of its admission to the Security Council. China flatly refused India's accession (and has been delaying consent since); Pakistan also opposed the measure, while India's smaller neighbours could not afford to speak out against it. In addition to the reform of the Security Council, India intends to strengthen the General Assembly and the ECOSOC. This is, at least, a policy more in accordance with the wishes of other developing countries.[68] The tactics of the Indian government in the Doha Round and in international climate negotiations demonstrate that India is only partly prepared to accept any shrinking of its national leeway for the benefit of global goods in matters where intense preferences of domestic constituencies are affected.[69]

The failure of the Doha Round has in no small part been the result of Brazilian and, more so, Indian resistance to concessions on their part. India's Minister of Commerce presented a long list of non-negotiable issues, including a negative list of sensitive imports. This was obviously intended to help India keep some leeway for ad hoc import restrictions on uncompetitive industrial sectors.[70] Other barriers to the successful conclusion of the Doha Round were anti-dumping regulations, used more by India than by any other state and directed mostly at other emerging economies such as China, Indonesia and South Korea,[71] as well as import duties for agricultural products. At the same time, the Indian government has demanded the complete removal of all agricultural export subsidies provided by developed countries. This obstinacy can hardly be explained by pressure from specific interest groups alone, as, for example, their access to the Indian delegation in Geneva was very restricted.[72] I would argue that the Indian government successfully internalised the potential repercussions of compromise on important constituencies and financiers and thus did not need to take specific advice from outsiders.

In international climate negotiations (especially in Copenhagen and Cancùn) too, India has been spotted as a troublemaker by the international press. Indian representatives repeatedly stated that India was falsely regarded as a major emitter of green house gases, as per capita emissions were only five per cent of those in the United States and every citizen of the earth should have, in principle, the same pollution rights. Reductions should be based on the Kyoto principle of

---

67. Cf. Manmohan Singh, "India and the US: Towards a New Partnership", *op. cit.*; Deepak Mohanty, *Global Financial Crisis and Monetary Policy Response in India* (New Delhi: RBI, 2009).
68. Cf. Stuenkel, *op. cit.*
69. Andrew Hurrell and Amrita Narlikar, "A New Politics of Confrontation? Developing Countries at Cancun and Beyond", *Global Society*, Vol. 20, No. 4 (2006), pp. 415–433; Narlikar, *op. cit.*
70. cf. Greg Rushford, "Elephant in the Room", *The Wall Street Journal* (14 December 2007).
71. World Trade Organization, *Trade Policy Review India. Report by the Secretariat* (Geneva: WTO 2011).
72. Hurrell and Narlikar, *op. cit.*

common, but differentiated, responsibilities.[73] This position, shared by all developing countries, means that no reduction commitments are accepted. The Indian government also insists that only a half of the Indian population are connected to the electricity grid and that this disparity has to be righted before asking for national energy-saving efforts. These efforts should, in addition, be financed by technology transfers from industrialised countries.[74] Last but not least, the international verification of emission reduction commitments was refused by the government.[75]

The official utterances show a certain bias: India's per capita emissions are certainly still low, but are also increasing rapidly in accordance with economic growth and accelerating vehicle production. Energy consumption is, in addition, not driven primarily by the needs of the poorer sections of society, but by capital- and energy-intensive production and – even more so – by the under-pricing and wasting of electricity and fuels to the benefit of relatively wealthy farmers, who absorb the lion's share of the respective subsidies. If China, India and the United States continue on their current development paths, efforts by all other countries to avoid global warming will be in vain. India's position is also not commensurate with the interests of quite a few island and low-lying developing countries, or those who are less in need of an increasing supply of fossil fuels.[76] India, in addition, will be affected disproportionally by climate change and should, therefore, be interested in a stark reduction of emissions. The government finally took a softer position in Copenhagen and negotiated with Brazil, China, Indonesia, South Africa and the United States over a non-binding resolution for reductions, complemented by a unilateral declaration to increase, by 2010, the reduction in emissions from 20 per cent to 25 per cent as compared to 2005.

In Cancún in October 2010—apparently under pressure from the other regional powers and African and island states—the Indian government announced its acceptance of binding commitments "in an appropriate form", its preparedness to finance climate mitigation actions without external assistance and its willingness to permit strict external scrutiny of its mitigation achievements.[77] The causes for this radical departure from the former course were the bolstering of energy security by saving, the support of the growing domestic sector of wind and solar power appliances, the shielding of India against the negative effects of climate change and – last but not least – the intention to project India as a responsible/alternative international power alternative.[78] We should add, in fairness, that the Indian government has launched a reasonable number of new domestic initiatives to lower the energy intensity of both production and household

---

73. Devesh Kapur et al., "Climate Change: India's Options", *Economic and Political Weekly* (1 August 2009), pp. 34–42; H.A.C. Prasad and J.S. Kochher, *Climate Change and India – Some Major Issues and Policy Implications* (New Delhi: Ministry of Finance, 2009).

74. Prasad and Kochher, *op. cit.*

75. Navroz K. Dubash, "Copenhagen: Climate of Mistrust", *Economic and Political Weekly*, Vol. XLIV, No. 52 (2009), pp. 8–11

76. Group Centennial, *op. cit.*; T. Jayaraman, "Will it be a US Endgame at Copenhagen?", *Economic and Political Weekly*, Vol. XLIV, No. 50, (2009), pp. 13–15.

77. David Wheeler and Saurabh Shome, "Less Smoke, More Mirrors: Where India Really Stands on Solar Power and Other Renewables", *Working Paper*, 204 (Washington DC: Center for Global Development, 2010).

78. Namrata Patodia Rastogi, "Winds of Change: India's Emerging Climate Strategy", *The International Spectator*, Vol. 46, No. 2 (2011), pp. 127–141.

appliances, to increase the efficiency of power plants and to modify the share of non-traditional sources in the energy mix – even before international pressure made itself felt.[79] So there is a certain contradiction between harsh, self-interested statements in international forums and a more progressive attitude on the ground. It should be noted, however, that important segments of civil society and of industry demanded a more progressive position in climate policies long before the official shift, but the resistance that remained against this shift was so strong that the climate-friendly Minister of the Environment, Jayram Ramesh, had to be replaced shortly after the Cancùn summit.

In energy policy, where there is currently no global governance architecture, self-regulation is called for. China and India, as latecomers among the large-scale consumers of fossil fuels have tried to carve out separate niches from Western and state-owned companies in the oil- and gas-producing countries and have tried to invest in oil and gas exploration and exploitation in neglected or newly-emerging regions (Africa and Central Asia), irrespective of their political nature. By this endeavour they have not only come into conflict with the United States, but also with each other – wherein China has most often managed to outbid India. This race for the remaining sources of fossil fuels was preceded and accompanied by a massive build-up of the naval forces of both countries, not least so as to secure the transport of vital energy imports, therein raising the danger of future clashes.[80] Finally, the larger the share that China and India are taking from the shrinking cake of fossil energies, the smaller the share that will be left for poorer developing countries less able to adopt to an oil- or gas-deficient environment. This was, however, never a topic of consideration in India.

To summarise, the Indian government has not challenged the existence, norms and operations of (most often market-friendly and oligarchic) global governance institutions and certainly has no intention of reforming them according to the 'one-state-one-vote principle'. The Indian government is insisting only that these institutions become more representative, in other words that India – along with other regional powers – should be co-opted into the exclusive club of the established powers on an equal footing.[81] That the government has no hesitation in following such a path could already be seen in the acceptance of the invitation to the discussions of the G8 or in its being a founding member of the G20, whose task is to discuss and decide on the reform of the international financial architecture, and in the separate negotiations of major emerging countries with the established powers during the final phases of the Doha Round as well as in Copenhagen. This preparedness does not change the fact that India is hiding behind other developing countries – playing the poverty card – when and only when concessions or financial contributions are demanded of India from developed countries, most notably the United States. In a certain sense, India and

---

79. Cf. Joachim Betz and Melanie Hanif, "The Formation of Preferences in Two-level Games: An Analysis of India's Domestic and Foreign Energy Policy", *GIGA Working Papers*, No. 142 (Hamburg: GIGA, 2010).

80. Cf. Anidita Chatterjee and Mohit Sinha, *Power Realignments in Asia: China, India and the United States, Report of a US-India Policy Dialogue* (Center for the Advanced Study of India, Philadelphia, PA, 2006); Sascha Müller-Kraenner, "China's and India's Emerging Energy Foreign Policy", *Discussion Paper*, Vol. 15 (Bonn: DIE, 2008); Shashank Joshi, "China and India: Awkward Ascents", *Orbis*, Vol. 55, No. 4 (2011), pp. 558–576.

81. Narlikar, *op. cit.*

other emerging economies, in this way, use the rest of the 'third world' as a shield to avoid major contributions to global problems, and will probably continue to do so for as long as this advocacy strategy is still able to bring influence and special treatment.

Apart from the instrumental use of poorer and less powerful states, the Indian position sketched out above is also a reflection of old foreign policy *leitmotifs* (the preservation of sovereignty, non-interference in internal affairs, the fight for a new economic world order, and so on) that will not be abandoned easily, even if India is prepared to come to club agreements with the established powers. Resistance to fully contributing to the achievement of global public goods (foremost in trade and climate matters) are, finally, also the expression of electoral compulsions. Even if farmers or consumers in India are not sufficiently organised to protest forcefully against any eventual concessions by the government in the international arena, they still have enough power to determine the result of both national and state elections. We should not forget that political office is a cherished career in India, not solely, but still significantly, for material reasons.[82] As such, in cases where voter preferences are very strong, even a government relatively insulated against societal pressures is forced to eventually give in.

Conclusion

One should not expect too much of the re-distributional efforts made by the Indian government at the national, regional and global levels. Domestically, there have been some steps to correct the overly capital- and skill-intensive development path and to try to make sure that the poorer states and sections of society are not completely excluded from economic and social progress. It might, however, be difficult for the government to stem the momentum generated by those private companies who favour the more well-governed and attractive states within India. It might also be difficult to rebalance the existing development model, which is highly path-dependent, and builds on traditional strengths and a certain structural heterogeneity in India's economy and society. In addition, the budgetary scope for corrective programmes is rather limited. It might, therefore, be expected that the government will continue only to rebalance the results of economic activities by private agents at the margins.

Regionally, efforts to build a prosperous South Asian community are motivated ultimately not by some altruistic re-distributional desire but mostly by fears of a spill-over, therein undermining India's security, and by the further advances of China within South Asia. A more proactive stance is obstructed far less by the protectionist interests of industry groups than it is by traditional patterns of enmity within the region, which are preserved not only by India but also by its neighbouring states.

Globally, there is still some ambivalence with regard to the Indian position. On the one hand, the country wants to be included in the club of established powers and thus does not really challenge the status quo concerning the distribution of power, wealth and influence. There is, therefore, no real commitment to a just

---

82. Cf. Kanchan Chandra, *Why Ethnic Parties Succeed. Patronage and Ethnic Head Counts in India* (Cambridge: Cambridge University Press, 2004).

global order but instead predominantly only a desire to move up the status hierarchy.[83] In several international forums (in the WTO, in trade, finance and climate negotiations), India increasingly engages with smaller groups of powerful nations to affect outcomes at the expense of a more broad-based universalist approach it traditionally espoused, showing a preference for "global governance by oligarchy".[84]

On the other hand, India often refuses to pay the necessary contributions expected from members of the club and is still posing as a poor country. This strategic positioning is reinforced by the remnants of traditional foreign policy preferences cherished by less dynamic states and is bolstered by the fear of antagonising important voter groups if concessions were to be made that would be costly for them. Examples might be the removal of energy subsidies and import duties, or non-tariff barriers on agricultural products. Farmers are politically a very powerful group (as nearly 60 per cent of the Indian working population is employed in agriculture), whose interests have to be taken into consideration during international negotiations even when they have no real collective organisation or representation, in the Western sense. The puzzle of why India is not embracing global governance without reservation can, therefore, ultimately be largely explained by the self-interest of the political elite.

---

83. Mehta, *op. cit.*
84. Malone; *op.cit.* p. 250.

Index

Note: Page numbers in *italic* type refer to tables

Abdelal, R.: *et al.* 92
Adeney, K.: and Lall, M. 94
Africa 7, 47
Africa-India Summit (2011) 47
African National Congress (ANC) 61–2, 62, 64–5, *65*, 66, 103
African Renaissance Fund (2000) 48–9
aid 47; donors 35, *35*
Albright, M. 43
Alden, C.: *et al.* 37, 42, 45; and Vieira, M.A. 22, 48, 49, 85
Amaral, A.D.: *et al.* 63
Amorium, C. 22, 81, 88, 89
Annan, K. 54, 71
Antkiewicz, A.: and Whalley, J. 23
Araujo Castro, J.A. de 35, 46
authority: political 13

Bachrach, P.: and Baratz, M.S. 5
balancing perspective 15–17; institutional 17; soft 16, 23
Baldwin, D. 20
Bandung Conference (1955) 42–5; principles 45; spirit 51
Baratz, M.S.: and Bachrach, P. 5
Barbosa, R.A.: and César, L.P. 83
Better World for All, A (2000) 60
Betz, J. 9, 109–27
Beus, J. de: and Koelble, T. 61
Bhattacharyya, B. 98–9
Bisley, N. 43
Black, D.: and Wilson, Z. 103
Bourguignon, F.: *et al.* 1
Bourne, R. 70
Branco, R. 73, 74
Brandt Commission (1977) 58
Brantner, F.: and Gowan, R. 29
Brasilia Declaration (2003) 24
Brazil 2, 9, 22, 61, 68, 70, 73–5; Agency for Development Cooperation 48; credibility 80; diplomats 73, 77, 79–80, 84–5; foreign policy 73, 89; goals/ambitions 84; government 47, 48; human rights 88; inequality 61; Institute of Applied Economic Research (IPEA) 47; *Itamaraty* (Ministry of External Relations) 74–81, 83–5, 87, 90; Worker's Party (PT) 61, 63, 65, *see also* Brazil's strategy; India, Brazil and South Africa (IBSA states)
Brazil, Russia, India and China (BRICs) 26, 28, 34, 44
Brazil's strategy 75–6; avoid mindless opposition (defensive/passive) 77–8; build new organisations (assertive) 83–5; collectivise (defensive/passive) 78–80; consensus creation (neutral) 80–1; principled presidential righteousness (aggressive) 87–8; propagate new thinking (assertive) 85–7; technocratic-speak (neutral) 81–3
Bretton Woods 27, 59, 60
British government 44
Brookings Institution 110
Bull, H. 33, 38
Burbach, R.: and Tarbell, J. 43
Burges, S.W. 9, 62, 69, 73–90
Burns, E.B. 73
Burns, J.M. 7
Bush, G.W.: administration 40

capitalism 55
Cardoso, F.H. 61–4, 67, 70, 74, 82, 85–6, 87, 88; and Faletto, E. 85
César, L.P.: and Barbosa, R.A. 83
Chandy, L.: and Gertz, G. 54
Chatterjee, P. 100
child support grant 70
Chin, G. 53
China 3, 6, 26, 69, 123; Development Bank 26; foreign policy 36
Chirac, J. 67
Cohen, J.C.: and Lybecker, K.M. 82

INDEX

Cohen, S.P. 94–5, 103, 107, 112
collectivisation approach 78–80
colonialism 94–100
commissions 58
Commuri, G. 94
constructivism 92
Cooper, A.F. 6, 42, 44
cooptation perspective 18–20, 28
coordination: South-South 33–5, 37, 51
Copenhagen Accord (2009) 5
Costa, D. 84
Cox, M. 43
Cox, R.W. 15, 104
currency 26, 28

Dahl, R. 5
Davies, R. 24
Deacon, B. 59
decolonisation 42
democracy 20, 87
dependency theory 41
Deutsch, K. 30
developing countries 6, 12, 22
diplomats: Brazil 73, 77, 79–80, 84–5
distributive justice 35–50; critical approaches 37, 41–2; realism 37, 39–40
Doha Round (2001) 123
dollar (US) 26, 28
Dos Santos, T. 41
Doyle, M. 38

Easterly, W. 49
economic growth 12
economic relations: South-South 24
energy 124–5
European Union (EU) 29, 42, 69

Faletto, E. 85; and Cardoso, F.H. 85
Farer, T.: and Sisk, T.D. 41
farmers 127
Feinberg, R. 77
Finnemore, M. 57
Flemes, D. 7, 17, 23
foreign policy: Brazil 73, 89; India 9, 91, 107, 111–26; US 38, 43
fossil fuels 125
framing 55
free trade agreements (FTAs) 121
Free Trade Area of the Americas (FTAA) 77, 78
Freitas, M.V. 87
Fukuyama, F. 38

G8 3, 68
G20 6, 22, 53, 68–9, 80–1
G24 6
G77 43
Gandhi, M. 95

Gandhi, R. 103
Ganguly, S. 106, 110–11, 115
Gertz, G.: and Chandy, L. 54
Gilpin, R. 7, 17, 18, 39, 83
Gini Inequality Index 61
Glenn, J. 27
global governance 5, 43, 73–4
global redistribution 1–2; inter-state 4–5, 4
global South 3, 8, 11
global warming 124–5
globalisation 113
Goldman Sachs 11, 31, 34
Goldstein, J.: and Keohane, R.O. 51
Gonzalez, F. 66
Gordhan, P. 6
governance: global 5, 43, 73–4
governments: Brazil 47, 48; British 44; India 36, 47, 110, 113, 114, 120, 124–6; South Africa 63
Gowan, R.: and Brantner, F. 29
grants: child support 70; social 69–71
Graz, J. 68
Green Climate Fund 5
Grotius, H. 38
growth: economic 12; India 109–10, 114–15, 119
Guimarães, S.P. 77, 84
Gumede, W.M. 61, 66

Hague, W. 44
Hall, A. 70
Hanif, M.: et al. 1–9, 30
Hart, A.: and Jones, B. 15
hegemonic stability theory 17
Held, D. 38
Hemerijck, A.: and Schludi, M. 59–60
Herrera, Y.M.: et al. 92
Hinduism 96–7
historic bloc 42
HIV/AIDS crisis 82
Hochstetler, K. 65
Hopf, T. 92, 93
human rights 88
Hunter, W. 63
Hurrell, A. 15, 17, 34, 100; and Narlikar, A. 22, 34

identity: India 91–4, 100–3, 107
Ikenberry, G.J. 12, 20, 34, 40; and Wright, T. 12, 19, 27
imperialism 43
India 2, 91–3, 106–7, 109; aspiration 96, 107; civilisation 94–100, 107; colonialism 94–100; competition 9; demography 95; economy 114; emerging power 93, 107, 109–11; farmers 127; foreign policy 9, 91, 107, 111–26; free trade agreements 121; global profile 105; globalisation

113; government 36, 47, 110, 113, 114, 120, 124–6; growth 109–10, 114–15, 119; Hinduism 96–7; identity 91–4, 100–3, 107; neighbouring countries 121, 123; nuclear power 100–1, 116, 122; poverty 119–20; public 120; strategy 120–1; and US 114–16; young politicians 103, *see also* India, Brazil and South Africa (IBSA states)

India, Brazil and South Africa (IBSA states) 1–9, 11–15, 30–1, 33, 44, 85; balancing perspective 15–17; cooptation perspective 18–20, 28; demand-size 3; global inter-state redistribution 4–5, 4; money 25–8; partnership 35, 46, 51; prestige 7; rising powers 14–15; security 28–30; spoiler perspective 17–18; trade 21–5, 81; Trilateral Forum 12, 23, 24, 25–6, 28; Trust Fund 8, 33, 46–8, 50, 71, *see also* Brazil; India; South Africa

India Development Initiative (IDI) 47
inequality: Brazil 61; wealth 1–2
inequities: international institutions 37
International Action against Hunger and Poverty 71
International Bank for Reconstruction and Development (IBRD) 27
international economic regimes 57
international institutions: inequities 37
International Monetary Fund (IMF) 6, 26–7, 58, 59, 63, 69; board 6
international order 42–5
international organisations 55–60

Jervis, R. 17
Jing Wang: *et al.* 4
Johnston, A.I. 31; *et al.* 92
Jones, B.: and Hart, A. 15
justice: distributive 35–50; international 38

Kagan, R. 40
Kai He 17
Kant, I. 38
Katzenstein, P. 93
Keohane, R.O. 19; and Goldstein, J. 51; and Nye, J. 38
Khilnani, S. 93–4
Khor, M. 5
Kingstone, P.R.: *et al.* 63
Koelble, T.: and de Beus, J. 61
Korea 53
Kragelund, P. 47, 48
Krasner, S. 12, 39, 58–9
Kratochwil, F.: and Lapid, Y. 92
Krieckhaus, J.: *et al.* 63
Krishna, S.M. 92, 95, 97–8, 99–100

Lafer, C. 74, 77
Lake, D. 18

Lall, M.: and Adeney, K. 94
Lapid, Y.: and Kratochwil, F. 92
leadership 2, 7, 68
Luke, S. 5–6
Lula, L.I. 68, 70, 74, 80, 86, 87, 88, 90
Lumumba, P. 41
Lybecker, K.M.: and Cohen, J.C. 82

Maastricht Treaty (1992) 59
McDermott, R.: *et al.* 92
McGrew, A. 19
McNamara, R. 57
Make Poverty History campaign 54
Malik, P.M.S. 99
Malone, D.M. 127
Manuel, T. 69
March, J.G.: and Olsen, J.P. 42
Mbeki, T. 61, 64, 66, 67
Medianu, D.: *et al.* 4
Mercosul 83–4
Mercosur 23
Michie, J.: and Padayachee, V. 63
Middle East 50
middle power 15, 89
Millennium Development Goals (MGDs) 60
Molina, A.C.: and Shirotori, M. 24
money 25–8; currency 26, 28; Special Drawing Rights (SDRs) 26, 28; US dollar 26, 28
Moravcsik, A. 76
Morphet, S.: *et al.* 37, 42, 45
Mukherjee, P. 98, 115, 121
Murphy, C.N. 54, 55–6, 57, 59

Nabers, D.: *et al.* 1–9, 30
Nandy, A. 100–1
Narlikar, A. 6, 102–3, 104, 105–6; and Hurrell, A. 22, 34
Nath, K. 24
Nayar, B.R.: and Paul, T.V. 96
Nehru, J. 95
Nel, P. 7, 15, 25; *et al.* 1–9, 30; and Stephen, M.D. 2, 14
neo-Gramscian tradition 42, 53, 55
networks 66–7
New International Economic Order (NIEO) 57, 58–9
New Partnership for Africa's Development (NEPAD) 71
Non-Aligned Movement (NAM) 43
non-governmental organisations (NGOs) 60
nuclear power 100–1, 116, 122
Nye, J.: and Keohane, R. 38

Odell, J.S. 75, 76
Ollapally, D. 96
Olsen, J.P.: and March, J.G. 42

INDEX

Organisation of American States (OAS) 79, 87
Organisation for Economic Co-operation and Development (OECD) 4–6, 11; Development Assistance Committee (DAC) 5, 35

Padayachee, V.: and Michie, J. 63
Palat, R.A. 43–4, 101–2, 105
Pant, H.V. 111
Pape, R. 16
Paraguassu, L. 88
Parekh, B. 99
Partido da Social Democratica Brasileira (PSDB) 62, 64, 65, 66
Patriota, A. 74–5
Paul, T.V.: and Nayar, B.R. 96
Payne, R.A. 55
peace 20
Phillips, A. 50
Pieterse, I.N.: and Rehbein, B. 13
Pilot, S. 103
political authority 13
poverty 53–72, 119–20; programmes 120; rates 54; rediscovery 54
poverty alleviation 69–71, 86; child support grant 70; programmes 70; social grants 69–71
power 5, 20; new regional 1; Western 44, 51
Power, T.J. 62, 64, 66
Prebisch, R. 57
Puri, L. 23

Rao, N. 99, 105
Raustiala, K.: and Victor, D.G. 21
realism 102; distributive justice 37, 39–40
Reconstruction and Development Programme (RDP) 63
redistribution: global 1–2, 4–5, 4
regional powers: new 1
Rehbein, B.: and Pieterse, I.N. 13
Rodrik, D. 24
Roett, R. 69
Rohter, L. 90
Russia 26

Sagar, R. 96, 97, 98, 104
Schludi, M.: and Hemerijck, A. 59–60
Scindia, J. 103
security 28–30
Sengupta, D.: and Chakraborty, D. 21
Shirotori, M.: and Molina, A.C. 24
Shome, S.: and Wheeler, D. 124
Sikri, R. 95, 104
Silva Paranhos Jr, J.M. da 73
Singh, M. 97, 98, 113, 114
Singh, N. 115, 120

Sinha, Y. 113, 118
Sisk, T.D.: and Farer, T. 41
Six, C. 49
Smith, K. 9, 91–107
Soares, M. 66
social forces 56
social grants 69–71
South Africa 2, 7, 48–9, 61, 62, 63, 68, 70; government 63, *see also* India, Brazil and South Africa (IBSA states)
South African Customs Union (SACU) 23
South America 84
South Asian Free Trade Agreement (2010) 121
South-South coordination 33–5, 37, 51
South-South economic relations 24
South-South initiatives 33–5, 41
South-South organisations 43, 44
Southern Common Market (Mercosur) 23
Southernisation 86
spoiler perspective 17–18; free riders 18
Stephen, M.D. 8, 11–31; and Nel, P. 2, 14; and Zürn, M. 30
Strange, S. 67
Sukarno 42
Suttner, R. 61

Tarbell, J.: and Burbach, R. 43
tax 67
Taylor, I. 3, 23
Techno-Economic Approach of the African-Indian Movement (TEAM-9) 47
Teivaninen, T. 81
Thérien, J-P. 56, 58
trade 21–5, 81; South-South 24; world flow 21

United Nations Conference on Trade and Development (UNCTAD) 23, 41, 57
United Nations Development Programme (UNDP) 46, 59
United Nations Relief and Rehabilitation Administration (UNRRA) 56–7
United Nations (UN) 28–30, 73; agencies 59; High Level Advisory Group on Climate Change Financing 5; Responsibility to Protect (R2P) doctrine 38; Security Council (SC) 7, 28–30, 47, 123
United States of America (USA) 11–12, 29, 30; dollar 26, 28; foreign policy 38, 43; and India 114–16

Vale, P. 27
Vickers, B. 68
Victor, D.G.: and Raustiala, K. 21
Vieira, M.A. 8, 33–41; and Alden, C. 22, 48, 49, 85; *et al.* 37, 42, 45
Virmani, A. 113

INDEX

Wade, R.H. 22
Waltz, K. 16
wars 43
Watson, A. 42
wealth: inequalities 1–2; shifting 4–5
Weldes, J. 92
Wendt, A. 93
Western powers 44, 51
Westhuizen, J. van der 8, 53–72
Whalley, J.: and Antkiewicz, A. 23; *et al.* 4
Wheeler, D.: and Shome, S. 124
Wilson, Z.: and Black, D. 103

Woods, N. 35, 48
World Bank 27–8, 57, 59, 69–71, 109–10, 119–20, 123; board 6n
World Economic Forum (WEF) 67–8
World Trade Organisation (WTO) 21–2, 24, 25, 77–8, 79, 82, 106, 123
Wright, T.: and Ikenberry, G.J. 12, 19, 27

Young, O.R. 9

Zoellick, R. 27, 28, 77, 78
Zürn, M. 13; and Stephen, M.D. 30